Governing Financialization

Governing Financialization

The Tangled Politics of Financial Liberalization in Britain

JACK COPLEY

UNIVERSITY PRESS

Great Clarendon Street, Oxford, OX2 6DP,
United Kingdom

Oxford University Press is a department of the University of Oxford.
It furthers the University's objective of excellence in research, scholarship,
and education by publishing worldwide. Oxford is a registered trade mark of
Oxford University Press in the UK and in certain other countries

Published in the United States of America by Oxford University Press
198 Madison Avenue, New York, NY 10016, United States of America

British Library Cataloguing in Publication Data
Data available

Library of Congress Control Number: 2021939029

ISBN 978-0-19-289701-5

DOI: 10.1093/oso/9780192897015.001.0001

Printed and bound in the UK by
TJ Books Limited

For Jimmy Copley and Bryn Gough

Acknowledgements

This book was many years in the making. It grew out of research that I conducted while doing my PhD at the University of Warwick—funded by the Economic and Social Research Council, to which I am grateful. I was lucky to be supervised by Mat Watson and Ben Clift, and I owe them both a great deal of thanks for their generosity, intellectual stimulation, and continuing mentorship. Many people have provided me with valuable feedback on the research contained in this book, but I want to extend my particular thanks to Andrew Gamble, Chris Rogers, Lorenzo Feltrin, and Te-Anne Robles. I am deeply grateful to Alexis Moraitis and Javier Moreno Zacarés for reading the entire manuscript and providing insightful feedback. Thanks are also due to the team at Oxford University Press, especially Dominic Byatt for his excellent editorial guidance, and to the anonymous reviewers for their comments. This book's argument has been honed over the years through countless discussions with brilliant students, and I would like to acknowledge in particular my 'Meltdowns' students at the University of Bath with whom I have had many fruitful conversations about the key themes of this book. To my parents, I owe so much. I thank them for their love, support, and encouragement. To Euge, te amo y gracias por todo.

Earlier versions of sections of Chapters 2 and 4 appeared in J. Copley (2017), 'Financial Deregulation and the Role of Statecraft: Lessons from Britain's 1971 Competition and Credit Control Measures', *New Political Economy*, 22(6): 692–708 and J. Copley and A. Moraitis (2020), 'Beyond the Mutual Constitution of States and Markets: On the Governance of Alienation', *New Political Economy*, DOI: 10.1080/13563467.2020.1766430. These articles can be accessed at https:// www.tandfonline.com/. Further, previous drafts of parts of Chapters 5 and 7 appeared in J. Copley and M. E. Giraudo (2019), 'Depoliticizing Space: The Politics of Governing Global Finance', *Environment and Planning C: Politics and Space*, 37(3): 442–60 and J. Copley (2019), 'Why Were Capital Controls Abandoned? The Case of Britain's Abolition of Exchange Controls', *British Journal of Politics and International Relations*, 21(2): 403–20.

Contents

List of Figures

Abbreviations

BOE	Bank of England
CBI	Confederation of British Industry
CCC	Competition and Credit Control
DCE	Domestic Credit Expansion
DoI	Department of Industry
DoT	Department of Trade
DTI	Department of Trade and Industry
EEC	European Economic Community
FCO	Foreign and Commonwealth Office
FSA	Financial Services Authority
GDP	Gross Domestic Product
GRG	Gower Report Group
IMF	International Monetary Fund
LSE	London Stock Exchange
MIB	Marketing of Investments Board
MLR	Minimum Lending Rate
MRC	Modern Records Centre
MTFS	Medium Term Financial Strategy
NYSE	New York Stock Exchange
OFT	Office of Fair Trading
PSBR	Public Sector Borrowing Requirement
RPC	Restrictive Practices Court
SIB	Securities and Investments Board
SRA	Self-Regulatory Agencies
TNA	The National Archives
TUC	Trades Union Congress
US	United States of America

1

Introduction

The cover of *Time* magazine in May 2016 was an image of the word 'capitalism' overrun and strangled by an invasive vine with leaves that resembled those found on a US dollar bill. The existential threat represented by these creeping money vines, the feature article explained, was 'financialization' (Foroohar, 2016). Financialization is a concept that began to bleed from a niche set of academic debates into broader usage in the 2000s and particularly in the aftermath of the 2008 global financial crisis. Its proliferation reflects the fact that it grasped a palpable transformation in the global political economy following the disintegration of the Bretton Woods system in the 1970s, namely the untrammelled ascendance of the financial sector. According to some accounts, the centre of gravity of the world economy had shifted from nation states to massive financial corporations that sit astride the globe, coordinating a web of money flows that penetrate national borders with little resistance. Despite the spectacular collapse and painful rescue of financialized capitalism, this bloated and unwieldy system staggered on. Yet politics was changed forever. The metaphor of the vine captured well the contemporary zeitgeist. Politics became pervaded by a deep anxiety with the unrivalled power of a global financial sector that had supposedly extended its parasitic grip over both the world economy and democratic processes.

The initial excitement with the alchemy of new financial engineering that in 1997 allowed Larry Summers, then Deputy Secretary of the US Treasury, to remark '[f]inancial markets don't just oil the wheels of economic growth—they are the wheels', largely evaporated following 2008 (Mirowski, 2013: 222). This was the greatest financial crisis in world history, destroying $50 trillion in asset values in a single year (equivalent to one year of world GDP), and generating shockwaves that reverberated out from the banking hubs of advanced capitalist nations to the global economy (Mogato, 2009). In the ensuing depression of economic activity, compounded by painful state-imposed adjustments, a growing chorus of voices in formal politics identified the disproportionate growth of global finance as a key pathology of twenty-first-century capitalism. This ranged from British Prime Minister David Cameron's empty call for a rebalancing of the UK's economy away from the financial sector (Telegraph, 2010), to scathing critiques by formerly fringe political figures such as Jeremy Corbyn and Bernie Sanders—building upon the momentum of the 2011 Occupy movement—of an economy that had been rigged in favour of the 'speculators and gamblers' (Pickard, 2017).

Governing Financialization: The Tangled Politics of Financial Liberalization in Britain. Jack Copley, Oxford University Press.
© Jack Copley 2022. DOI: 10.1093/oso/9780192897015.003.0001

Such critiques also gained traction, in a warped form, on the far right. For France's Marine Le Pen, the key political battle was between patriots and globalists, with the latter embracing the erosion of nationhood by the combined forces of '[f]inancial globalisation and Islamist globalisation' (Melander, 2017). Hungarian Prime Minister Viktor Orbán too capitalized on the political fallout from the devastating effects of the financial crisis on Hungary's economy by reinvigorating anti-Semitic tropes about a 'crafty', 'international' enemy that 'speculates with money', embodied by the Jewish Hungarian businessman George Soros (Walker, 2018). Beyond the electoral sphere, a new impetus was given to unusual and often conspiratorial critiques of financial power. Calls for a return to the Gold Standard spread in the US, yet rather than articulating the typical fiscal conservative stance, they were increasingly pitched as an anti-establishment strategy to rein in the financial elite by tying the economy to a real, tangible form of wealth (White, 2015; Benko, 2011). In the depths of the Internet, a matrix of websites and blogs launched fantastical critiques of so-called 'money power', piecing together a garbled assault on bankers and their political lapdogs by drawing from the Federal Reserve conspiracy, notions of the deep state, or veiled claims of Jewish world domination.

Like all disasters, financialization has several competing origin stories. Most accounts, however, give a central role to the actions of powerful states beginning in the 1970s. Athanasios Orphanides (2015), MIT economist and former governor of the Central Bank of Cyprus, expressed this argument succinctly in a *Foreign Affairs* piece on the causes of the financial crash: 'It's politics, stupid'. Through policies of deregulation, the institution of light-touch financial oversight, and the construction of technocratic and marketized forms of economic governance, states acted to propel the tremendous growth of global finance and in turn disempower themselves. The most popular explanation of states' support for financialization pointed to two factors. The first was the nefarious power of finance capital to influence the political process. '[B]anks had invested well', Nobel laureate economist Joseph Stiglitz (2010: 326) argued, 'not in the housing or the real sector, but in politics . . . they had bought deregulation'. The second was the enduring strength of neoliberal ideology. A new consensus had emerged in both national policymaking circles and international organizations, extolling the benefits of financial liberalization—driven in part by a well-connected network of intellectuals such as Milton Friedman and Friedrich Hayek (Metcalf, 2017). Variants of this explanation enjoyed wide support on diverse parts of the political spectrum in Europe and the US following the global financial crisis.

The British state's role in propelling financialization has often been held up as the archetypal case of the combined power of financial lobbying and laissez-faire ideas. As the *Guardian*'s senior economics commentator Aditya Chakrabortty (2011) wrote: 'Britain is ruled by the banks, for the banks'. The intimate, centuries-old connections between the British state and the world-leading financial sector located in the City of London (referred to hereafter as the City) had long been a topic of debate (see Ingham, 1984). Indeed, since the nineteenth century, it had been common to suggest that vast political power was wielded by City bankers—'those real potentates of modern times who sway the destinies of nations with a rod of gold, and issue their decrees in bank notes and Exchequer bills' (Gore, 1854: 31). Yet many accounts insisted that a fundamental change occurred in state-City relations under the governments of Margaret Thatcher. Thatcher and her acolytes—dedicated free market ideologues, many of whom had previous careers in finance—supposedly embraced the City and committed themselves to promoting its interests on the global stage, regardless of the negative effects. As one assessment of Thatcher's project put it: 'whatever happened to manufacturing, the City was intended to flourish' (Coakley and Harris, 1992: 37). It was this reckless pro-City policy agenda, according to this explanation, that drove the expansion of the UK financial sector to its pre-eminent global position and meant that Britain acted as a falling domino, provoking a chain reaction of financial liberalization around the world that eventually culminated in the 2008 crisis.

This book challenges this conventional wisdom through an in-depth analysis of declassified state archives. By exploring why the British state pursued four pivotal financial liberalization measures—the 1971 Competition and Credit Control (CCC) policy, the 1977–79 abolition of exchange controls, the 1986 Big Bang, and the 1986 Financial Services Act (FSA)—this book argues that the political roots of financialization do not lie primarily in the overwhelming political influence of the financial sector nor the power of neoliberal ideas. In fact, during the critical years of the birth of financialization, British governments did not implement a coherent, intentional strategy to favour finance capital. Instead, these governments were desperately navigating a series of political binds and economic precipices that had their origins in the coming apart of the post-war global order. As the profitability of capital fell worldwide (though geographically unevenly) from the late 1960s, the phenomenon of simultaneously worsening economic stagnation and rising inflation—known as 'stagflation'—put terrible strain on the post-war institutional arrangements of many advanced capitalist countries. Britain was among the worst affected, due to its relative lack of economic competitiveness. As this book will explain, financial liberalization was deployed in an ad hoc manner either to postpone the worst effects of the crisis, so as to maintain governing legitimacy, or to enact painful economic restructuring in a manner that shielded the state from political backlash. The British state pursued such policies in an attempt to reconcile the demands of domestic civil society with the suffocating, impersonal pressures of the global economic crisis on Britain's balances with the rest of the world. Financialization was an accidental result, not an intended outcome.

Financialization, Stagnation, and States

If the rise of global finance and its collapse in 2008 provoked an inquest in both popular and elite circles, it also gave rise to a burgeoning social science literature that has addressed the concept of financialization. From the start, this literature has been profoundly interdisciplinary, drawing from international political economy, political science, heterodox economics, sociology, and geography—yet with common roots in an older, pre-disciplinary political economy tradition. As academic interest in financialization proliferated, it came to be used in divergent ways and perhaps stretched too thin in the process.

This chapter will explore three strands of this vast literature. First, the broadest approaches conceptualize financialization as the general growth of financial actors, practices, and discourses, and seek to apply this understanding to particular cases, such as the car industry or housing markets. Second, a more precise branch of this literature understands financialization to denote a causal relationship between financial sector expansion and 'productive stagnation', which refers to the faltering economic growth across various advanced capitalist countries since the 1970s. Third, a limited number of accounts have focused explicitly on the *politics* of financialization, examining the role of states in navigating the twin phenomena of financial expansion and productive stagnation.

The Financialization of...

As Brett Christophers (2015: 186) argues, if the various accounts of financialization share anything in common, it is 'perhaps only the hazy conviction that "finance"...today enjoys a historically unique significance'. Indeed, the most commonly cited definition casts the analytical net particularly wide: 'financialization means the increasing role of financial motives, financial markets, financial actors and financial institutions in the operation of the domestic and international economies' (Epstein, 2005: 3). This broad conceptualization has generated an expansive research agenda that has sought to trace the creeping financialization of industry, government, and everyday life.

Perhaps the most important factor driving the financialization of the contemporary social world, according to this literature, is the rise of shareholder value. Originally developed by agency theorists such as Eugene Fama and Michael Jensen in the 1970s, shareholder value theory emphasizes that corporate managers tend to pursue their own selfish ends if they are not exposed to the whip of market discipline (Van der Zwan, 2014: 107). This inefficiency could be rectified, it was proposed, by transferring greater corporate control to shareholders, through a variety of mechanisms. As the shareholder value principle was widely adopted in corporate boardrooms, companies began to transform their business strategies along distinctly financial lines. This was epitomized by General Electric, as the technology manufacturing company founded by Thomas Edison had by 2008 become one of the largest financial services companies in the world, offering personal, mortgage, and commercial loans (Foroohar, 2017: 152). This reorientation around the imperative of shareholder value maximization spread to various industries around the globe, from US timber companies (Gunnoe and Gellert, 2011) to Japanese pharmaceuticals (Montalban and Sakinç, 2013) to British water providers (Bayliss, 2014). Relatedly, different economic sectors became penetrated by an array of financial actors and instruments, from the growing role of banks and investment funds in the global food system (Clapp, 2014) to the increasing practice of securitization in national mortgage markets (Langley, 2008) to the use of derivatives by universities (Engelen, Fernandez, and Hendrikse, 2014).

Financialization has not been limited to the private sector, but rather a number of accounts have tracked how mechanisms of government have come under the sway of financial logics. Ian Hardie (2011), for example, has argued that as investors increasingly trade risk in emerging economy bond markets, governments in the Global South face rising borrowing costs and, in turn, higher risk of sovereign debt crisis. Other scholars insist that the state itself has become an object of financialization, with Yingyao Wang (2015) arguing that even the Chinese state, which not only coordinates but owns much of the Chinese economy, has increasingly relied upon financial instruments to govern the market. This financialization of government extends from the heights of central government to regional and local politics. Indeed, particular attention has been paid to the financialization of urban governance (Lake, 2015; Weber, 2010).

A different strand of financialization research shifted focus from business and government to the sphere of 'everyday life', analysing the manner in which the expansion of financial practices amongst non-elite sections of the population has led to transformations in the lived experiences of contemporary capitalism. As Paul Langley (2004: 554) argued, such scholars understand financialization as a 'set of processes constituted in practice through discourses of economy'. This approach emphasizes the instability, uncertainty, and unevenness of financialization, rather than characterizing it as a coherent and all-encompassing stage of capitalism. Rob Aitken (2007) analysed how various strategies employed by US banks, businesses, and even government agencies have attempted to draw large sections of the population into the realm of private finance, and have attempted to construct the notion of the US citizen as a prudent saver and investor. Leonard Seabrooke (2006) similarly examined how the US state attempted to imbricate low income groups into credit networks as a strategy to boost the US' position in global financial markets. With a particular focus on changing class relations, Randy Martin, Michael Rafferty, and Dick Bryan (2008) conceptualized financialized capitalism as a sort of contemporary dystopia, in which the pressures unleashed by financial innovation have both intensified competition between capitals and forced workers to approach their everyday life as a balance sheet.

Financial Expansion, Economic Stagnation

While the aforementioned approaches to financialization shine an important light on the expansion of financial practices at the corporate, state, and everyday level, they have in general avoided directly linking these processes with a second glaring feature of contemporary capitalism: the relative stagnation of growth in advanced capitalist economies since the 1970s (OECD, 2020). Concepts have abounded to capture this phenomenon, from discussions of Japan's 'Lost Decade(s)', to 'Eurosclerosis', to debates among economic policymakers and commentators about the possibility that we are living through a period of what US economist Alvin Hansen termed 'secular stagnation' (Hansen, 1939; G. Davies, 2017; Summers, 2013). While economists have pointed to a range of factors to explain this stagnant economic performance, particularly slowing population growth (Teulings and Baldwin, 2014), certain scholars working within the broad rubric of financialization studies have instead sought to conceptualize the tremendous growth of global finance since the 1970s as internally related to the atrophy of the 'productive economy'. These approaches have thus contributed to a more precise definition of financialization, whereby the term denotes the interrelated development of two phenomena: financial expansion and productive stagnation. However, there is no consensus on the direction in which causality operates between these two phenomena. While certain accounts argue that the growing financial sector has directly reduced growth in the underlying economy, opposing accounts insist that pre-existing weaknesses in the productive economy have spurred financial expansion.

The former explanation—that financial expansion has caused productive stagnation—is well captured by the title of *Financial Times* editor Rana Foroohar's popular book on financialization: *Makers and Takers: The Rise of Finance and the Fall of American Business* (Foroohar, 2016).[1] Fundamentally, financialization is said to constitute the expropriation of the makers (non-financial capital) by the takers (finance capital). This explanation points to the importance of the rise of shareholder value, which has not only led to the reorientation of corporate strategy around financial objectives but has also discouraged companies from making long-term investments, thus contributing to the stagnation of economic growth (Crotty, 2000; 2003). From the 1980s, companies began to increase dividend payments to shareholders and plough earnings

---

[1] See also Mazzucato (2018).

back into their own stock in order to keep its price rising, thus draining the reserves available for future investment (Stockhammer, 2004; Lazonick, 2013). In addition, Gérard Duménil and Dominique Lévy (2002: 61) argue that a significant fraction of non-financial corporate profits has been paid to financial actors in the form of interest, such that 'the profits pumped out of the productive sector of the economy do not return to it'. Corporate earnings that *were* invested became increasingly directed towards short-term financial assets, including securitized debt. Income streams based on this interest-accruing activity began to outpace traditional returns from real investment (Orhangazi, 2008a). The net result of these developments has been the restructuring of the non-financial corporation from 'an integrated combination of illiquid real assets' to a '"portfolio" of liquid subunits that...management must continually restructure to maximise the stock price' (Crotty, 2003: 2).

The cause of this shift in corporate strategy is disputed, but several explanations have been offered. Englebert Stockhammer argues that the answer can be found in a power struggle taking place within firms, between managers and shareholders. While managers seek 'power and prestige...in high market share and fast growth, luxurious offices and many subordinates', shareholders are motivated by a singular desire for profit (Stockhammer, 2004: 724). In the last forty years, the post-war fetters on the shareholding class have been gradually repealed, allowing them to subordinate management's plurality of interests to profit-driven, finance-oriented strategies. Two mechanisms were particularly important in effecting this shift in corporate strategy: stock options, which link managerial pay to the company's stock price, and the threat of hostile takeover, whereby unprofitable companies are acquired by other firms. William Lazonick and Mary O'Sullivan (2002), on the other hand, argue that US corporations in the 1960s and 1970s became too large, with managers becoming divorced from the production process and thus lacking the technical know-how to make informed investment decisions. This, coupled with the challenge posed by formidable Japanese manufacturing competitors and the gnawing effects of inflation, meant that US corporate strategy shifted from 'retain and invest' to 'downsize and distribute', whereby companies' labour forces were reduced and profits increasingly distributed amongst shareholders. Finally, Duménil and Lévy (2004, 2002) relate the financial sector's 'parasitic' behaviour towards real economy firms to the neoliberal revolution of the 1980s, during which financial rentiers used the stagflation crisis to seize both economic and political power. These approaches, then, insist that financial capital has systematically expropriated the wealth produced by productive capital through mechanisms related to shareholder value and rent-seeking, resulting in the simultaneous ballooning of the financial sector and paltry real economy performance.

The latter explanation, in contrast, argues that underlying problems with productive capital accumulation have given rise to financial expansion. This explanation has rather unsettling political consequences, as it suggests that attempts to quash contemporary financial excesses—through, for example, the imposition of a strict regime of financial regulations—would not necessarily reignite economic growth, but instead reveal the unresolved problems in the productive sector. As Harry Magdoff and Paul Sweezy wrote:

> There is no reason whatever to assume that if you could deflate the financial structure, the talent and energy now employed there would move into productive pursuits...What growth the economy has experienced in recent years...has been almost entirely due to the financial explosion.
>
> (quoted in Bellamy Foster, 2007: 4)

While such accounts share a common causal narrative—that financial market growth emerged as a response to protracted economic crisis—there is significant divergence regarding the definition of the underlying crisis, and the sustainability of financial expansion as a resolution.

Giovanni Arrighi (1994) was among the first political economists to employ the term 'financialization', which he used to refer to a recurring process that coincides with the decline of a hegemonic capitalist power. Arrighi and Beverly Silver (1999: 32) argue that during periods of hegemonic decline, in which the world capitalist system is cast into deep crisis, capital reacts by 'shedding its commodity form in favor of its money form': non-financial corporations respond to the dearth of profitable productive investment opportunities by investing in financial assets, which offer higher rates of return (Orhangazi, 2008b). This results in a worldwide growth of financial markets. Building upon Arrighi's insights, scholars associated with regulation theory and the social structures of accumulation approach have conceptualized financialization as part of a new 'regime of accumulation' that emerged in the 1970s to resolve the crisis of the post-war 'Fordist' accumulation regime (Jessop, 1997: 503). As slowing productivity and accelerating inflation undermined the Fordist growth model, financial speculation and the holding of liquid financial assets became an increasingly profitable alternative to productive investment (Boyer, 2000: 112; Tabb, 2010: 148; Becker et al., 2010: 227). Indeed, several Marxist scholars have focused on how the weak rate of profit on productive investments since the 1970s has provoked capital to flee to the financial realm (Brenner, 2006; Kliman, 2012; Shaikh, 2011). This resulted in what Samir Amin (2003: 43) termed 'financial hypertrophy', whereby capital markets inflate, there is a proliferation of financial instruments, a growing financial influence over corporate decision-making, and the simultaneous globalization of these processes. Lastly, a number of approaches, employing the terms 'privatized Keynesianism' or 'house price Keynesianism', similarly identify financial expansion as a remedy to the breakdown of the post-war growth model (Crouch, 2009; Hay et al., 2008; Watson, 2010). Such accounts argue that while Keynesian state policies of demand stimulus boosted consumption in the post-war era, this framework was dismantled during the stagflation crisis. In the absence of state-led demand creation, *private* credit expanded in order to enable mass consumption. Fundamental to all such approaches is the notion that financial expansion simply papers over the cracks in the underlying productive structure, without offering a lasting solution.

Financialization and the State

The debate on the relationship between financial expansion and productive stagnation has advanced this literature beyond the shortcomings of the 'financialization of' approaches. However, as a whole, this literature has tended to neglect the high politics of financialization, in terms of the role of states in mediating the twin phenomena of a ballooning financial sector and an anaemic economy. As Eric Helleiner (1995: 315) argues, the increasing scale and global character of financial markets is not simply 'a product of unstoppable technological and market forces'; rather, state policy initiatives have been of 'central importance in encouraging and permitting the process'. While much of this literature implicitly acknowledges the importance of states, state action in propelling financialization tends to be theorized in either pluralist or functionalist terms. Simply put, the state is conceived of either as a mere conduit for different elite factions and competing ideologies or as a reflexive, automatic regulator of capital accumulation. In both cases, little space is left for an analysis of the political and strategic dimensions of state behaviour in relation to financialization (Van der Zwan, 2014: 114).

Explanations that insist financial expansion has caused productive stagnation tend to adopt an interest-based and ideational lens to understand the state's role in financialization. The state is understood as another instrument wielded by financial elites in their expropriation of productive capital in the neoliberal period. This capture of the reins of state power was effected in two ways: directly, through political lobbying; and indirectly, through the propagation of pro-finance ideas. The 'radical deregulation' of the 1970s and 1980s, Crotty (2009: 564) argues, was 'pushed by financial institutions and justified by efficient financial market theory'. Duménil and Lévy (2004: 69) are even more explicit, labelling US Federal Reserve Chairman Paul Volcker's drastic 1979 interest rate increase as a 'coup' to restore 'the hegemony of finance': 'One should not see here the hand of a mysterious market, but, in fact, a centralized decision, a deliberate policy.' Thomas Palley (2013: 7) differs from Duménil and Lévy in this respect, insisting that financial deregulation 'was not part of a grand plan'. Instead, it was the '*laissez-faire* financial ideology' associated with the ascendant financial elite that created a political climate favourable to deregulation (ibid.: 8; emphasis in original). The state, as such, is conceived of as a more or less passive vehicle for specific group interests, depending on the balance of class forces, or as a receptacle for economic ideologies.

Several accounts have taken steps to bolster these claims with historical evidence, with specific attention paid to the UK case. An important early intervention, in this regard, was made by Frank Longstreth (1979: 160), who argued that the 'state can be, and in the case of Britain has been, dominated by a particular fraction of the dominant class'. This fraction was identified generally as financial capital, and specifically the City. Explicitly drawing from Longstreth's work, Leila Talani (2012: 65–6) claimed that the City's 'institutional nexus with the Bank of England and the Treasury' has meant that British policy favours the financial sector, resulting in 'the definitive submission of productive capital to financial capital'. Indeed, Aaron Davis and Catherine Walsh (2016: 679) argued that the British state's pro-finance stance in the 1980s was a constitutive element of the City's 'slow, staged coup' against domestic industry. The 'exogenous shocks' of the 1976 International Monetary Fund (IMF) bailout and 1979 Conservative election victory meant that 'senior ministerial positions in the Treasury were taken by a succession of politicians with City backgrounds and/or networks' (Davis and Walsh, 2017: 37). The result was that this 'dominant elite in government actively organized the economy according to a particular financialized economic epistemological framework', and thus 'its interventions were in favour of global finance and financial elites and against national industry and industrial elites' (ibid.: 45). In addition to its instrumental power over the British state, the City is said to wield '*ideational power*', which Scott James and Lucia Quaglia (2020: 38; emphasis in original) define as 'the narratives and discourse that the financial industry articulates over time to shape the broader policy agenda'. Yet Jonathan Hopkin and Kate Alexander Shaw argue that, in the case of Thatcher's liberalization of the City, the power of laissez-faire ideology actually ran counter to the interests of City elites. In pursuing the Big Bang, they claim, Thatcher demonstrated a willingness to disrupt the City's protectionist arrangements so as to boost the UK finance industry's long-term 'ability to compete with rival financial centers such as New York' (Hopkin and Shaw (2016): 352). Financial liberalization, according to this account, was thus pushed through by an 'ideologically motivated [political] elite that was ahead of the domestic business lobby in its commitment to free markets' (ibid.: 364).

Alternatively, explanations that understand financial expansion to be a symptom of productive stagnation tend to adopt a functionalist approach to the state, emphasizing the state's role in automatically facilitating capital accumulation. Just as these approaches tend to view the capitalist order as a jigsaw puzzle in which different pieces fit together more or less snugly, the state is understood as the referee of this game, intervening to remove obstacles to capitalist reproduction. In the face of the crisis of productive capital, states acted instinctively to provide capital with escape routes to more profitable investment opportunities through financial liberalization. In the process, states themselves became transformed, with their various agencies and functions becoming streamlined to the needs of the new pattern of financial capital accumulation. As John Bellamy Foster (2007: 6) explains, the 'role of the capitalist state was transformed to meet the new imperative of financialization'. For Colin Crouch too, advanced capitalist states deregulated finance because it was functional to the formation of a new privatized Keynesian model. Peripheral states that resisted had such policies 'imposed as conditions for assistance from or membership of such international bodies as the International Monetary Fund, the World Bank, the Organisation for Economic Co-operation and Development (OECD) or the European Union' (Crouch (2009: 388).

Such functionalist approaches have put forth significant historical accounts of the state's role in financialization, with a particular focus on the US. Arrighi argued that the Reagan administration sought to respond to its declining economic hegemony by establishing the US as the global centre for 'privately controlled world money', through a variety of policy measures. These included the 'Volcker shock' interest rate hike, a spate of financial deregulations designed to attract mobile capital, and the expansion of government debt linked to an escalation of the Cold War (Arrighi (1994: 326–8). Robert Brenner (2006: 276) too argued that as the US manufacturing sector continued to founder in the 1970s,

> the late Carter and especially the Reagan administrations...moved decisively toward financial deregulation, breaking down hitherto existing barriers that confined financial institutions to specialized functional and geographic spheres. They also adopted a series of policies designed to raise the rate of return on financial activity...The Reagan regime, in its early years, could hardly have catered more directly to the needs of financiers.

More specifically, Volcker's monetarist experiment in the late 1970s and early 1980s, alongside financial liberalization and corporate tax breaks, constituted part of an intentional policy 'to detonate a major restructuring of the US economy' that would eliminate unprofitable industrial capitals, crush unions, and lead to 'a reallocation of means of production out of industry into financial services' (ibid.: 271). The state, according to this functionalist interpretation, is a rational watchdog of capital accumulation, which acted mechanically to rescue the ailing productive sector through the facilitation of financial largess.

As demonstrated, explanations of the role of states in propelling financialization have tended to be grounded in interest-based and ideational or functionalist understandings of the capitalist state. In the former, policy outcomes reflect the warring social factions attempting to capture state power and the competing ideologies of economic governance. The latter conceptualizes state behaviour as a functional, automatic response to blockages in the accumulation of capital— framing the state as a superstructural functionary of the capitalist system. However, several scholars have advanced a more convincing, distinctly political, account. This account conceptualizes the state's role in boosting financial growth not simply as a result of certain fractional interests or a mechanistic response to economic crisis, but as a strategic initiative to negotiate the social conflict and political upheaval arising from the breakdown of capital accumulation.

Wolfgang Streeck (2011: 10) suggested that the 'post-war settlement between labour and capital' began to come apart at the seams in the late 1960s due to the irreconcilable contradiction at the heart of democratic capitalism, between the principles of marginal productivity and social need. States in 'wealthy capitalist democracies' found it politically impossible to contain rising wage demands by allowing unemployment to rise, and thus instead crafted monetary policy so as to allow accelerating inflation to artificially inflate corporate profits and thus delay the necessary restructuring (Streeck, 2014: xv). Yet this pacification strategy became unsustainable as inflation spiralled out of control, provoking the monetarist pen-ance unleashed by Volcker and Thatcher in the early 1980s. In place of inflation, states expanded public debt as a strategy to reconcile the social conflict arising from productive stagnation by 'introduc[ing] resources into the distributional conflicts of the time that had not yet in fact been produced' (Streeck, 2011: 14). Finally, following the exhaustion of the strategy of rising public indebtedness, states boosted private credit and debt through policies of financial deregulation, in order to 'make future resources available for securing present social peace' (ibid.: 20). Financial expansion is thus more than a functional response to productive stagnation—it is a political strategy to assuage the social dislocations arising from the crisis.

Similarly, Greta Krippner (2011) explored the motives underpinning the US state's fostering of financial growth through an analysis of the development of the US Federal Reserve's monetary policy and financial deregulation from the 1970s to the 2000s. Rather than highlighting a coherent ideology of 'Reaganomics', Krippner (ibid.: 140) argued that monetarism and financial deregulation consti-tuted trial-and-error responses to a series of profound governing dilemmas:

> The state faced three interrelated difficulties as the era of post-war abundance came to an end: a social crisis associated with increased distributional conflict as growth slowed, a fiscal crisis that resulted from policymakers' attempts to meet proliferating demands with ever more limited resources, and a legitimation crisis that reflected sinking public confidence.

The US state strategized to delay this unfolding crisis by pursuing domestic financialization and a transformation in monetary policy, which 'removed internal and external constraints on the expansion of credit in the US economy' (ibid.: 139). Facing demands from various sectors of society for increasingly scarce resources, this strategy of boosting credit expansion appeared to policymakers as a depoliticized mechanism that could postpone economic catastrophe while pro-tecting state legitimacy.

This political account of the state's role in financialization understands financial expansion as ultimately deriving from the deep-seated crisis of post-war capitalism. Yet Streeck and Krippner push beyond the functionalism of other accounts by bringing the messy politics of financialization to the fore. States did not propel financial expansion as an automatic response to crisis, but rather financial liberalization is conceived of as a political strategy, without being necessarily coherent, to delay the myriad social and political quandaries arising from economic stagnation.

Financialization and the Contradictions of Liberal Governance

Existing accounts of financialization have, for the most part, inadequately framed the state's role in mediating processes of economic stagnation and financial expansion. For approaches that insist that the tremendous growth of the financial sector has come at the expense of the productive sectors of the economy, the state is understood through an interest-based and ideational lens as a tool wielded by financiers for their own ends or as an entity beholden to neoliberal ideology. For approaches that posit causality in the opposite direction—productive stagnation spurred financial growth—the state is a functional regulator of capitalist dynamics, mechanistically removing blockages to the circuit of capital. The state is either a vessel for factional interests/ideas or a rational automaton: in both cases, the politics of state governance matter little.

The path towards a better understanding of the governance of financialization must instead lie in the political account advanced by Streeck and Krippner. This approach takes the state seriously as a strategic actor, bringing into view the frenetic, haphazard nature of policymaking. However, while Streeck and Krippner provide rich insights into the politics of financialization, and thus point in the direction of a better conceptualization of the role of the state in this process, this theorization is incomplete. Krippner puts forward an extremely convincing empirical explanation of the US state's motivations in pursuing financial liberalization, yet this is not couched in a systematic theory of the capitalist state. The overriding emphasis throughout her account is on the dilemmas of governing the 'distributional struggle' over 'resources' between various social groups. The peculiar nature of this universal resource—capitalist money—and the contradictory imperatives entailed in the state's management of it, are not explored.

Streeck (2014: xv) too prefers to 'travel light in terms of theory', drawing from an array of schools of thought, from Jurgen Habermas's and Claus Offe's work on legitimation crises to Michał Kalecki's account of the political business cycle. Eschewing Karl Marx's insistence that capital is a social process, Streeck understands capital as an empirical class of people defined by their income and thus as a strategic political actor. This personalization of capital results in his troubling identification of the disciplinary mechanism of global markets with what he calls the *Marktvolk*, or people of the market—an inconspicuous, international community of investors that wields power over national states' finances (ibid.: 80–1). Further, against Marx, capitalism itself is not understood as inherently contradictory, but rather it runs up against something outside of itself: the principle of democracy. The governance challenge to which financial liberalization was a palliative response was, for Streeck, the capitalist class's rebellion against the encroachment of national democratic mechanisms into the private, profit-making sphere. As such, the piercing empirical insights of this political account of financialization are not developed into a critical theory of the fundamental structure of capitalist society nor the form of liberal governance that emerges to manage it.[2]

This book carves a new path to understanding the role of the state in propelling financialization. By examining perhaps the most iconic case of financial liberalization—Britain in the 1970s and 1980s—through an exploration of declassified government and Bank of England (hereon referred to simply as the Bank) documents, this account interrogates the practical dilemmas faced by policymakers in a way that interest-based, ideational, and functionalist accounts do not provide space for. In order to theorize this phenomenon, the book draws from the 'value-form' interpretation of Marx's critical project (see Pitts, 2019). In contrast to Streeck and Krippner, the governing dilemmas that policymakers faced are traced back to a contradiction that lies at the heart of capitalist society, and thus the challenges of governing financialization are framed as a particular expression of a more general paradox of liberal governance.

For Marx, capitalism is a profoundly dominating and contradictory social system. The structure of capitalism is such that people have no direct obligations to one another—they are formally autonomous, private individuals. Yet they also lack direct access to the means of subsistence. To survive, people are thus forced onto the market to socialize with one another through money-mediated commodity exchange. However, this form of human socialization accidentally unleashes a powerful logic of economic competition, compelling the members of capitalist society to produce more goods and services in less time. The 'law of value' is what Marx (1976: 294) terms this dominating pressure exerted upon all market participants, forcing them to raise their labour productivity or else face collapse. While this dynamic results in a growing abundance of material wealth, it tends to plunge the social system into crisis by flooding markets with commodities and driving down prices and profitability. Such crises ultimately occur, Marx insists, because in capitalist society value does not equal material wealth—value

---

[2] See Jerome Roos's critique of Streeck's work (2019).

instead represents the labour time required to produce that wealth. Faced with this impersonal form of domination, which derives not from any elite group but from the basic money relations of capitalist society itself, people rebel. Humans prove to be imperfect capitalist subjects, regularly rejecting the dictates of the law of value, as it places socially synthetic restrictions on the meeting of human needs, demands, and aspirations (Holloway, 2015). The actual development of capitalist society, then, is not the execution of predetermined social laws, but rather an everyday struggle between the abstract imperatives of value relations and concrete assertions of human need.

The reproduction of such a society is a matter of state (Bonefeld, 2014; Clarke, 1991). By policing property rights, providing the institutional framework for market competition, and managing money, states prove themselves to be constitutive of capitalist society—not perched outside of it, smoothing out its inconsistencies. Further, through the creation and governance of international monetary regimes, states establish the law of value as a *global* logic that in turn imposes itself back upon them with crushing force. Governments occupying the state apparatus are therefore subject to a decentred, dominating pressure that, while it appears external, is in fact self-generated. The fundamental contradiction of capitalist society—the contradiction between the impersonal pressure to continually raise labour productivity and real human needs—therefore appears to policymakers as a scalar contradiction between the world economy and national politics (Bonefeld and Holloway, 1995).[3] States must ensure the competitive viability of the national economy on world markets, yet they must simultaneously maintain their political legitimacy by addressing their domestic population's concerns. This is a perennial antinomy of capitalist state governance, reflected within the canon of liberal political economy, from Adam Smith onwards, as a deep anxiety about the socially disruptive effects of unfettered market competition.

In attempting to navigate this impasse, this book argues that states necessarily have recourse to two types of strategy. The first, *depoliticized discipline*, seeks to rationalize domestic social relations in line with world competitive dictates in a manner that shields policymakers from popular backlash (Burnham, 2001). This is achieved by establishing 'automatic rules or pilots' for economic governance, so as to grant the state autonomy from political pressures and legitimacy concerns (Bulpitt, 1986: 28). This strategy finds its clearest theoretical expression in the neoliberal claim that the process of market adjustment must be insulated from popular interference by a strong, depoliticized state (Slobodian, 2018). The second strategy, *palliation*, entails a recognition that questions of legitimacy cannot simply be banished through clever legislation. If discipline is the only weapon in its arsenal, the state flirts with provoking mass upheaval that could threaten what

---

[3] Streeck takes the latter tension at face value, rather than understanding it as 'mode of existence' of a deeper contradiction within capitalism itself (Marx, 1976: 255).

John Maynard Keynes (2013: 380) called 'the destruction of existing economic forms in their entirety'. As such, states must often 'buy time' by employing palliative measures that violate the norms of rules-based governance in order to delay global competitive pressures, with the ultimate objective of warding off the spectre of popular revolt. Of course, this strategy of postponement also has its limits, as the necessity to compete on global markets cannot be delayed indefinitely without resorting to autarky. Consequently, state authorities tend to employ both depoliticized discipline *and* palliation strategies—in sequence or simultaneously—in an attempt to reconcile the adherence to the autonomous logic of capitalism with the creation of a legitimate national political project.

Through an extensive analysis of declassified state archives, this book argues that British financial liberalization during the critical period of the 1970s and the 1980s can best be understood through this lens. During these years, the profitability crisis that plagued global capitalism was expressed in many advanced capitalist nations as the paradoxical phenomenon of stagflation. British stagflation began to accelerate in the late 1960s, exacerbating Britain's already uncompetitive position in the world economy, and resulting in worsening balance of payments crises and speculation against the pound. From the late 1970s until the early 1980s, Britain's experience of the profitability crisis took a new form, as the IMF's bailout and North Sea oil generated inflows of foreign currency that inflated the price of sterling. The strong pound ensured that Britain no longer faced repeated currency crises, yet it worsened the recessionary conditions at home by making exporters even less competitive, with profit rates remaining desperately low and inflation high. This intractable, drawn-out downturn was experienced by successive British governments as what Offe (1976) usefully terms a 'crisis of crisis management'. The usual policy levers of post-war governance proved less and less effective, yet attempts to mount a radical break with the so-called 'post-war consensus' brought governments into direct conflict with an increasingly militant trade union movement. As Prime Minister Edward Heath's special adviser commented in 1971, 'our present situation is one which, almost by definition, conventional measures cannot resolve'.[4]

Financial liberalization policies constituted attempts to navigate this unknown territory and the political challenges it presented. It is important to note that the term *liberalization* is preferable to *deregulation* for capturing the nature of the policy changes that unleashed financial expansion (Cerny, 1993; Vogel, 1996). Taken as a whole, such policies did not constitute the abandonment of state regulation but rather a change in the *form* of regulation—from one that seeks to bend financial markets to serve various predetermined ends to one that promotes the organization of financial activity around the principles of competition and profitability. This book studies four of the most important financial liberalizations

---

[4] TNA T338/39, Comment by Reading, 10 February 1971.

during this period: the 1971 CCC measures, the 1977–79 abolition of exchange controls, the 1986 Big Bang, and the 1986 FSA. These liberalizations were part of broader strategies pursued by British governments, from Heath to Thatcher, to respond to the national manifestations of the global profitability crisis. They were attempts to manage both the impersonal domination of a system of perpetual competition mired in deep crisis, and the political imperative to placate a population that was unwilling to sacrifice its needs at the altar of national competitiveness. Financial liberalization measures were elements of wider strategies intended to either discipline national social relations in line with world market standards, while neutralizing domestic political backlash, or postpone these competitive pressures into the future in order to maintain governing legitimacy. These measures were sometimes relatively successful and other times woeful failures—yet they always generated unintentional knock-on effects and new patterns of development that governments would later have to reckon with.

This book emphasizes the short-term orientation and fundamentally pragmatic nature of the British state's role in propelling financialization. This stands in contrast to functionalist approaches that insist on the state's automatic mediation of the dual processes of economic crisis and financial expansion. There is very little evidence to suggest that the British state intended to forge a new, long-term growth paradigm centred around financial accumulation. Such perspectives fail to grasp the conflictual pressures upon the state generated by the dynamics of capitalist society, and thus overlook the messy strategizing that is inherent to liberal governance. Yet neither was financial liberalization chiefly designed to benefit the City's global business prospects. The City's flourishing was a concern of the state insofar as it contributed to Britain's economic balances with the rest of the world. The interest-based and ideational approaches—which suggest that financial liberalization was an expression of the state's capture by financial elites and imbuement with neoliberal ideas—do not fully capture the state's role in financialization. Such personalized critiques of the politics of financialization are inadequate to their object. Many of them interpret the abstract, impersonal domination of capitalist social relations as the personal domination of a nefarious class of financial actors, and thus their theory of the state's propulsion of financialization is a theory of a corrupted state. This book puts forward a more troubling contention: the politics that drove financialization were a conjunctural expression of the more general dynamics of governing capitalism's foundational contradictions.

Plan of the Book

In order to grasp the broader role of states in spurring processes of financialization, this book explores the governing motivations that underpinned the British state's policies of financial liberalization in the 1970s and 1980s. The bulk of the book therefore consists of a fine-grained historical analysis of archival documents. This includes declassified government files held at the UK's National Archives, which detail policy debates taking place within the Prime Minister's office, the Treasury, and various branches of the British state during this period of transformative change. Further, the Bank's declassified archives shed new light on the discussions occurring within the central bank's Court of Governors, as well as this institution's relationships with other parts of the state apparatus, while crucial financial liberalization measures were being formulated. To supplement the analysis, the Confederation of British Industry (CBI) and Trades Union Congress (TUC) archives, housed at the University of Warwick's Modern Records Centre, were also explored. By carefully tracing the archival record, alongside an examination of a wealth of secondary sources, this book reveals novel insights into the manner in with British policymakers pursued financial liberalization in an attempt to traverse the various obstacles generated by the profitability crisis.

Before proceeding with the empirical discussion, this book sets out the theoretical framework in Chapter 2. This chapter argues that the form of social domination peculiar to capitalism does not simply emanate from a particular elite group or institution, but rather derives from the very monetized social relations that constitute capitalist society. Averages of labour productivity come to dominate market participants, pressing them to produce more in less time—a decentred social logic that Marx terms the law of value. This dynamic creates powerful pressures for the classification of society into flexible, market-dependent producers, while simultaneously creating a tendency towards falling average profitability and thus crisis. The actual course of capitalist development is characterized by a violent struggle between this impersonal form of domination and people's everyday affirmation of their social needs.

States actively establish this system on a global scale through the creation and governance of national money and international exchange rate regimes. Despite reproducing world market relations, these same relations in turn force national policymakers to maintain their territories' competitiveness or face a range of impersonal sanctions. Yet state authorities must also maintain their political legitimacy by responding to the wishes of their domestic polities. This contradiction between world market viability and national legitimacy is heightened in moments of global crisis. Policymakers, this chapter argues, manage this dilemma by employing governing strategies that fall on a spectrum between palliation and depoliticized discipline. Much can be learned about these opposed governing strategies from an engagement with the neoliberal and Keynesian strands of liberal political economy, which articulate well the deep-seated tension between continual market adjustment and social stability, and the need for political authorities to reconcile the two. The financial liberalizations studied in this book should be understood as elements of these broader governing strategies.

Chapter 3 acts as a bridge between the theoretical lens described above and the in-depth archival analysis in the subsequent chapters. This chapter puts forward a novel historical categorization of British stagflation, by identifying two distinct phases within Britain's experience of the global profitability crisis. The first, from 1967 to 1977, was characterized by low rates of profit, rising inflation, and repeated current account imbalances that resulted in currency crises. The second, from 1977 to 1983, still saw low profitability and high inflation, but the rising price of sterling ensured that there were no sterling crises. The chapter then details how governments combined governing strategies of depoliticized discipline and palliation in different ways during these two periods in order to navigate the contradictory imperatives of global competitiveness and domestic legitimacy. Policies of financial liberalization constituted attempts to support these strategies.

Chapter 4 explores the 1971 CCC measures, which saw the scrapping of most of the state's direct controls over credit creation within the economy. Following the 1967 sterling devaluation, Harold Wilson's government sought to launch a sustained recovery in the balance of payments by depressing domestic consumption and boosting exports, in order to bring UK competitiveness in line with world averages during the early stages of the profitability crisis. Monetary policy was enlisted in support of this strategy, as the state authorities sought to restrict credit for personal consumption and extend credit to exporters—a mix of disciplining and palliation measures. Yet the existing monetary toolkit, which relied on the state authorities more or less directly intervening in the allocation of private credit, provoked a growing backlash from broad swathes of British society. This politicization of monetary policy compounded the functional inadequacies of the existing system, which was becoming increasingly antiquated as new forms of banking institutions emerged. The CCC proposals—a brainchild of the Bank— sought to resolve these problems by giving the market mechanism a much greater role in credit allocation and thus allowing the state to govern at arm's length. Despite initial reservations, this policy gained the support of the Treasury and the Conservative government, partly because they believed it would allow them to enforce the painful shift of credit resources from persons to exporting companies while veiling the state's hand in the process. CCC can thus be understood as a measure to depoliticize the state's enforcement of disciplining and palliation measures so as to better navigate the accelerating stagflation crisis.

Chapter 5 tackles the abolition of exchange controls in the years 1977–79—a liberalization that powerfully propelled the increase in global capital mobility. Following the IMF's 1976 loan to Britain, accompanied by a package of conditionalities, and the discovery and marketization of North Sea oil, the pound rapidly rose in price, which helped to combat inflation while further exacerbating the squeeze on exporters' profitability. With Britain's export sector facing disaster, this chapter demonstrates that the governments of James Callaghan and Thatcher endeavoured to gently depreciate sterling through exchange control relaxation and provide palliative relief to British firms. However, while the Callaghan government was ultimately impeded by their tense relations with the TUC and the possibility of a run on sterling orchestrated by flighty currency markets, the Thatcher administration was able to fully abolish exchange controls by emphasizing that this policy was not a beggar-thy-neighbour attempt at currency manipulation, but was rather motivated by laissez-faire conviction. The dismantling of exchange controls can thus be understood as a palliative measure to stave off the worst effects of the profitability crisis, masked with free market rhetoric.

Chapters 6 and 7 explore the liberalization of the London Stock Exchange (LSE) in 1986 that facilitated its transformation into a truly global financial centre. An anti-monopolies court case had been brought against the LSE in 1979 for its restrictive practices. Despite requests from the LSE's chairman, Thatcher refused to exempt it from this case, because this would clash with the government's pro-competition rhetoric. However, Chapter 6 argues that the government's stance changed following the implementation of the Medium Term Financial Strategy (MTFS)—Thatcher's monetarist experiment. MTFS, launched in 1980, was an attempt to defeat stagflation and reignite profitable capital accumulation by locking the government into a radically disciplinary policy straitjacket. However, this strategy of depoliticized discipline was reliant on a deeply ideological faith in the government's own ability to reduce the monetary aggregate £M3, which in reality proved extremely difficult. As such, MTFS resulted in an unprecedentedly deep recession without the commensurate fall in £M3 that would justify the economic pain. In order to rescue this strategy, the Thatcher administration relied on increasingly large debt sales on the LSE in order to soak up liquidity and artificially reduce the money supply. This in turn required that the normal functioning of the LSE was not interrupted by the anti-monopoly case. As such, in 1983, the government exempted the LSE from this case, on the condition that it voluntarily abolish certain restrictive practices—thus beginning the countdown to the 1986 Big Bang. The Thatcher government's liberalization of the LSE, then, was in large part a desperate attempt to rescue their failing strategy of depoliticized discipline.

Chapter 7 examines the 1986 FSA, which swept away much of the City's cartelistic, informal governance structure and instead instituted a comprehensive statutory framework that promoted global competition. Following a series of City scandals, the government commissioned legal expert Laurence Gower to assess the UK's securities regulations. His initial proposals for a statutory system of self-regulation, presided over by a government body, was received with anxiety by the government and Bank due to the increased political intervention in financial affairs that it would imply. However, following the 1983 decision that set in motion the Big Bang, it became clear to the government and Bank that the impending globalization of the City required a commensurate system of clear and impartial regulation. The fear remained, nevertheless, that in case of a financial crash in the City, a statutory regulatory system would leave the govern-ment on the hook for this crisis, potentially shattering its political legitimacy. The government and the Bank thus endeavoured to depoliticize Gower's proposals by inserting a non-governmental body between the government and the City, which would both absorb the blame for future financial crises and impede political intervention in informal Bank–City relations. The resultant FSA was thus an attempt to institute a form of depoliticized financial governance appropriate to the preceding fifteen years of financial liberalization.

Chapter 8 reiterates the key arguments and findings of the book. In addition, this chapter explores how the four liberalizations examined here impacted upon the trajectory of financialization in the late twentieth and early twenty-first centuries. Britain's liberalization of its financial sector boosted global capital mobility, and thus created powerful pressures on other states to follow suit, contributing to a dynamic of competitive deregulation that spread around the world. Further, the arm's-length, depoliticized design of the 1986 FSA generated an institutional path dependency, whereby future British systems of financial governance would take a similarly light-touch form. This meant that London would incubate a series of banking scandals in the 1990s, as well as being home to some of the riskiest financial practices exposed by the 2008 crisis. Finally, the growing financial flows unleashed by the liberalizations of the 1970s and 1980s were increasingly channelled into the housing market, resulting in Britain's particular dynamic of housing-centric financialization.

2

Framing Financialization and the State

'Liberalised finance tends to metastasise, like a cancer', wrote Martin Wolf (2019), the *Financial Times*'s chief economics commentator, in an extended assault on what he termed 'rigged capitalism'. Employing a similarly medical metaphor, another vivid account of financialization points to the growing control of financial logics over capitalist society: 'twenty-four-seven news broadcasts run a visual ticker-tape of stock prices at the bottom of their broadcast screens as if the modulations of equity prices were an EKG to the global body' (Martin, Rafferty, and Bryan, 2008: 124). Indeed, for critiques of financialization, the concept of *domination* is a recurring theme—that is, the domination of contemporary society by a rogue financial sector. The state too has fallen captive to the forces of financial domination, according to the interest-based and ideational approach to the politics of financialization. As the forces of financialization gathered pace, the halls of political power became subordinated to (and often populated by) an ascendant class of financiers and beholden to the policymaking norms that serve their interests. The British state, supposedly, is a case in point. As one account claims, during the Thatcher years 'City personnel, norms and practices came to dominate the main UK departments of economic management at every level' (Davis and Walsh, 2017: 40).

The functionalist approach to the state's role in financialization also puts the notion of domination at the centre of its analysis—not domination by one fraction of capital, but the dominating power of the capitalist class in general. In the context of economic crisis, policymakers automatically liberalized their financial sectors in order to allow capitalists to earn profits through speculative ventures. According to such accounts, states' propulsion of financialization can be explained by recognizing that capitalists have an effective 'veto over state policies in that their failure to invest at adequate levels can create major political problems for the state managers' (Block, 1987: 58). This leads to a conceptualization of the state as the cockpit of capitalism, with policymakers helping to steer the system towards a financialized mode of accumulation in order to avoid a capitalist investment strike. As Brenner (2009: 2–3; emphasis in original) tellingly commented, 'the continuation of capital accumulation has come *literally* to depend upon historic waves of speculation, carefully nurtured and publicly rationalized by state policy makers'.

The historical evidence presented in this book does not support either of these explanations. In fact, pulling back the veil on political decision-making processes

Governing Financialization: The Tangled Politics of Financial Liberalization in Britain. Jack Copley, Oxford University Press.
© Jack Copley 2022. DOI: 10.1093/oso/9780192897015.003.0002

in relation to financialization is startling in what it *does not* reveal. The archives do not reveal the cunning power of financial elites, the coordinated strength of the capitalist class, nor the ideological coherence of neoliberal strategies. Instead, the state appears as an ensemble of actors desperately responding to a series of real dilemmas through haphazard and often contradictory strategic initiatives. The concept of domination, as such, appears to be an unsuitable tool for examining the politics of financialization. If we can speak of it at all, the state appears dominated, simply put, by the chaos of modern economic life.

Yet this need not be the case, so long as domination is understood not simply as direct relations of coercion wielded by one group or institution over another, but as abstract relations of coercion wielded unintentionally by society against itself. It is this form of impersonal domination that Marx's value theory attempts to grasp. According to the value-form interpretation, Marx sought to explain how peoples' everyday social interactions, when mediated through capitalism's monetized relations, accidentally give rise to a dynamic system of crushing social constraints. More specifically, the subjects of capitalist society are pressed to continually augment their labour productivity or face personal ruin by powerful competitive forces that emerge from their individual market interactions. Attempts to reveal the source of such tyranny by seizing hold of the industrialist, the banker, or the politician reveal these people to be mere 'character masks' that are worn and discarded by an impersonal social force (Marx, 1976: 757). There are parallels here with Michel Foucault's theory of power as 'rooted deep in the social nexus' (2001: 343), with disciplining effects that circulate through society in a horizontal, 'capillary' manner, rather than being imposed from above (1995: 198). Yet while Foucault associates this form of domination somewhat ambiguously with Western modernity, Marx rigorously grounds it in capitalism's peculiar social relations (Postone, 1993: 159).

This chapter will argue that this theory of domination can best explain the British state's actions in furthering processes of financialization. The cash nexus that forms the substance of capitalist society is a political construction. States produce and police the web of capitalist money relations, both nationally and through the creation of international exchange rate systems. Yet in constructing the fabric of capitalist society, states unconsciously produce a competitive logic that imposes itself back upon them as a seemingly external economic imperative. States are not simply dominated by financial elites or the coordinated actions of the capitalist class. Rather, states are forced by the global monetary relations of their own making to continually augment the competitiveness of their territory or face a range of impersonal sanctions. Yet this unending pressure runs up against the need for the state to address the needs, demands, and aspirations of civil society. When this system lurches into deep crisis, as during the stagflation era that birthed financialization, the contradiction between the economic and political reproduction of the state intensifies.

The politics of financialization in Britain should be understood as the politics of navigating this dilemma—the counterposed pressures of capitalist competition and social needs—which appears to policymakers as a scalar tension between global market viability and national political legitimacy. The financial liberalizations that were deployed by the British state in this era formed part of two larger governing strategies: depoliticized discipline, which sought to restructure domestic social relations in line with the impersonal dictates of world capitalist relations; and palliation, which sought to temporarily hold these market pressures at bay in order to maintain domestic social order. As this chapter shows, much can be learned about these two strategies from a critical engagement with the canon of liberal political economy, beginning with Smith. Liberal thought contains a gnawing anxiety that the need for perpetual economic adjustment under capitalism may produce an unmanageable social order. While neoliberalism articulates the need for the state to restrain popular democratic forces through institutional design in order to enforce market adjustment, Keynesianism recognizes the limits of such depoliticized disciplining measures and advocates that the state ease people's suffering through palliative policies to keep them from dismantling the market itself. This chapter argues that both neoliberal and Keynesian thought partially express a fundamental truth about the contradictory pressures exerted upon the state in capitalist society. In other words, states do not simply employ strategies of depoliticized discipline and palliation because of the influence of neoliberal or Keynesian ideas respectively. Instead, neoliberal and Keynesian ideas articulate the real necessity for states to wield these strategies to manage the impersonal pressures of global competition and domestic political demands.

This theoretical lens throws into sharp relief the British state's pursuit of financial liberalization in the period under study. Various governments, forced to reconcile the abstract domination of the world market in a period of severe crisis with the need to maintain domestic legitimacy, turned to financial liberalization measures in an ad hoc fashion. These policies cannot be deduced from the lobbying or ideological forces exerted upon particular governments, nor did they form part of a coherent blueprint to financialize the British economy. Financial liberalizations instead constituted elements of wider strategies of depoliticized discipline and palliation, which themselves had unforeseen effects that later governments would have to navigate. Financialization is a retrospective characterization of the broad tendencies that emerged from this messy, contradictory governing process.

Money and Impersonal Domination

Sharp disagreements exist not only over the intricacies of Marx's value theory, but even over the sort of social puzzle that it seeks to address. For Hayek (1982b: 170),

Marx's adherence to a 'physical cause of value', namely labour, meant that he remained oblivious to the 'self-directing order' that characterized market activity, and instead wrote erroneously of the '"chaos" of capitalist production'. This is not simply a neoliberal smear, but in fact chimes with a prominent strand of Marxist thought that understands value as a transhistorical category, synonymous with wealth: 'historically in all forms of society it is labour that is the active creator of wealth' (Gamble and Walton, 1976: 113). Value, according to this reading, is a physiological substance—it represents humans' exertion of effort during the labour process (Carchedi, 2009: 150). Under capitalism, the bourgeoisie rigs this system, and seeks to wring unremunerated *surplus* value from the working class. According to this interpretation, Marx's theory serves as a transhistorical political slogan that demands the return of value back to its producers. Reflecting this commonly held notion, the economist Joan Robinson (1960: 23) commented: 'Marx believed that, under socialism, the labour theory of value would come into its own'.[1]

The value-form approach,[2] which this book adopts, turns this interpretation on its head. Value and wealth are not synonymous: value is one *form* of wealth that predominates in the fully monetized relations of capitalist society. Rather than a physical substance, value is a social web of interdependence formed when people exchange the products of their labour on the market. It is this social nexus—value—that subjects all actors in capitalist society to a decentred form of domination, pressing them to raise their labour productivity. People's monetized relations with one another give rise to a social universe that in turn directs their activities in an automatic fashion. According to this reading, Marx's value theory is designed to interrogate precisely the 'self-directing order' that Hayek castigated him for ignoring. Yet in contrast to Hayek's vision of capitalism as a seamless coordinating mechanism, Marx depicts an autonomized social system that is profoundly dominating, fundamentally contradictory, and that generates tendencies which erode its own foundations. Marx therefore provides a theory of social domination that can capture the nebulous yet binding pressures exerted upon the British state in the late postwar period, which policymakers responded to by employing financial liberalization measures.

---

[1] Postone (1993: 7) refers to this reading as 'Traditional Marxism', yet it is debatable whether this transhistorical interpretation could accurately be described as the dominant current within Marxist scholarship at any point.

[2] This book uses the label 'value-form' as shorthand for a diverse body of Marxist scholarship, including Isaak Rubin's early exegesis of Marx's value theory, certain scholars associated with the Frankfurt School, particularly Alfred Sohn-Rethel and Theodor Adorno, and various authors working within the broad milieu of the New Reading of Marx (Neue Marx-Lektüre), the Value Criticism (Wertkritik) group, and Open Marxism.

Value and Competition

The social fabric of capitalism is made up of money relations between private, market-dependent commodity owners. For Marx, this apparently innocuous fact entails a sort of social alchemy, whereby quality is reduced to quantity. During the process of commodity exchange, a product is equated with a certain amount of a generic substance: money. Money abstracts from the particular qualities of this product and the labour that produced it. As Georg Simmel (1971: 330) observed, money 'hollows out the core of things ... their uniqueness and incomparability ... They all rest on the same level and are distinguished only by their amounts'. The distinctive characteristics of goods (their size, weight, colour, etc.) and the unique attributes of the labour that created them (the rhythm of the work, the skills and tools employed, etc.) fall away and are replaced by a number. Indeed, through the lens of money, commodities are merely different crystallized quantities of 'human labour in the abstract' (Marx, 1976: 128). The social consequence of this process of abstraction is that types of human labour that would be otherwise incommensurable are rendered commensurable and their products exchangeable. Money thus provides a common language for the private producers within capitalism, uniting these formally independent units into a coherent society (Rubin, 1978). Crucially for Marx, this remarkable social mechanism emerges as the accidental result of the private endeavours of the atomized subjects of capitalist society when mediated through money (Marx, 1976: 167).

However, if money relations integrate the independent members of capitalist society, they also unleash a runaway dynamic that dominates them. In addition to equalizing different forms of labour, the social technology of money compares these working activities *in terms of time* (Bonefeld, 2010). When producers bring their commodities to market, they collectively and unconsciously establish average prices for particular commodities that reflect market-wide labour productivity averages. These productivity averages are then communicated back to individual producers by the market performance of their commodities. Those that produce above the mean pace and sell their commodities at the average market price will enjoy an above average profit rate; or, alternatively, they can set their commodity prices below the market average and capture greater market share, while still remaining profitable. Yet those that fall behind in the productivity race and continue to sell their commodities at the market average price will struggle to make a profit. They may consequently set their commodity prices above the market average in order to cover their costs, but in doing so they risk ceding market share to their competitors and thus flirt with economic ruin. While such productivity norms are mere abstractions that arise from the monetized working practices of the whole community, they nevertheless confront each market participant as a binding regulative law that impels them to speed up or perish: 'this abstraction has the same ontological rigor of facticity as a car that runs you over'

(György Lukács quoted in Lotz, 2014: 53; Sohn-Rethel, 1978). For this reason, the clock looms large over the capitalist workplace.

Governed by these seemingly independent forces of their own creation, the members of capitalist society are thrown into an unending competitive struggle for economic existence. This temporal imperative presses the owners of society's productive capacities to attempt to wring every possible moment of labour time from their workforce while holding their wages at subsistence level. Recognizing that the economic viability of this society is proportional to the disempowerment of its labouring population (Marx, 1976: 1062), states and political authorities at various scales are compelled to continually mould people into a malleable, market-dependent proletariat. This is pursued through the disruption of non-waged, non-marketized forms of subsistence, the commodification of social goods, the imposition of competitive wages and terms of employment, and manifold other mechanisms. John Holloway (2002: 42) insightfully terms this process 'class-ification', indicating that this regimentation and disciplining of the population is never an achieved fact, but must be consistently undertaken anew in response to competitive dictates and social struggles.

It is this dynamic that Marx sought to capture with his theory of value. Qualitatively, value denotes the relationship of radical equality between diverse types of human labour that emerges when the products of labour are exchanged for money. Quantitatively, the value of a particular commodity equals the average time necessary for its production within the entire market nexus. Surplus value refers to the time that the working class spends producing commodities *in excess of the time they spend producing the commodities that they consume*—a surplus of capitalist society's total labour time that is distributed among competing firms as money profits. The 'law of value' signifies the motion of this system: by socializing through the market, the atomized agents of capitalist society accidentally create an inter-dependent social web in which labour productivity averages act as a whip, forcing them to produce more in less time. This dynamic pressure finds its full realization as capital: the continual expansion of value based upon the exploitation of the popu-lation's labouring capacity. Marx's value theory is therefore a theory of a peculiar form of self-imposed, temporal domination. This domination does not ultimately derive from any particular institution or elite group, but rather emanates imperson-ally from the monetized social relations themselves. The agents of capitalist society unwittingly create a social logic that constrains them: 'Their own collisions with one another produce an alien social power standing above them' (Marx, 1993: 197).

Wealth and Crisis

This theory of impersonal domination implies a radical rethinking of the concept of wealth in capitalist society. As mentioned earlier, wealth and value are not synonymous for Marx. Rather, he insists that 'use-values'—tangible, useful things—'constitute the material content of wealth, whatever its form may be' (Marx, 1976: 126). Wealth exists in every type of society: it is the result of the 'richness of human creativity' exercised upon nature (Holloway, 2015: 8). In contrast, value is the historically peculiar form that wealth takes in the fully monetized social relations of capitalist society. More specifically, value signifies the labour time required on average for the production of wealth under capitalism. For example, if labour productivity doubles in the furniture industry, then the value of a table will fall by half, yet the physical qualities of the table as an item of wealth will be unchanged. Wealth and value are therefore in contradiction with one another. Rising labour productivity creates ever more wealth in terms of useful goods, but it diminishes the value of each good in terms of the labour required to produce it and thus the money it can command on the market. Moishe Postone (1993: 289) usefully terms this capitalism's 'treadmill effect', whereby the wealth-producing capacities of society speed up while the magnitude of value created stays the same. Like someone running on a treadmill, capitalist society accelerates in terms of the scale of material output but remains glued to the spot in terms of the production of value. This contradiction is the basis of capitalist crises.

As already established, capitalism's very monetized social relations let loose an autonomous logic that sets individual producers against one another in a battle to raise their labour productivity. While productivity increases can be secured through the intensification of the work process, this strategy runs up against the physical limit of human exhaustion. Technological innovation, however, can unleash potentially limitless productivity gains. For this reason, the general trajectory of capitalist production entails an increase in the value of fixed capital and material inputs relative to the value of wages (Marx, 1976: 762). Capitalist development is therefore synonymous with automation. This results in unimaginable increases in material affluence, yet it generates dire problems for the inner workings of this social system. Although labour-saving technology boosts the competitiveness of the firms that first introduce the new machinery, when these productivity gains are widely adopted the result may be a depression in the average profit rate across the economy. This is because rising labour productivity means that more commodities can be produced in the same amount of time, leading to falling commodity prices as firms compete for market share through price-cutting and rising supply outstrips demand. This may result in a rising *mass* of profits, as more commodities are produced and sold, but a declining *rate* of profit, as the price of each commodity declines relative to production costs. Ultimately, what Marx (1981: 319) called the 'tendency of the general rate of profit to fall' is a reflection of the decline in the labour time expended, per commodity, within the whole economy.

If this dynamic is left unchecked, and the profit rate continues to trend downwards, conditions of stagnation emerge. The heightened labour productivity results in an oversupply of commodities that tests the limits of market demand, all except the most competitive firms are incentivized to reduce their investment and capacity utilization, and market laggards may take on a growing volume of debt or be pushed into bankruptcy. This may not directly result in financial crises, characterized by a sharp contraction in credit, but these stagnant conditions do increase the likelihood and destructiveness of such crashes as dwindling profits call into question the solvency of debtors (Clarke, 1994: 59). However, Marx (1981) identified several counter-tendencies that can arrest falling profitability. These include the cheapening of labour, machinery, and input materials due to rising productivity, the heightened exploitation of workers, the expansion of global trade that provides access to cheap resources and new markets, the increase of capital's turnover time, or the large-scale devaluation of capital and immiseration of workers through crisis. The interaction of the tendency and its counter-tendencies means that the falling profit rate is not a mechanical 'law'. It is rather an explanation for the frenzied struggle of capitalist production, whereby enterprises battling to raise their individual profitability tend to undermine general profitability, forcing them to further intensify their pursuit of profit through myriad strategies, in an unending 'cumulative spiral' (Clarke, 1994: 242).

The fact that there exists a tendentially inverse relationship between capitalist productivity and profitability hints at a deep social paradox. Driven by an impersonal logic of their own accidental creation, the private agents of capitalist society chase the expansion of value and in the process threaten to erode it. Counterintuitively, tremendous increases in human ingenuity and productive potential jeopardize the production of value. Capitalist crises therefore occur alongside enormous stocks of unsold goods, left to gather dust because they cannot be translated from mere material wealth into money. Value, as a principle of social organization, becomes increasingly inadequate to the world of tremendous material abundance that it has produced.

The Antagonism of Value

This value-form interpretation of Marx's project tends to portray a society in which meaningful human agency is foreclosed. In their attempts to address their needs and realize their ambitions through the market, people create their own social straitjacket. Yet in contrast to this closed system—as it is portrayed by scholars such as Postone (1993)—the actual trajectory of capitalist development is not simply characterized by the working out of 'value logic', with real people dragged in tow. Instead, people continually challenge this impersonal form of domination, and in its place assert other principles of social organization and alternative types of social wealth.

To live in capitalist society is to confront both the tremendous productive capacity and the fundamental social inadequacy of value as a form of wealth. Capitalist society produces a dazzling abundance of material wealth, yet the very condition for its production—the profitability of capital—dictates that people have their access to these things restricted in the form of competitive wages. Capitalism tantalisingly offers the realization of all worldly aspirations, but the price of admission is the subordination of human autonomy to the dictates of the law of value. This price is too high, and, as such, value is regularly shrugged off as an ill-fitting form of wealth (Holloway, 2015). People in their everyday lives refuse to be classified into mere producers of profit for a blind social imperative, and more generally refuse the transformation of various social goods into vessels for the realization of profit. This takes a variety of forms: from struggles for a living wage and public services, to demands that the environment be protected from resource extraction, to chauvinistic attempts to defend the national or racial community against economic globalization. Anti-value, then, can have a progressive or regressive bent—it is not the monopoly of any particular political tendency.

This dynamic of struggle rears its head at every level and every moment of capitalist reproduction. Yet periods of crisis intensify this antagonism. As crises accelerate, the contradiction between value and wealth contained within the commodity is expressed on the surface of society as a series of paradoxes: the need for mass redundancies counterposed to the intensification of labour for those who keep their jobs; dwindling profits counterposed to enormous productive capacities; homelessness counterposed to empty, unsaleable housing stock; hunger counterposed to the overproduction of food. Pressures to discipline society, so as to raise the profit rate and rekindle investment, run up against the real needs and aspirations of society in all its diversity—aspirations that cannot be synchronized with the booms and busts of capitalist development. As David McNally (2004: 202) observes, the antagonism that marks capitalist society is a 'fundamental conflict between different life-projects': the project of capital—'accumulation as an end in itself'; and the project of human beings—concrete needs, wants, purposes.

In sum, domination in capitalist society is not simply exercised by powerful social groups, whether finance capital in particular or the capitalist class in general. Rather, the agents of capitalist society accidentally create a rod for their own backs. By forging capitalist social relations, they unleash a dynamic of impersonal domination that compels them to compete over labour productivity, inadvertently drives the social system into crisis, and provokes backlash as people reject the market's dictates and instead assert their needs. Thus far, this dynamic has been discussed in abstraction from the international state system. The following section will show that states do not stand outside of capitalism, administering it from on high, but instead the global domination of the law of value is reproduced precisely *through* the actions of states.

The Political Constitution of the Law of Value

Global capitalism appears to states as an external force. Foreign trade, investment, and speculative flows buffet national economic indicators, pressing policymakers to adjust the national economy in accordance with changing world market circumstances. Yet despite this appearance of externality, global capitalism is fundamentally a political creation. Via the construction and governance of monetary relations at the world scale—from the policing of territorial currencies to ensuring their mutual exchangeability through international monetary regimes—states forge and manage the infrastructure of the law of value. Global capitalism thus simultaneously relies upon states for its functioning *and* subordinates states to its impersonal dictates. The state's relationship to the world capitalist market is one of an institution that loses control of the very creature it gives life to. It is in this sense that we can speak of the domination of states under capitalism—not domination by an elite faction (finance capital or otherwise), but the domination of the state by an automatic social mechanism of its own making.

If the law of value is established and communicated through money relations between private, market-dependent commodity owners, then in concrete terms these monetary relations are constituted by an extensive quilt of different forms of money, stitched together into a single financial network. As Perry Mehrling (2013a) correctly observes, on the national scale, money refers to a hierarchy of social commitments, from financial securities, to bank deposits, to the state-issued currency. While not all of these money-forms are directly issued by the state, their credibility and their acceptance as money relies on their relationship to political authority. Law casts 'the benevolent glow of coercive enforceability' over different types of money (Pistor, 2013: 323). The state polices this hierarchical money chain, which forms the connective tissue between the disparate parts of the economic whole. Value is in a very real sense 'a practice of government' (Bonefeld, 2014: 183).

Yet the state's currency is not the final rung in the money ladder. In order to integrate the national territory into the global market, territorial currencies must be made commensurable with one another. Through the system of international exchange rates, the various national money hierarchies are finally linked together on the world stage, forming one global force field of labour equalization and competition (Burnham, 1990: 1). Through the commensurability of the Renminbi and the Real, for example, the labour of an electronics manufacturing worker in Guangdong, China and the labour of a combine harvester operator in Mato Grosso, Brazil become instantly comparable in purely quantitative terms. By equating these two currencies (at a specific ratio), the computer hard drive and the bushel of soybeans become equated as different quantities of generic wealth, and the diverse types of labour that produced them are equated as merely different amounts of abstract labour. Such equality brings about a radical socialization of people at opposite ends of the globe, resulting in a 'butterfly effect' of sorts, as an increase in labour productivity in one Chinese factory exerts pressures (however small) upon other market participants to boost their own productivity. People become socialized under conditions of desperate competition—a kind of anti-social socialization. A world community is forged, but one of mutual anxiety and solipsism. Value is thus established as a global form of time-based wealth consti-tuted by a colossal money network with no definite locus.

The intercourse of different territorial currencies sets their corresponding political territories against one another in unrelenting economic competition. Through the exchange rate, the weight of global productivity averages directly presses down upon national economies: 'just as the value form transmits the competitive discipline of capitalist relations to individual capitals through the role of money, it also transmits global capitalist discipline to national states through the international system of exchange rates' (Kettell, 2004: 23). For states, the balance of payments acts as a crude indicator of the competitive viability of their territory in relation to world market norms. If a national territory falls behind in the global productivity race and fails to maintain average profitability of capital, exports from this territory will be harder to competitively price, the current account of the balance of payments may fall into deficit, and the stock of foreign currency reserves will be gradually depleted. This 'reserve constraint' ultimately 'disciplines the behaviour of the deficit country' (Mehrling, 2013b: 357). The generation of foreign currency inflows through national economic competitiveness is a necessary prerequisite to enjoy the fruits of global capitalism. If the balance of payments falls further into deficit and foreign reserves dwindle, the likelihood grows of a 'sudden speculative attack' against the national currency that 'eliminates the last of the reserves' as the state attempts to defend the price of its currency (Krugman, 1979: 311–12). The national territory thus stands at the precipice of a total halt to its international payments, the collapse of its territorial money, and a fundamental crisis of political authority.

Confronted by these impersonal world market sanctions, the government of the day comes under tremendous pressure to wield the state apparatus to ensure average profitability within its territory. Failure to do so can result in the govern-ment's discrediting or a deeper crisis of the state's ability to 'define and enforce collectively binding decisions on the members of a society in the name of their common interest' (Jessop, 1990: 341). As Benjamin Cohen (1982: 460) writes, 'national governments have two basic policy options' when faced with a payments disequilibrium: pursue what is called 'adjustment' in the sterilized language of economics, or secure external financing. Adjustment implies the painful discip-lining of domestic social relations in line with global competitivity standards. The various institutions of the state apparatus are required to leap into action to secure national economic viability. This may include attempts to disorganize and cheapen labour, cut state spending that is not directly aimed at boosting the profitability of capital, tighten monetary policy to create a deflationary economic climate, or produce a culture of civic responsibility premised upon the acceptance of economic discipline in the name of national prosperity. Discipline may also be pursued through the devaluation or depreciation of the national currency, which Fred Hirsch (1965: 77–80) terms a 'hoax on the public at large', as it promotes 'a tightening of belts by every family in the land' without having to impose an unpopular 'straight cut in wages'. Yet if adjustment proves too painful and politically toxic, the state may be forced to finance its current account deficit through inflows of foreign currency. While this can take the form of inward portfolio and foreign direct investment, territories suffering from low profitability will be less likely to attract these flows. In such cases, the state may be forced to rely on borrowing from global financial markets, international organizations, or foreign central banks. The costs of securing such financing 'are borne not in the present but in the future', which allows national governments temporary reprieve from the political implications of failure to achieve global competitiveness (Cohen, 1982: 460). However, this strategy also implies rising national indebtedness and the state's increasing subjection to the metrics of financial credibility. Ultimately, the wolf returns to the door.

In periods of global crisis, as individual firms' quest for profit through the introduction of labour-saving technology erodes general profitability, these constraints upon states intensify. The costs of falling behind in the competitive race increase, the necessity for the state to discipline society according to the imperatives of world value relations becomes more desperate, and the state consequently risks shattering the illusionary basis of its own ideological reproduction, namely that it is a malleable reflection of the democratic will of society. As discussed earlier in this chapter, the contradiction at the heart of capitalism between the production of material goods and the production of value drives this form of society towards crisis. The necessity for firms to increase productivity generates tendencies towards the overproduction of commodities, general price deflation, and a decline in the average rate of profit. This mechanism is not a pure market phenomenon, but rather it plays out through the actions of states (Hirsch, 1978). Under competitive pressure to raise national productivity through labour-saving innovation, policymakers strategize to boost national productivity through various mechanisms, including the shift of state financial support from low to high productivity sectors, the development of labour-saving technology through the public education system, or the creation of economies of scale through state-backed mergers. While this may succeed in boosting the productivity of a particular economic territory, it results in downward pressure on profitability for the system as a whole. As the global downturn gathers pace, states are pressed to respond by enhancing their national competitivity to keep their territory's head above water, which further exacerbates the crisis on the world scale. Territories with particularly low profitability are faced with a widening gap between popular economic expectations and existing market conditions. As such, political compromises come under growing strain and the state's tools of macroeconomic management become rapidly antiquated. The crisis of capitalist social relations is expressed in the state sphere as a 'crisis of crisis management' (Offe, 1976).

The law of value, as it operates on the world stage, is a fundamentally political construction. States and state-delegated political authorities are responsible for the construction of the global monetary relations that instantaneously communicate changes in labour productivity to all world market participants and in turn set them against one another in desperate competition. However, it is important not to confuse this 'market making' role of the state with the notion of state *control* over the capitalist market. While states directly produce certain forms of money and regulate all other forms, their actions create an alienated logic of economic competition that in turn dominates them.[3] By governing the domestic chain of money-forms that ends with the national currency, and in turn plugging this national currency into the global system of exchange rates, states subject their territories to the impersonal dictates of the law of value and its built-in crisis tendencies. It is this compelling force—fundamentally more constraining than the lobbying efforts of financiers or the veto power of capitalist investors—with which the British state struggled during the period of financial liberalization studied in this book. The following section will explore how states battle to reconcile compliance with this form of intangible domination with the need to respond to the very tangible demands of their citizenry.

The Paradox of Liberal Governance

How should states govern this autonomous logic of their own creation? This question is a central preoccupation of liberal political economy, defined by Smith (1999: 5) as 'a branch of science of a statesman or legislator'. Indeed, a continuous vein of trepidation runs through the liberal canon regarding the counterposed needs for the state to both manage the perpetual economic adjustments required by market competition and construct a legitimate national political order. As such, this book argues that a critical reading of the liberal tradition offers piercing, if partial, insights into the contradictory nature of capitalist state governance and in turn the form of politics that birthed financialization.

Awed by capitalism's productive potential, Smith argued that the wealth of nations is achieved through the ever more exact division of labour and application

---

[3] Chartalist approaches that insist money is a 'creature of the state' thus articulate a half-truth: see Beggs (2017) and McNally (2014).

of machinery in production, which is itself propelled by the competitive impulses of the market mechanism. Society is regimented and set in motion towards a world of universal opulence, not by the commands of a central authority but by the self-interested endeavours of countless private actors, acting as if directed by an 'invisible hand' (1999: 32). Yet as Max Weber (1978: 336–7) highlights, this market system 'could not develop except in the frame of a public legal order' emanating from the 'universalist coercive institution' of the state. The 'free economy', according to the liberal tradition, 'amounts to a political practice' (Bonefeld, 2016: 9). For Hayek (1982a: 109), the unconscious coordination of the market system, which he called the 'catallaxy', can only operate within a state-policed legal framework: 'A catallaxy is thus the special kind of spontaneous order produced by the market through people acting within the rules of the law of property, tort and contract.' The establishment of such a self-organizing market society, 'bound only by abstract rules of conduct' laid down by the state, was 'the greatest discovery mankind ever made' (Hayek, 1982a: 136).

Despite this triumphalism, liberal political economy is also characterized by a gnawing anxiety concerning the problem of the integration of the human subject into this self-moving system. The functioning of the market depends on people's continual willingness to adjust their activities to its competitive dictates, regardless of the lived consequences. Against the meritocratic rhetoric of capitalism's more crass defenders, Hayek (1982a: 72; emphasis in original) writes that often in a 'market order ... the return of people's efforts do *not* correspond to recognizable merit'. Whether an individual's economic efforts are rewarded with income or not is determined by the relationship between their activities and the conditions established on the market, about which 'they could not have known' in advance (ibid.). The subjects of market society must therefore accept the possibility of personal economic ruin, 'in spite of the best efforts of which they were capable', and react stoically by adjusting their actions in accordance with the directions communicated to them through market signals (ibid.). The 'content of market ethics', for Weber (1978: 636), is one's acceptance of the market's 'matter-of-factness' and the disciplining of one's behaviour 'according to rational legality and ... respect [for] the formal inviolability of a promise once given'.

Humanity has proven consistently unworthy of this lofty ideal. People regularly refuse to remould their lives in accordance with the unending competitive dictates of the market—they are 'sticky', in the language of Keynesian economics. Hayek (1982a) attributed this refusal to adjust to a hangover from what he called 'tribal society'. Keynes (2019: 176), however, offered a more incisive reflection on this mismatch between ideal market ethics and real human behaviour: 'Men will not always die quietly.' The dark underside of the clinical workings of the invisible hand is the immiseration of great swathes of people who fail the test of market viability. The existential danger for liberal political economy is that these people 'in their distress may overturn the remnants of organization, and submerge civilization itself in their attempts to satisfy desperately the overwhelming needs of the individual' (ibid.). Liberalism is haunted by 'the poverty, the looming disorder ... the revolutionary or chaotic popular menace' that is produced by the normal functioning of capitalism (Mann, 2018: 210). The challenge that the liberal tradition sets itself, as a policy science, is to theorize how the state should construct the institutional conditions for the operation of world market forces without generating an ungovernable social order.

This governance paradox identified by the liberal canon is real and intractable. Further, it *appears* to state policymakers in the form of a conflict between two different scales: global economy and national politics (Bonefeld and Holloway, 1995). States are not simply hemmed in by the global imperatives of the law of value—they must also respond to the wishes of their citizens. Whether by direct or indirect sanction, electoral defeat or riot, the state is pressed to live up to its image as 'the embodiment of the general interest of society and as the neutral arbiter of all particularistic claims' (Clarke, 1988: 128). Governments are thus torn between constructing domestic political projects that can win elections and ensuring the viability of the national economy on the world stage, without which electoral promises are meaningless. During global profitability crises, this dilemma intensifies. As policymakers struggle to rationalize domestic capitals, discipline the national labour market, and retrench state expenditure, society attempts to evade this counter-intuitive 'belt-tightening' by asserting heterogeneous needs, expressed as growing industrial unrest, protest, political support for populist parties, increasing demand for credit, etc. The need for the state to confine 'the production of use values within the bounds of profitability' becomes increasingly difficult to reconcile with its ostensible role as the political medium through which society advances its real aspirations and needs (Burnham, 2006: 75).

Liberal political economy correctly articulates a fundamental tension at the heart of capitalist society, one that policymakers perceive as a conflict between global economy and national politics. Yet for the Marxist tradition, this apparent mismatch between global market forces and domestic political obligations is but the surface appearance of a deeper contradiction between capitalism's impersonal, competitive dictates and tangible human needs—between value and wealth. In place of a genuine accommodation of these contradictory imperatives, states develop governance strategies that allow them to construct a facade of reconciliation, which will be examined next.

Between Depoliticized Discipline and Palliation

Hemmed in by the global workings of the law of value and the need to maintain a stable domestic social order, particularly in moments of generalized crisis, states have recourse to two forms of governing strategy: depoliticized discipline and palliation. While the former seeks to impose economic adjustment upon the national territory while strategically neutralizing popular backlash, the latter recognizes the need to meet domestic political demands by temporarily holding world market pressures at bay. The policies of financial liberalization studied in this book constituted elements of these broader strategies.

This chapter argues that these strategies are well articulated by two divergent strands of liberal political economy: neoliberalism/ordoliberalism and Keynesianism. This argument draws from the work of Werner Bonefeld (2016) and Geoff Mann (2018). Bonefeld argues that the ordoliberal call for a strong, depoliticized state to enshrine market competition contains fundamental insights into the political underpinnings of the capitalist economy. In a similar fashion, Mann (2018: 258) claims that Keynesianism should be understood as 'the scientific form of a political anxiety endemic to modernity'—that is, the Keynesian impulse to alleviate the pain generated by capitalism expresses a broader liberal concern about the long-term sustainability of a market-based social order. Both scholars, this chapter contends, are correct. Neoliberal and Keynesian reason reflect the double-sided nature of capitalist society, whereby the state is buffeted by the contradictory forces of incessant economic competition and tangible human demands that in turn express the abstract value and concrete usefulness of the commodity form itself.

For the neoliberal tradition, the successful governance of the market requires a depoliticized state. As Hayek (1945: 527) writes, the 'marvel' of the price mechanism is its ability to connect dispersed parcels of knowledge scattered across the globe into a single social system. This 'system of telecommunications . . . enables individual producers to watch merely the movement of a few pointers, as an engineer might watch the hands of a few dials, in order to adjust their activities to changes' (ibid.). The problem, as mentioned earlier, is that faced with personal economic ruin, people refuse to adjust to these price pointers. Whether domestic industrialists seeking protection from foreign competitors or workers unionizing to resist downward pressure on wages, society's tendency to shrink from the unrelenting discipline of market competition constitutes a profound threat to the market system in which 'order *is* adjustment' (Jan Tumlir quoted in Slobodian, 2018: 223; emphasis added). Confronted by the unmalleability of the subjects of capitalist society, neoliberals advocate the establishment of a powerful state that can undergird and police capitalist competition (Gamble, 1994b; Bonefeld, 2016; Slobodian, 2018; Biebricher, 2018). Such a state must 'not allow itself to become the prey of the competing social interests', each of which seeks to have its factional demands translated into state policy, nor be beholden to a 'mass democratic citizenry' that asks for the suspension of market order so that immediate social needs can be met (Bonefeld, 2016: 3). Rather, an impartial state must provide the legislative basis for markets to function, protect them from the distortions of monopoly and democracy, and enforce market outcomes. In practice, this suggests a 'rule-based (constitutional) framework' in which governments' discretionary power to deviate from market dictates is limited by institutional safeguards (Feld, Köhler, and Nientiedt, 2015: 2). These safeguards should not simply be forged at the national level; rather, neoliberal thinkers advocate a multi-tiered system of international treaties and supranational institutions that can override national democratic forces and protectionist tendencies, thus fully 'encasing' the wiring of global capitalism—a project that Quinn Slobodian (2018) usefully terms 'ordoglobalism'. In this way, whether one chooses to 'marvel' at the signals of the price mechanism or not, the state can compel one to obey them.

Neoliberal thought gives voice to a political strategy long employed by states to achieve national economic competitiveness without haemorrhaging popular support: depoliticized discipline. This strategy requires the construction of subtle governing devices that allow policymakers to impose market discipline on domestic populations while veiling the state's hand in the process. If successful, this grants state authorities autonomy from legitimacy pressures by establishing 'automatic rules or pilots' that allow for the 'euthanasia of politics' (Bulpitt, 1986: 28–32). As Matthew Flinders and Jim Buller (2006) pointed out, three forms of depoliticization can be identified: institutional, whereby politicians delegate governance to ostensibly non-political institutions; rules-based, whereby decision-making discretion is curtailed by explicit rules; and preference-shaping, whereby rhetorical strategies are employed that portray specific social issues as outside of the state's jurisdiction. The goal of depoliticization is to place 'at one remove the political character of decision-making' so as to allow the state to govern capitalism in a more insulated manner (Burnham, 2001: 128). These strategies are especially important during periods of economic downturn, such as the profitability crisis of the late postwar period, because the state must both manage a lacklustre economy and avoid blame for this poor performance in the eyes of the electorate (Krippner, 2007: 479). Depoliticized discipline, a mode of governance that finds its clearest articulation in the neoliberal tradition, thus offers policymakers a way to impose painful domestic adjustment to world market averages without paying severely at the polls or provoking a more fundamental crisis of state legitimacy.

However, such a strategy has definite limits. The question of human needs cannot be banished altogether through legislative innovation, because people ultimately refuse to passively observe their own immiseration. Indeed, as one contemporary commentator put it, politicians that tried in vain to maintain the depoliticized disciplining mechanism of the Gold Standard during the Great Depression, and recognized 'no end to the amount of punishment that the people could take', found themselves 'run over by a steam roller they had not seen coming, namely, the human equation' (Lionel Edie quoted in Eichengreen and

Temin, 2000: 207). Keynesianism,[4] in contrast, admonishes the neoliberal impulse as a form of dangerous idealism, and instead expresses both an awareness of the spectre of popular revolt and a political will to suspend market norms in order to soothe unrest. For Mann (2018: 95), this liberal tradition understands well that the politics of necessity always burst through their institutional shackles: 'The people must be fed, or they will do what is necessary to feed themselves'. Capitalism necessarily generates both destitution and historically unprecedented opulence, yet the former always threatens to spill out of its confines and flood the latter. This requires a pragmatic, discretionary state that can act to alleviate the worst destitution so as to preserve social order. However, this by no means suggests a sympathy for mass politics (Dunn, 2018). Rather, Keynesianism shares with neoliberalism a desire for a depoliticized mode of economic governance, advocating that the levers of demand management be operated by 'an insulated and bureaucratic élite' (Bulpitt, 1986: 27). This vein of liberal thought, then, entrusts to enlightened technocrats the power to resist the impersonal pressures of the law of value, at certain crucial moments, in order to stave off popular upheaval.

The Keynesian tradition expresses an important political reality: the need for states to postpone the bite of global competition through palliation strategies. Palliation, in Streeck's memorable words, allows the state to 'buy time', without addressing the fundamental competitive mismatch between the national territory and the world market. By taking 'flight from the present', the state can maintain domestic political legitimacy by kicking the economic can down the road (Bonefeld, 1995: 40). For neoliberals, palliation is the strategy of the weak state—overrun by popular forces and beholden to the whims of mass democracy (Bonefeld, 2016). Yet faced with the social unrest generated by the dislocating effects of market competition, particularly during global profitability crises when the social fabric itself threatens to pull apart, policymakers often have little choice but to adopt 'the activist, rationalist, crisis-fighting mindset of Keynesianism' (Tooze, 2018a). While such palliation strategies may temporarily alleviate the contradiction between the imperatives of value and human need, they risk damaging national credibility on global financial markets. It is therefore important that crisis delaying measures do not appear as such. They must be dressed up for global audiences as sober evidence-, theory-, or conviction-based policies.

Depoliticized discipline and palliation should be conceptualized as two ends of a governing spectrum, upon which particular policies may lie. Indeed, a policy may constitute a hybrid governing strategy, to the extent that it contains measures that discipline certain parts of the economy while offering palliative relief to politically sensitive groups. Which strategy takes precedence at any given moment

---

[4] This book refers to Keynesianism not as a strict economic doctrine, but rather follows Mann's brilliant analysis of Keynesianism as a distinctly anxious strand of liberal thought that emerged from the French Revolution (2018).

is strongly influenced by the limits placed on state action by the imperatives of value and human need. If the weight of the crisis threatens to push the national economy over the brink, and policymakers discover a mechanism that can veil the state's hand in the necessary restructuring, then depoliticized discipline may be pursued. Yet if the political backlash is too strong, if society proves too resistant to its own recreation as an aggregation of single-minded producers, then policy-makers may be forced to buy time through palliation. The framework of action within which state actors strategize is thus not a structural given, but is rather determined by social struggle.

This book's understanding of state behaviour shares affinities with Jim Bulpitt's 'statecraft' approach. Against accounts that frame policymaking as the execution of political elites' ideological convictions, Bulpitt (1986: 21) conceptualizes state governance as the art of 'winning elections' and maintaining a 'degree of govern-ing competence in office'. This approach focuses on governments' pragmatic decision-making and tactical manoeuvring as they seek to successfully plot a course through the structural constraints imposed upon the state (James, 2018). There are clear overlaps with this book's understanding of policymaking as determined not chiefly by ideology or lobbying pressures but by the need to strategically respond to real governing dilemmas, often in an ad hoc fashion. Nevertheless, Bulpitt's approach remains quite narrow and superficial. Statecraft is oriented towards maintaining party unity, winning elections, transforming a government's rhetoric into common sense, and achieving governing competence—a somewhat arbitrary list of objectives (Bulpitt, 1986: 21–2). In addition, Bulpitt limits his analysis to what he terms the 'Court', defined as the Prime Minister and their friends and advisers (Buller, 1999: 694). Peter Burnham (2001), however, overcomes these weaknesses by marshalling Bulpitt's concept of statecraft as part of a wider Marxist theory of the political management of capitalism's contradict-ory and crisis-ridden development. This book draws inspiration from Burnham's approach. Further, the analysis presented in the following chapters expands the analytical lens beyond the 'Court' to examine the strategic machinations of less senior politicians and even unelected officials operating within the civil service. Finally, this book explores how, in seeking to negotiate the counterposed impera-tives of global competition and domestic legitimacy, different branches of the state apparatus—from the executive to the treasury to the central bank—often formulate divergent strategies that reflect their unique institutional trajectories. The final policy product, then, is frequently an awkward amalgamation of these different strategic initiatives.

The four financial liberalizations examined in this book, which cumulatively acted to propel processes of financialization in Britain and on the world stage, should be understood through this conceptual lens. These policies were not designed solely to address problems within the financial sector. Rather, financial liberalization was a tool of macroeconomic management—an instrument for the governance not just of finance but of the broader contradictory dynamics of capitalist society. Each of these four policies constituted elements of wider strategies to respond to both the sputtering performance of Britain's economy in the context of global crisis and the intensifying demands of British people that their tangible needs should not be sacrificed at the altar of capital accumulation. Financial liberalization was employed in a pragmatic and often haphazard manner to provide support for state governance strategies of depoliticized discipline, palliation, or a hybrid of the two. These policies in turn had unintentional knock-on effects that constrained future governments in various ways.

*   *   *

To live in the era of financialization is to feel palpably subject to a kind of domination. People are pressured into shouldering unbearable debt burdens, sovereign nations in the Global South and European periphery are plunged into poverty by credit markets, and states appear unwilling or unable to rein in financial markets despite the patent madness of the status quo. Because states have been complicit in unleashing the forces of financialization, much of the academic literature has understood policies of financial liberalization to have resulted from states' direct domination by financial elites or the coordinated power of the profit-hungry capitalist class.

This book, in contrast, attempts to understand the *indirect* domination of policymakers by a social logic of their own accidental creation, via an examination of Marx's value theory. Through the seemingly innocuous practice of money-mediated commodity exchange, the market-dependent agents of capitalist society produce a dynamic social imperative that forces them to continually compete to raise labour productivity. Heterogeneous forms of wealth become mere vessels of value—a homogenous, temporally-constituted substance—and human productive activities become geared towards the production of tangible goods only insofar as they embody this intangible value. This principle of production as a 'means to a means' (Postone, 1993: 181) drives itself into regular crises and provokes people to continually rebel against the imperatives of value and assert a variety of needs and aspirations in its stead.

States do not stand outside this system of wealth, governing it and smoothing out its wrinkles. Rather, through the creation and governance of a world network of money relations, states directly contribute to the formation of the law of value as a global system of radical commensurability and crushing competitive pressures. As a consequence, policymakers are forced to maintain their national territory's world market viability or face external imbalances, while simultaneously being seen to respond to their citizenry's demands. This dilemma is heightened during periods of global economic downturn, when the frenzied drive by companies to raise their individual productivity accidentally undermines general profitability. In order to successfully govern this conflictual and contradictory form of social relations, states recur to two forms of strategy: depoliticized discipline, which aims to restructure domestic social relations in line with global market imperatives, and palliation, which attempts to postpone these market imperatives in the name of rescuing governing legitimacy. As this chapter has discussed, these two governing strategies are well articulated by the neoliberal and Keynesian strands of liberal political economy respectively. While the neoliberal school insists on the need for the state to insulate the painful process of market adjustment from the passions of an enfranchised electorate, Keynesianism recognizes that the state must intervene to relieve the most severe suffering, so as to keep the masses from destroying the market mechanism itself.

The financial liberalization measures spurring the processes that we have since come to label as financialization are best understood through this conceptual lens. These policies constituted pragmatic strategies designed to traverse the contradictory pressures imposed upon the state by capitalist social relations in a moment of profound global crisis. Transformations in financial regulation were pursued as strategies either to delay the impending crisis and assuage social upheaval, or to restructure the economy in line with global averages, while shifting the blame away from the state authorities. Before examining these liberalizations in detail, the following chapter will provide a broad historical introduction to the profitability crisis in Britain—the period during which these measures were implemented.

3

The Political Economy of the Profitability Crisis in Britain

In contemporary British politics, commentators on the left and right wrestle over the legacy of the 'postwar consensus'. While the left points to rising living standards, growing political participation, and the state's provision of a range of social goods, the right reminds them of rampant inflation, industrial strife, and the politicization of every aspect of economic governance. Both accounts contain important truths. In the thirty years or so after World War II, an informal social contract was formed that allowed for a degree of human flourishing that was simply unimaginable during the miserable interwar years or the strict deflationary regime of the Gold Standard—a social contract that favoured those who found themselves on the right side of Britain's racialized, colonial social hierarchy (Jacobs, 1985; Shilliam, 2018). These stratified social improvements, however, were underpinned by a historically unprecedented global economic boom. This boom gradually came to an end, reaching a point in the late 1960s where both the national policy framework of demand management and the global infrastructure of Bretton Woods were becoming patently unsustainable. '[I]t was not Keynesian policies that sustained accumulation' during this period, as Simon Clarke (1988: 283) insightfully observed, 'but rather it was sustained accumulation that permitted the pursuit of Keynesian policies'.

The financial liberalization measures introduced in the 1970s and 1980s, this book contends, were part of the British state's broader attempts to come to terms with the growing gap between the postwar policy paradigm and its weakening economic basis. As the global boom slowed, with Britain particularly badly affected due to its relatively poor competitiveness, successive governments were forced to reconcile the growing tension between global economic viability and national political legitimacy. This particular policy dilemma reflected a fundamental antinomy at the core of the political governance of capitalist society: the contradiction between the continual competitive pressure to augment labour productivity, emanating from capitalism's monetized social relations, and people's assertion of their needs. Nevertheless, before moving from this level of conceptual abstraction to the archival examination of particular financial liberalizations, it is important to introduce an intermediate level of historical context. This chapter will thus present a stylized history of Britain's experience of the crisis that gripped the global capitalist system in the late postwar period, as well as discussing the

Governing Financialization: The Tangled Politics of Financial Liberalization in Britain. Jack Copley, Oxford University Press.
© Jack Copley 2022. DOI: 10.1093/oso/9780192897015.003.0003

broad strategies governments pursued to manage it. This historical narrative will in turn form a solid basis for the more detailed analysis in the following chapters.

The global capitalist economy entered a period of remarkable expansion following World War II. This Golden Age of capitalism was powered by the high profitability that resulted from the devastation of two world wars and the Great Depression, the drawing of new resources and populations into capitalist social relations, and the spread of US production technologies around the world. However, from the 1960s, this postwar boom began to lose steam, as the growing adoption of labour-saving machinery by leading economies fostered overproduction, the cheapening of commodities, and a fall in global profitability. The chief symptom of declining profitability was stagflation. This accelerating world downturn intersected with the long-term deterioration in Britain's relative economic competitiveness, resulting in a worsening national crisis that British governments in this period were forced to reckon with. This book divides the era of stagflation in Britain into two distinct phases: the first, from 1967 to 1977, saw falling profitability, rising inflation, and repeated balance of payments and currency crises; while the second, from 1977 to 1983, was characterized by low profitability and high inflation, but with a strong currency, which further exacerbated the recessionary conditions.

Governments in this first phase faced a dilemma. Their attempts to postpone the worst effects of the profitability crisis through palliative measures—and thus ensure their continued political legitimacy—tended to worsen Britain's balance of payments performance and thus increase speculative pressure on sterling. This would force governments to retreat from palliation and instead impose discipline, often masked by depoliticization devices. During the second phase, the problem of currency crises was alleviated by the appreciation of sterling, due to the flow of North Sea oil and the 1976 IMF package. Yet policymakers faced another problem: the strong pound helped to discipline British social relations and thus bring the national economy in line with world market standards, but it also threatened to shatter governments' legitimacy because of the ensuing recession. Governments were thus forced to deliberate between employing strategies that, on the one hand, enforced economic discipline, and, on the other hand, alleviated this disciplinary pressure through palliative measures.

This chapter will demonstrate how, in the years 1967–77, the governments of Wilson, Heath, and Wilson (again) fluctuated between palliative and disciplining governing strategies, in line with the opposing pressures of external economic imbalances and domestic political agitation. In contrast, the Callaghan and Thatcher governments, in the period from 1977 to 1983, operated forms of hybridized governing strategies, which simultaneously sought to work *with* the strong pound to purge inflation from the British economy and rekindle profitable capital accumulation, and *against* the strong pound by attempting to provide politically important domestic constituencies with temporary respite from the worst of the crisis. The four financial liberalizations studied in this book—CCC, exchange control abolition, the Big Bang, and FSA—were intimately related to these wider governing strategies employed to navigate the political and economic perils of the profitability crisis. That these policies together unleashed dynamics of financialization on the national and global scale was an unintended consequence.

From the Golden Age to Stagflation

The period from 1950 to 1973 is commonly referred to as capitalism's Golden Age. The postwar economic expansion saw unprecedentedly high growth rates across the capitalist world, uninterrupted by a major global recession (Vonyó, 2008: 221). Although this was truly a global boom, it was geographically uneven. Japan and West Germany—two countries that emerged prostrate from World War II—became among the world's most dynamic exporting economies. Europe and Asia as a whole registered impressive per capita growth, while Latin America and Africa underperformed relative to the global average (see Maddison, 1995, table 3-1). Finally, the US and Britain—pioneering capitalist economies—fell behind in the competitive race, despite still growing at a rapid pace. The postwar boom was made possible by a spike in the profitability of capital, which was itself the legacy of the dislocation, destruction, and destitution bequeathed by two world wars and an intervening global depression. Protracted economic crisis and conflict had resulted in a drastic devaluation of capital and the physical destruction of factories, transport infrastructure, and residential property (Kliman, 2012: 22–4; Vonyó, 2008). The working class in many countries—their organizations undermined by mass unemployment and in some cases crushed by fascism—saw their wages held down by a significant swelling of their ranks in the early postwar years. Japan, for example, repatriated more than six million people from its former colonial possessions between 1945 and 1948, while West Germany accepted around nine million people from the east in the period 1945–50 (Abramovitz, 1994: 121). Labour similarly flowed into the Netherlands and France from their colonial territories of Indonesia and Algeria (Eichengreen, 1997: 227). These additions to the labouring classes were augmented by the shift of agrarian populations into industrial employment—a process that had been delayed by war and depression (Temin, 2002). In sum, this meant that postwar reconstruction would see cheap capital set in motion by an inexpensive and politically contained labour force. The stage was set for an investment boom driven by massive profitability.

In order to realize this growth potential, it was crucial that the major economies could embrace international trade and investment without generating domestic political instability. Otherwise, their growth would have been limited by the size of their domestic markets. Global integration was eventually achieved through various mechanisms of economic cooperation, conducted under the umbrella of US hegemony. One such mechanism was the Bretton Woods system. At the 1944 Bretton Woods conference, delegates from forty-four nations—led by the US, with Britain playing a secondary role—sought to forge a monetary system that could avoid both the breakdown in world trade that characterized the interwar years and the Gold Standard's rigid adjustment mechanism that had generated great political turmoil (Cohen, 1977: 90). The goal of the conference, in other words, was to create an 'international monetary constitution' that could marry trade liberalization with the national policy autonomy necessary to meet the demands of enfranchised electorates (Bordo, 1993: 28). The resulting system differed from the Gold Standard in three important ways. First, under fixed-adjustable exchange rates, countries would peg their currencies to the dollar at a given ratio, but their currencies would be allowed to fluctuate within limits. The dollar in turn was convertible to gold at $35 an ounce. Second, strict controls on international capital flows would limit destabilizing speculation against national economies. Third, the IMF was created to monitor national economic performances and provide financing to countries in balance of payments troubles (Eichengreen, 2008: 91).

On its own, however, the Bretton Woods Agreement was insufficient to alleviate barriers to international trade and investment. In the immediate postwar years, growth failed to take off. Many major economies, with the exception of the US, 'were simply too devastated by the war—their export capacities damaged, their import needs enormous, their monetary reserves exhausted'—to embrace free trade and currency convertibility (Cohen, 1977: 94–5). The fundamental problem was that war-ravaged economies had insufficient foreign currency reserves, particularly dollars, to import the necessary food and capital goods to build up their exports that would in turn allow them to earn foreign currency. To make their currencies convertible in such conditions was to welcome waves of devastating speculation. Britain made sterling convertible in July 1947, at the insistence of the US, but was forced to suspend convertibility in August after a run on sterling drained $1 billion in Bank reserves (Bordo, 1993: 44). The scale of the world economy's dollar shortage was too great to be solved by the IMF's limited coffers. Instead, it required massive, direct provision of dollars by the US state, which had a clear interest in stimulating demand for US exports. From 1948 to 1951, the Marshall Plan injected $13 billion into European economies in return for their commitment to trade liberalization (Crafts and Toniolo, 2012: 370). The Korean War performed the same function for Japan. From 1950 to 1953, the US procured huge volumes of industrial goods from Japan at guaranteed prices (Chuǎng, 2019: 62–3). The creation of the European Payments Union in 1950, under US guidance, saw members agree to accept other members' currencies in exchange for exports, deficit countries were provided with credit to alleviate trade imbalances, and members were encouraged to liberalize trade and move towards currency convertibility (Toniolo, 2005: 327). Finally, the project of constructing the European Economic Community from 1957 began to further eliminate barriers to trade, boosting commercial relations among members. By 1958, Western European economies had achieved currency convertibility (Eichengreen, 1997: 224). During the 1950s, then, such cooperative initiatives secured an increasing degree of international economic integration, allowing economies to take advantage of sky-high profitability and setting the postwar boom in motion.

As global trade and investment rose, growth came to be powered not simply by the immense profit margins of postwar reconstruction, but by the spread of advanced US industrial technologies (Crafts and Toniolo, 2012: 363). The US had exited the war as the clear leader in technological capacities (Nelson and Wright, 1994: 148). However, from the 1950s on, the productivity gap between the leading industrial nations began to narrow (ibid.: 153). As Europe and Japan opened up to global markets, they began to import 'continuous flow production' methods and technologies from the US (Schwartz, 2018: 184–5). First developed in Henry Ford's car factories before being generalized across various manufacturing sectors, this mass production method involved the introduction of advanced industrial machinery and minute sequencing of every stage of the work process, such that production could be undertaken by less skilled labourers on a continuous assembly line (Link, 2020: 30–3). When this form of production was adopted globally the result was a rise in the ratio of fixed capital to labour, as companies undertook large capital investments to boost the productivity of their workforces and remain competitive (Dollar and Wolff, 1994). Between 1950 and 1973, the stock of machinery and equipment in Europe and Japan grew by roughly 8 per cent each year, compared to just 3.5 per cent in Europe from 1973 to 1991 (Maddison, 1997: 54). This process was reflected in the eventual decline in the share of the total workforce employed in manufacturing across advanced economies. The industrial employment share of the US, as an early industrializer, had reached its highest point in 1953; in France it peaked in 1964, in West Germany in 1970, and in Japan in 1973 (Eichengreen, Perkins, and Shin, 2012: 87). As global productivity converged with that of the US, the tremendous output flooded world markets with commodities and tested the limits of demand, firms cut prices to capture or retain market share, and there was a precipitous fall in global profitability.[1] Profit rates fell unevenly across the capitalist world, with market laggards like Britain suffering early, while leading economies like Japan and West Germany were able to withstand the price competition and maintain healthy profitability for

---

[1] While Brenner (2006) argues that the crisis was rooted in falling profitability, he rejects Marx's theory of the tendential fall in the profit rate. In contrast, Shaikh (1992), Carchedi (1991), Moseley (1991), McNally (2011), Mattick (2011), Kliman (2012), Smith (2019), and others have convincingly demonstrated that some variation of this theory is the best framework for understanding the profitability crisis.

longer (Shaikh, 1987: 115). Regardless, as Brenner (2006: 37) argues, the years 1965 to 1973 saw the world economy transition from 'long boom to long downturn'.

The most prominent symptom of the profitability crisis was the peculiar phenomenon of stagflation: stagnation in business investment, output, and employment accompanied by rapid inflation. As profitability declined, companies were deterred from expanding their production operations and instead sought to raise prices in order to boost profit margins. This crisis was exacerbated by the policy frameworks and international institutions of the postwar period. Keynesian demand stimulus, designed to maintain full employment, began to instead pro-voke price hikes without a commensurate increase in output and employment, because profitability was too low to justify businesses responding to a rise in demand with greater investment (Brenner, 2006: 159; Moseley, 1997: 26; Carchedi, 1991: 169–74). Further, inflation within particular national economies was transmitted abroad through the Bretton Woods fixed exchange rate system: 'tradable-goods price increases in the largest of all trading nations were immedi-ately radiated outward to the rest of the world economy' (Cohen, 1977: 102).

In turn, the crisis of falling profitability exacerbated existing deep-seated problems of the Bretton Woods arrangements. One contradiction of the system made worse by the profitability crisis was the Triffin dilemma. As discussed above, in order for economies devastated by war to open up to world trade, they needed massive injections of dollar liquidity, which in turn required the US to run balance of payments deficits. However, such US deficits undermined confidence in the dollar's convertibility into gold at $35 an ounce, which resulted in increasing speculation against the dollar (ibid.: 98–9). As the profitability of US capital fell in the 1960s, this combined with the inflationary pressures generated by President Lyndon B. Johnson's Great Society programme and the Vietnam War to further undermine the US balance of payments (Bordo, 2020: 199).

As a result of the worsening external position of the US, speculation against the dollar began to mount through the Eurodollar markets. 'Eurodollars' was the name given to accumulations of dollars in London banks that could be used to conduct lending, investment, or speculative activities out of the purview of both British and US banking regulations (Strange, 1994: 106–7). Created in 1957, this market effectively 'punctured a hole' in the Bretton Woods order, which had been predicated upon strict controls of global financial flows (Burn, 1999: 226). The US state supported the Eurodollar market's development because by offering higher interest rates on dollar deposits than were allowed by domestic US banking rules, foreigners would be incentivized to hold dollars and thus finance the US balance of payments deficit—delaying the need for the US to impose painful domestic adjustment (Helleiner, 1994: 90–1). However, as the global competitiveness of the US declined, this market came to function as a disciplinary mechanism against the dollar (Green, 2020: 116). In 1971, investors began moving their money from dollars to deutschmarks via this unregulated market, leading US

President Richard Nixon to suspend the dollar's convertibility into gold (Eichengreen, 2008: 130–1). The Smithsonian Agreement of late 1971 sought to rescue the system of fixed-adjustable rates by instituting new exchange rates, including a modest devaluation of the dollar. However, speculation soon undermined this agreement too.

This heralded the end of the Bretton Woods era and the beginning of the era of floating exchange rates. As global profitability continued its downward march through the 1970s, the world economy plunged deeper into recession and inflation became the scourge of governments everywhere—a situation now worsened by the erratic movements of floating currencies. The 1973 oil shock, when the Organization of Arab Petroleum Exporting Countries announced an oil embargo following the Arab–Israeli war, supercharged this dynamic of falling profitability and rising prices. Yet neither this discrete event nor other contingent factors constituted the root cause of the crisis. Instead, falling profitability was ultimately driven by the normal dynamics of capitalist development, whereby the intangible domination of world value relations created a frenzied struggle for market survival, leading individual firms (aided and directed by states) to boost productivity through the adoption of labour-saving technologies, accidentally resulting in generalized overproduction, downward pressure on commodity prices, and the erosion of profitability. As discussed in Chapter 2, this crisis expressed the fundamental contradiction at the heart of capitalist society between the production of tangible wealth and the production of value.

Britain's Crisis: National, Global, or Both?

The postwar boom transformed Britain. Between 1950 and 1975, as Britain's formal empire disintegrated, real GDP more than doubled (Edgerton, 2018: 283). Incomes rose, allowing working class households to acquire consumer durables previously restricted to the middle classes, from the personal car to the colour television. Infrastructure was revolutionized, with the construction of motorways, a massive increase in the public housing stock, and the achievement of self-sufficiency in food. This period also saw the consolidation of the Beveridgean welfare state, which secured the extension of public provision of health, education, and benefits (ibid.: 283–306). At the same time, however, the postwar era was marked by rising national anxiety over Britain's perceived economic decline. Decline had been a topic of concern amongst commentators and policymakers since the late nineteenth century, but this transformed into an obsession with impending ruin as postwar growth slowed (Supple, 1994: 441). During this period, there was a proliferation of literature focusing on various aspects of Britain's lagging performance, leading Jim Tomlinson (2001: 1) to speak of 'declinology' as an important narrative on Britain's experiences in the twentieth century.

The debate on British decline at times took on a distinctly partisan dynamic, with the political right placing blame upon Britain's rigid trade union movement and the left pointing the finger at the parasitic City (see Coates and Hilliard, 1986). However, Andrew Gamble (1994a: 30–5) usefully identified four key theses on British decline that underpinned this debate. The first focused on the negative effects of empire, particularly the overextension of British military power, British manufacturers' reliance on imperial export markets, and the outdated use of sterling as a secondary international reserve currency. The second addressed the 'anti-industrial and anti-business' culture of the British elite, which posited 'business life and the pursuit of profit as vulgar and distasteful activities, unsuitable for the well-bred' and which thereby impeded Britain's industrial modernization (Rubenstein, 1993: 2; see also Anderson, 1964). The third pointed to the failure of British governments to promote a dynamic manufacturing sector. This had two dimensions: governments in the postwar period considered full employment to be of equal importance to price stability and global competitiveness, thus allowing Britain's economic performance to atrophy; while the British state simultaneously proved incapable of creating a lasting economic development plan, which could have forged the necessary cooperative relations between the City, industry, and the trade unions to ensure economic competitiveness. The last thesis places the blame with Britain's political elites and institutions, which were also accused of capitulating to special interests, such that political business cycles began to develop whereby politicians would routinely inflate the economy in the run-up to elections. Such a perception of UK politicians was well expressed by US President Johnson in 1965, who, in a private message regarding Wilson's unwillingness to exercise domestic economic restraint, compared Wilson to 'a reckless boy that goes off and gets drunk and writes checks on his father' (Schenk, 2010: 162).

David Edgerton (2018: 391) has argued that this obsession with decline amidst postwar plenty should be seen as a 'form of jingoism, a delusion about inherent superiority, dressed up as critique'. Whether this assessment applies to all declinist literature is debatable, but certainly accounts of decline have tended to exaggerate Britain's twentieth century economic failings by contrasting them with its nineteenth century might, as well as overstating the scale or the unique Britishness of domestic impediments to growth. It is true that during the Golden Age, Britain fell behind its competitors in terms of productivity and GDP growth—but much of this is attributable to other economies 'catching up' to Britain's position as an advanced capitalist power, rather than the result of profound British failings (Crafts, 1995: 441–5; Tomlinson, 2005: 175).

Nevertheless, in debating Britain's decline in the postwar era it is important not to lose sight of the bigger picture, namely the *global* economy's gradual descent into crisis during this period. From the 1960s to the 1980s, Britain did not simply experience the effects of national decline in relation to its competitors—it faced a specific national manifestation of the global profitability crisis. As Gamble

(1994a: xix) commented: 'Some observers argued that there was no general crisis of capitalism, only a crisis of capitalism in Britain. But general crises always take the form of national crises'. Capitalism is a world system constituted by a global web of money relations that ties disparate communities into intimate economic dependency—yet it is a system that develops unevenly in space, displaying great variations in national and regional patterns of accumulation (Smith, 2010). Capitalist crises too exhibit this unevenness across various national contexts, unfolding 'in different countries with a different rhythm and in the context of different social and political institutions' (Clarke, 1988: 341). The crisis that British policymakers were forced to navigate in the late postwar period certainly had peculiarly British features, but its fundamental cause can only be located at the level of the totality of capitalist social relations, that is, at the scale of the world market.

Before the onset of the profitability crisis and the accompanying stagflation, Britain's postwar economic development had already taken on a lurching gait, referred to as 'stop-go' (Cairncross, 1995: 14). During the 'go' phase, the British state acted to inflate the economy through demand stimulus in order to maintain political legitimacy. However, without an increase in national competitiveness, this higher level of demand would tend to draw in imports, threatening the balance of payments and the foreign currency reserves. This would often be accompanied by speculation against sterling. At this point, the 'stop' phase would begin, with the authorities tightening monetary and fiscal policy and creating an economic contraction. While this would provide relief to the balance of payments, it would damage political legitimacy, and thus the cycle would begin again. As Samuel Brittan (1971: 455) observed, during the boom years 'Chancellors behaved like simple Pavlovian dogs responding to two main stimuli: one was "a run on the reserves" and the other was "500,000 unemployed"'. In the theoretical language employed in this book, the stop-go pattern of development emerged from policymakers' attempts to steer between the abstract imperative of world market viability and the concrete imperative of national political legitimacy—a contradiction inherent to the liberal governance of capitalist society. However, this dynamic became more severe from the late 1960s as global profitability plummeted. As the misery index (the sum of inflation and unemployment) rose across the advanced capitalist world during this period, British policymakers' tolerance for unemployment was forced to evolve: 'In the early 1970s, the alarm bells rang at one million [unemployed]; in the late 1970s, at one and a half million' (Brittan, 1995: 130).

British profitability fell sharply from 1950 to the early 1980s (see Figure 3.1). The Bank's own calculations at the time painted a grim picture, demonstrating that 'before 1965 the rate of return was well above the cost of capital, that the margin between the two was much narrower...between about 1965 and 1973, and that since then the rate of return has been consistently lower than the cost of

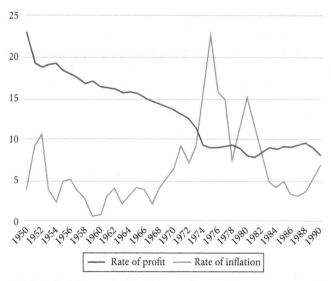

Figure 3.1. UK profitability and inflation rate (per cent), 1950–90. Rate of profit is taken from the Penn World Table's real internal rate of return (Feenstra, Inklaar, and Timmer, 2015). Rate of inflation is taken from Bank of England's Consumer Price Index, annual inflation rate (Bank of England, 2018).

capital' (Wilson Committee, 1980: 145). Facing this mounting threat to its members' survival, the CBI began to sound the alarm publicly. In a 1973 press release, the CBI claimed 'industrial profitability in this country has been steadily declining to the point where it is now at an historically low level... *[P]rofits measured in relation to capital employed now stand at just over one-third of what they were in 1955* (CBI, 1973: 2; emphasis in original). It was low profitability, not the unwillingness of City financiers to lend to industry, that was the cause of stagnant investment, wrote the CBI's Sir Arthur Knight in 1977: 'If profitable sales... were in reasonable prospect, suppliers of funds would not be so stupid as to hold back. If they were not, the suppliers would not be so stupid as to waste their money' (CBI, 1977: 39).

As a consequence of falling profitability, company liquidity collapsed, hovering around zero in 1965 before plummeting to a deficit of more than £1 billion in 1970 and £8 billion in 1974. In response, companies enacted two strategies to stay afloat. First, they took on increasing debt burdens. Manufacturing companies' debt-to-equity ratios rose from 20 per cent in 1960 to 49 per cent in 1970 and 59 per cent in 1975 (CBI, 1977: 15–17). Furthermore, in 1956–60, 90 per cent of industrial and commercial companies' funds came from internal sources (chiefly retained profits) and just 10 per cent came from external sources (bank borrowing, government grants, etc.); by 1966–70, the ratio had changed to 80 per cent and 20 per cent (Thomas, 1978: 310). Second, businesses cut back investment plans and raised prices in order to reverse the decline in their profit rates. This dynamic, combined with rising world prices, resulted in the rate of inflation creeping upwards. While the annual inflation rate had not exceeded 5.2 per cent since the Korean War, it rose to 9.4 per cent in 1971 before skyrocketing to 22.7 per cent in 1975 following the oil shock (Bank of England, 2018). These trends, combined with innovations in the financial sector that will be discussed in Chapter 4, began to distort and make increasingly volatile the money supply aggregates—indicators that with the rise of monetarism would come to play an important role in policymaking. Finally, this spiralling economic performance, generated by falling profitability, resulted in an increasingly precarious external position, as Britain's export capacity eroded relative to its competitors. The current account of the balance of payments was in deficit for four of the six years from 1964 to 1970, before plummeting to a deficit of more than £3 billion in 1973 and remaining in deficit until 1978 (Bank of England, 2019). Britain was repeatedly punished for its balance of payments troubles by speculative flows of unregulated Eurodollars, which Denis Healey termed an 'atomic cloud of footloose funds' (quoted in A. Davies, 2017: 196).

As British policymakers desperately attempted to restore something like normality to an economy that was shuddering and lurching out of control, their arsenal of received wisdoms and inherited common senses came under growing scrutiny. In 1971, Heath's special adviser, Brian Reading, wrote a fascinating note that captured the intellectual crisis of this period.[2] Reading imagined a hypothetical government meeting that took place in 1968, in which an 'intrepid forecaster' predicted that by 1970 there would be high unemployment, rapidly rising wages and prices, a balance of payments *surplus*, and the bankruptcy of Rolls Royce. 'At the very least', Reading muses, this forecaster 'would have been persuaded to go away and do his sums again—with a new slide rule. For . . . it was clearly impossible to combine 2.75 per cent unemployment [high by postwar standards] with 15 per cent wage increases'. Yet such stagflation was precisely the economic situation that Britain faced in 1971. This, for Reading, 'illustrate[d] the fundamental weakness of conventional economic wisdom': 'our present situation is one which, almost by definition, conventional measures cannot resolve'.

The period of stagflation was therefore also a period of continual policy innovation. Governments began to desperately experiment with the levers of incomes policy, price controls, industrial relations reform, exchange rate management, and financial regulation in an attempt to drag Britain out of its malaise. Yet the key transformation with regards to macroeconomic policy during this period was the shift from Keynesian demand management to monetarism (Hall, 1993). Significant academic debate exists over the nature and timing of this policy

[2] TNA T 338/39, Comment by Reading, 10 February 1971.

change. As Jacqueline Best (2004) points out, it was not a pure form of Keynesianism that had predominated in the postwar period, but rather what the influential economist Paul Samuelson termed the 'neoclassical synthesis' of Keynesian macroeconomics and 'neoclassical microeconomic principles' (see Backhouse and Boianovsky, 2013: 41). Monetarism, in turn, is a term that covers a variety of different economic theories, all of which focus on the achievement of price stability and market equilibrium through the implementation of an appropriate monetary policy (Clarke, 1988: 323). Regarding the chronology of the Keynesianism–monetarism transition, certain scholars have argued that the story does not in fact begin with Thatcher but rather with her predecessors, highlighting Chancellor Healey's 'unbelieving monetarism' in the 1970s (Dow, 2013: 69) or even the early monetary targeting imposed upon the British state by the IMF in the late 1960s (Clift and Tomlinson, 2008, 2012). What remains uncontested is that the deterioration of economic dynamism from the 1960s to the 1980s shook the foundations of Britain's postwar political order, rendering existing policy wisdom increasingly redundant and provoking a realignment of economic orthodoxy, whereby the governance of money came to occupy a more important position in the state's regulation of capital accumulation.

The following section will provide an overview of how the different governments in the period from 1967 to 1983 experienced and responded to the global profitability crisis and its British manifestations. This discussion will in turn provide a historical basis for the proceeding archival analyses of particular financial liberalizations—as these transformations in regulatory policy cannot be understood separately from the broader macroeconomic strategies taking place at the time.

Governing Stagflation

Stagflation in Britain was not experienced by policymakers as a homogeneous period, nor was this era simply one of ever deepening economic decay. Instead, for the purposes of this book's argument, it is useful to split Britain's experience of the crisis into two periods. The first, from 1967 to 1977, was characterized by falling profitability, rising inflation, and periodic currency crises related to poor export performance. The second, from 1977 to 1983, was characterized by low, stagnant profitability, high inflation, and a strong pound (propped up by North Sea oil and the IMF's seal of approval) that resulted in deeply recessionary domestic conditions. Thus, while policymakers in the first period were plagued with concerns over current account deficits, runs on sterling, and the level of the foreign currency reserves, policymakers in the second period were somewhat insulated from such external crises—creating a superficial air of economic recovery. Yet the positive external position masked the real emaciation of the non-oil economy and the strong pound further exacerbated the effects of the profitability crisis, plunging the British economy into an unprecedentedly deep recession.

The administrations that governed during this period relied on myriad policy instruments to manage the conflicting imperatives of the crisis of value production and stubborn human needs. Yet these various policies should be understood as existing on a spectrum between strategies of palliation and depoliticized discipline. Governments in the period 1967–77 tended to oscillate between these two strategies: the political pressures arising from stagnating living standards and trade union agitation pressed governments to delay the crisis through expansionist policies, until pressures on the currency became so great that governments' popular legitimacy concerns were sacrificed to rescue the immediate external position. In the 1977–83 period, governments were torn between embracing the deeply deflationary effects of the strong pound because of its disciplinary effects on the British economy, and resisting sterling's appreciation due to the ensuing recession's erosion of governing legitimacy. In some respects, this mirrors the stop-go development pattern of the broader postwar boom years, yet it also took on a new dynamic. Policies that would have previously resulted in a 'go' period began to amount only to a partial easing of the deeply stagnant character of British economic development. By contrast, the 'stop' periods resulted in such economic pain and social strife (while having limited success in reducing inflation) that policymakers increasingly sought to depoliticize these disciplinary measures through a range of mechanisms. As such, this era was characterized by governments' repeated employment of palliation strategies, depoliticized disciplining strategies, or some hybrid of the two, in order to navigate Britain through a system of global value relations in deep crisis.

From One Currency Crisis to the Next, 1967–77

Wilson took office in 1964 with grand ambitions for British economic development. He promised 'to create a New Britain, pulsating with the energies of the white heat of the new scientific revolution' (Edgerton, 2018: 282). Labour's 'National Plan' included the creation of the Department of Economic Affairs and later the National Board for Prices and Incomes (NBPI), which together attempted to generate an environment conducive to industrial investment by investigating the problems in specific sectors, assisting the private sector in formulating investment plans, and creating greater coordination between the state, private employers, and unions (A. Davies, 2017: 14). Meanwhile, the Ministry of Technology, the Industrial Reorganisation Corporation, and the Industrial Expansion Act sought to jump-start the modernization of British industry and propel higher productivity growth (Cairncross, 1995: 171). The National Plan was an attempt to transcend the tired back and forth of stop-go and set Britain on a growth-led path of institutional coordination, technological modernization, and global competitiveness. However, instead of being able to dedicate its term to pursuing this proactive scheme, Wilson's administration was rocked by three major sterling crises—November 1964, July 1965, and July 1966—and spent much of its remaining years entangled in 'a day-to-day struggle to support the pound' (ibid.: 150).

The source of such speculative attacks on sterling was the large balance of payments deficit that Wilson faced upon arriving in power in 1964. However, motivated by concerns that devaluation would be perceived as a damaging admission of failure on Labour's part, and aware of the government's slim majority in Parliament, he was determined not to give in to pressures to devalue the pound (Schenk, 2010: 155). As such, Wilson set about deflating domestic demand and seeking financial aid from the IMF and foreign central banks. The US discouraged British devaluation and provided funds to support sterling, fearing that sterling devaluation would ratchet up speculation against the dollar and that Britain's exchange rate problems would undermine British military support for the US imperialist project in south-east Asia (ibid.: 157).

Nevertheless, in November 1967 Wilson capitulated to speculative pressure and announced a downward step-change in the pound's price from $2.80 to $2.40 (Needham, 2014: 21). Consequently, the government agreed a standby arrangement with the IMF and foreign central banks in order to support the pound's new level, and introduced the most deflationary budget since the war, which included tax increases, public expenditure cuts, and a tightening of monetary policy. Furthermore, a series of changes in industrial relations were pursued. In 1965, Labour established the Donovan Commission to investigate the state of Britain's fractious industrial relations. The Commission's 1968 report, which identified the threat of a shift in power from official collective bargaining mechanisms to shop-floor agitation, resulted in a 1969 government White Paper, *In Place of Strife*. This proposed that the state should have power to impose penal sanctions on unofficial strikes, require compulsory ballots before official strikes, and order pauses to unconstitutional strikes (Thorpe, 2001: 152). The goal was to disrupt shop floor organizing as a way of tackling inflation and restoring the profitability of capital (Clarke, 1988: 302). With the National Plan in tatters, Wilson pressed ahead in late 1967 with an application for European Economic Community (EEC) membership as an alternative strategy for British economic regeneration—but this too was nixed by French President Charles De Gaulle's veto (Parr, 2006).

The objective of the Wilson government's disciplinary programme, former Treasury official Peter Browning (1986: 20) wrote, 'was to deflate home demand to release resources for the growth of the exports which would, in due course, flow from devaluation'. It was hoped that these measures would help Britain to break free from the trajectory of worsening competitiveness that was plunging the economy into repeated currency crises. By enforcing strict financial discipline, somewhat depoliticized by IMF conditionalities and the threat of sterling crises, the government intended to restructure British social relations in line with slowing global capital accumulation. To a degree, this was successful. Labour Chancellor Roy Jenkins presided over a £1 billion reversal in the balance of payments between 1967 and 1970 and a Public Sector Borrowing Requirement (PSBR) that turned negative (ibid.: 24).

It was this relatively positive outlook, in the context of a weakening global economy, that Heath inherited when he defeated Wilson in the 1970 general election. Indeed, it was this firm economic basis from which Heath intended to launch a radical break with his predecessor's struggle to reconcile the pressures of militant domestic unions and external constraints. As Heath himself argued: 'We were returning to office to change the course of history of this nation—nothing less' (Blackby, 1979: 52). The plan was to institute a form of 'liberal Keynesianism', which consisted of abandoning Wilson's industrial policy, disengaging from the system of industrial relations while reforming the trade unions, reducing state expenditure, and tightening monetary policy (Clarke, 1988: 307-8). In addition, Heath would seek Britain's entry to the EEC so as to 'open the British economy to fiercer competition from European industries', making 'the achievement of higher levels of investment and productivity in British companies essential for survival' (Gamble, 1994b: 74). A core tenet of this administration's 'Quiet Revolution', Martin Holmes (1997: 37) has argued, was that 'less government interference with market forces would help to restore competition and profitability to British industry after the years of inefficient socialist planning and indiscriminately wasteful subsidies'. In a sense, this was a project of economic disciplining without a depoliticization mechanism.

Yet, much like during the Wilson years, such ambition faded in the face of the accelerating stagflation crisis. The passing of the 1971 Industrial Relations Act, which sought to bolster the structures of official trade union bureaucracy at the expense of the shop floor, met instant and fierce backlash from the labour movement (Holmes, 1997: 19-20). The TUC launched a series of demonstrations under the banner of a 'Kill the Bill' campaign and encouraged its affiliated unions not to register with the new industrial relations system in order to reduce its effectiveness (Dorey, 1995: 72). Furthermore, the Heath administration's moderate denationalizations and discontinuations of state support for ailing firms were shaken by legitimacy concerns as the economy entered deeper into crisis. The government responded to the bankruptcy of Rolls Royce with a large package of state subsidies, and despite initially refusing to extend the same support to the foundering Upper Clyde Shipbuilders, was forced to rescue the company in February 1972 after a wave of industrial action by shipyard workers (Holmes, 1997: 42-4). More important than any particular event, however, was the level of unemployment, which breached one million in January 1972 (ibid.: 46). As a result, Chancellor Anthony Barber's March 1972 budget consisted of the so-called 'Dash for Growth', whereby a five per cent growth rate was projected, accompanied by an expansionary fiscal policy. This U-turn also included a relaxation of monetary policy, despite the government's 1971 implementation of the CCC measures (which will be examined in Chapter 4) that the Bank had hoped would allow the authorities to more easily *tighten* monetary conditions (Needham, 2014: 50–1). Demonstrating the government's new-found commitment to postponing the crisis through palliative measures, despite their initially anti-interventionist rhetoric, Barber claimed in a speech to Parliament that he was willing to sacrifice the exchange rate in order to hit the growth targets (Browning, 1986: 35–6).

The result of this shift from *politicized* discipline to an expansionist, palliative programme was the intensification of the dynamics of stagflation. In addition to fuelling a rise in imports and inflation, the 'Barber Boom' led to a spike in investment in the property market, rather than in export-oriented industries—a dynamic that was exacerbated by the CCC deregulation (Scott, 1996: 187; Needham, 2014: 52). In the summer of 1972, as the balance of payments began to deteriorate and inflation continued rising, there was a substantial move out of sterling by global investors (Cairncross, 1996: 132). The Bank responded by purchasing sterling, with the aid of foreign central banks (Needham, 2014: 56). Yet this put unsustainable pressure on the foreign currency reserves and the pound was ultimately floated in June (Cairncross, 1995: 192), contributing to the collapse of the Smithsonian Agreement and the deterioration of the European exchange rate regime—the 'snake'—that had been launched to stabilize Europe's currencies only two months prior (McNamara, 1999: 107).

These expansionary policies also did little to dampen wage claims. After the Heath government's initial attempt to reduce public sector pay awards was shaken by the 1972 miners' strike, an attempt was made to negotiate a voluntary incomes policy with the TUC; when this too failed, the government unilaterally imposed a three-stage incomes policy that sought to freeze wages and prices (Woodward, 2004: 138). The March 1973 budget nonetheless restated the five per cent growth target, and by the middle of the year the balance of payments was £1.5 billion in deficit—*before* the oil shock (Cairncross, 1995: 192). The final stage of Heath's incomes policy, which came in to force in November 1973, promised that total pay bills could rise by up to seven per cent (Woodward, 2004: 139). Yet this too was rejected by the National Union of Mineworkers, who began an overtime ban. The resulting sharp reduction in coal output, coinciding with the oil price hike and a record trade deficit, led to growing pressure on sterling and ultimately pushed Heath to enact a 'reverse' budget in December, which saw cuts of £1.2 billion in public expenditure (Holmes, 1997: 106–8). The property bubble—which had been developing since 1972—subsequently burst, leaving the secondary banks discussed in Chapter 4 highly exposed to falling property prices and forcing the government to launch a 'lifeboat' operation to rescue them (Needham, 2014: 191). Finally, in early 1974, following another miners' strike during the government's three-day week measures, Heath called a general election on the question of

'Who governs Britain?', failed to get a parliamentary majority, and consequently resigned.

Heath's government had initially attempted to address directly the snowballing stagflation crisis through a radical disengagement from cooperative forms of industrial relations and state support of industry: the discipline of the market would be brought to bear upon Britain's rigidified and uncompetitive economic relations. Yet this disciplining project became rapidly politicized, as it was neither justified by an immediately treacherous external position (considering the circumstances inherited from Wilson) nor underpinned by a coherent intellectual defence (as opposed to Thatcher's monetarist experiment) (Hall, 1993). Instead, Heath's economic tightening resulted in bankruptcies and growing unemployment, which directly challenged the government's legitimacy. The resulting policy U-turn consisted of selective palliation measures, designed to assuage the most militant fractions of the working class while simultaneously attempting to kickstart growth in an uncompetitive national economy within a context of global crisis. Such expansionary measures, in the absence of adequate profitability, acted to expand imports faster than exports, thus undermining the balance of payments, boosting inflationary pressures, and contributing to a growing property bubble (Clarke, 1988: 310).

Following Heath's defeat, Wilson returned to office, but without the far-reaching ambitions that had characterized his previous administration's National Plan. Nonetheless, the Wilson government did formulate, through the TUC/Labour Party Liaison Committee, a scheme to create a 'self-reinforcing spiral of disinflation' called the Social Contract (Britton, 1994: 19). Labour attempted to distance themselves from Heath's incomes policy by committing to voluntary collective bargaining and suggesting that the government would enact price controls and expand welfare subsidies in exchange for wage restraint on the part of the unions (Rogers, 2009: 638). The Social Contract was, to a degree, all things to all people, and was thus a useful instrument to reconcile the right and left wings of the Labour Party. Traditional social democrats within the party understood it as a means to better effect Keynesian demand management (Thompson, 2004: 59). Party radicals—who since 1970 had begun articulating an Alternative Economic Strategy (AES) through the National Executive Committee that sought to rejuvenate the British economy through an extension of economic planning, nationalization, and industrial democracy—could interpret the Social Contract as a step in the direction of socialist planning (Callaghan, 2000: 108). However, once it was required to be implemented on the ground, this policy framework quickly ran up against the reality of rapidly rising inflation and a growing external deficit, and the Social Contract transformed into what Britton (1994: 20) called 'frustrated Keynesianism'.

In 1974, demand remained depressed, investment was slowing, and the current account deficit stood at £3.3 billion (Rogers, 2009: 639). Simultaneously, from July

1974 to July 1975, wages rose by 33 per cent and retail prices by 26 per cent (Cairncross, 1995: 203). The government responded with a mildly contractionary budget that attempted to shift resources from the personal sector to the corporate export sector. Yet by December 1974, Permanent Secretary of the Treasury Douglas Wass observed that 'the economic costs of clinging to the existing [Social Contract] policy outweigh the political costs of abandoning it' (quoted in Rogers, 2009: 641). As Chris Rogers (2009) has shown, Healey's Treasury used the twin 'non-crises' of 1975—namely the fall in sterling's price and the government's drawing from the IMF credit facility—to justify cuts in public expenditure and a pivot towards a disciplinary incomes policy. Consequently, the Wilson government's pay policy was announced in July 1975, whereby a ceiling of £6 on weekly wage increases was implemented in order to reduce the rate of inflation (Needham, 2014: 88); while in November, following the application to the IMF, Healey announced that 50 per cent of state spending would be subject to cash limits (ibid.: 182). Although this succeeded to a certain extent in tackling inflation, which fell from 22.7 per cent in 1975 to 15.7 per cent in 1976, unemployment began to increase to politically difficult levels (Bank of England, 2018). The government's answer was not reflation, but rather to support ailing firms through the establishment of the National Enterprise Board. As Britton (1994: 28) writes, there was a 'political and social need for government to do something about unemployment, even though its hands were tied for the present on macroeconomic policy'.

The Wilson government's reversal, which Peter Jay of *The Times* called one of the most 'painful re-examinations of cherished commitments that any Government has ever undertaken in peacetime', had some success in combating the worst of the profitability crisis (quoted in Browning, 1986: 71). Inflation fell, investment began to increase, and the balance of payments deficit reduced in size (ibid.). In order to further alleviate British exporters' lack of competitiveness, and thus aid the balance of payments recovery, Healey sought a depreciation of sterling. Nevertheless, when sterling indeed began to slide downwards in March 1976, the government used this to create an air of crisis of confidence in the pound, thus justifying public spending cuts in the April budget (Rogers, 2013: 14). Following Wilson's resignation, Callaghan became Prime Minister in April and by June had negotiated a $5.3 billion loan from foreign central banks in order to support sterling. It was stipulated that if this loan was not repaid by December 1976, Britain would apply for a further loan from the IMF that would come with conditionalities—a strategy by which the US and West Germany sought to impose financial discipline upon Britain (Harmon, 1997: 9). Indeed, after sterling fell to nearly $1.50 in October, Callaghan announced an application to the IMF. The resulting $3.9 billion loan, agreed upon in December, was attached to a range of conditionalities, including a two-year ceiling on PSBR, £1 and £1.5 billion in public spending cuts over two years, domestic credit expansion targets, and the sale of state-owned petroleum shares (ibid.: 12–13). Yet this cannot be understood simply as the imposition by the US of economic stringency upon the British state through the instrument of the IMF: the 'IMF deal merely codified a change of political course well under way and proceeding under the stewardship of British social democracy' (Ludlam, 1992: 727). The Callaghan government found it 'politically expedient' to use the IMF bailout to depoliticize the unpopular discip- lining measures that it privately acknowledged were necessary, particularly given the rising influence of the leftist AES within the party, espoused by figures such as Tony Benn (Rogers, 2013: 15). By appealing to the IMF for conditional assistance, the government sought to limit its own 'freedom of action', and thus reassure global markets of Labour's economic credibility, while simultaneously allowing it to pursue domestic disciplining without shattering its popular legitimacy (Britton, 1994: 32).

Although it was not immediately clear at the time, the Callaghan government's rescue by the IMF would usher in a new phase of the profitability crisis. The periodic oscillation between palliative and disciplining strategies, in rhythm with the recurrent sterling crises, would give way to a different dynamic. With the pound set on a path of appreciation, British governments were faced with a dilemma: support the rise in sterling's price due to its deflationary, disciplining effects; or attempt to relieve the pressure of the strong pound on the domestic economy in order to preserve governing legitimacy. The crisis governing strategies that emerged in this period attempted to do both simultaneously.

The Strong Pound and the Deep Recession, 1977–83

The British experience of the global profitability crisis had, until 1977, been characterized chiefly by a periodic struggle to defend the price of sterling in the context of a deteriorating balance of payments performance. Foreign currency reserves, as such, were rarely in abundance, and had to be periodically run down in order to prop up the pound. Following the IMF's intervention, however, this situation changed dramatically. The sharp appreciation of sterling allowed the Bank to 'cream off' foreign currency and replenish the reserves, which reached £20.2 billion in November 1977 (Dow, 2013: 281; see Figure 3.2). Furthermore, North Sea oil, which started to flow in 1975, began to constitute a significant proportion of British exports in 1977, which further boosted sterling (Booth, 1995: 78).

This loosening of the external constraints on British policymakers did not imply their complete insulation from the global crisis. The strong pound both masked and exacerbated the decimation of non-oil industrial companies' rates of profit, and the rate of inflation remained high despite the disinflationary pressures of the exchange rate. The dilemmas created by the profitability crisis were not

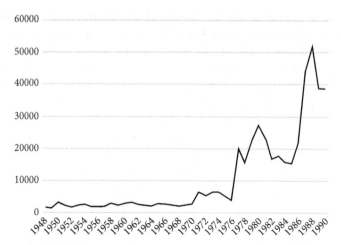

Figure 3.2. UK official international currency reserves ($US million), 1948–90 (Howson, 1994: 232).

resolved—they simply changed form. Rather than finding themselves pressed by the tangible demands of their electorate for the maintenance of living standards, on the one hand, and the threat of currency crises, on the other, the British state was now forced to reconcile the disciplining effects of the strong pound and the growing resistance from various sections of society to the resulting recessionary conditions.

In order to repay the IMF loan, the Callaghan government needed to ensure economic growth. Yet this could not come by way of demand stimulus reflation without sacrificing the IMF-imposed monetary targets. Export-led growth appeared to be the only solution, but the rising price of sterling made this difficult (Britton, 1994: 33). In order to achieve an increase in exports, then, the Callaghan government attempted to purchase the TUC's acquiescence to wage restraint through a series of tax cuts announced in July 1977. An expansionary mini-budget was also announced in October, in reaction to the increase of unemployment to over 1.2 million. In addition, the government sought to reduce the upward pressure on sterling by lowering interest rates and liberalizing exchange controls (to be examined in Chapter 5), which were partially dismantled in December 1977 and January 1978. Following the revelation that the PSBR had actually been below the IMF target in 1977, the government launched another moderately expansionary budget in April 1978, which led to an erosion of the balance of payments recovery as demand increased (Needham, 2014: 183).

At this time, fears within the government began to intensify that the recent confidence in sterling might not last, and that by the time the post-IMF boost in sterling wore off, the non-oil exporting sector of the economy would have already been decimated and deindustrialized. In July 1978, Callaghan consequently published a White Paper called *Winning the Battle Against Inflation*, which set a five per cent guideline for wage increases (Britton, 1994: 319). This strict incomes policy would, it was hoped, allow the government to increase the competitiveness of British industry by combating inflation, without the need to increase interest rates and thus further exacerbate the rise in sterling. This was not to be. The TUC rejected the five per cent guideline in September, and the Labour Party rejected any form of pay restraint at their party conference in October (Needham, 2014: 125). This paved the way for a devastating wave of industrial action, known as the 'Winter of Discontent', which began with Ford workers winning a 17 per cent wage hike in November 1978 and peaked with a one-day strike by 1.5 million public sector workers in January 1979 (Cairncross, 1995: 223). Labour subsequently lost the May General Election to Thatcher's Conservative Party.

The Thatcher governments have been subjected to intense academic scrutiny (Jessop, 1988; Hall, 1988; Kavanagh, 1990; Gamble, 1994a). Perhaps the phase of Thatcher's reign that has provoked the most debate was her first government's monetarist experiment in the early 1980s, which saw interest rates raised to politically painful heights with the aim of tackling inflation—mirroring the actions of the US Federal Reserve under Volcker (Thain, 1985; Bulpitt, 1986; Tomlinson, 2007). An important point of contention regarding this issue is the degree of intentionality behind the deep recession that resulted from this monetary policy stance. While Eric Evans (2004: 21) suggests that the Thatcher government purposefully plunged the British economy into a deep recession in order to 'kill inflation', Duncan Needham (2014) insists that the economic shock was a 'mistake' deriving from the government's unfamiliarity with monetary targeting. Yet rather than relying on this 'intentional versus accidental' schema, this period can be better understood by grasping the contradictory role of recession in the governance of capitalist society. The Thatcher administration's contractionary stance, alongside privatizations of nationalized industry and an assault on organized labour, was intended to restart profitable capital accumulation through the imposition of strict discipline. Yet the ensuing recessionary conditions also threatened to undermine the government's legitimacy. The result of these conflicting pressures was a fundamentally non-committal brand of monetarism. Thatcher's monetarist experiment can thus be understood as a negotiated attempt to reconcile the contradictory imperatives of value and human need through a hybrid governing strategy that fused elements of both palliation and depoliticized discipline.

Chancellor Geoffrey Howe's first budget in July 1979 was quite inconsistent, comprising deep counter-inflationary expenditure cuts and an interest rate hike, as well as inflationary VAT increases. In addition, the government removed the remaining exchange controls in July and October, in an effort to ease sterling's rise. Howe's second budget, on the other hand, was unambiguously contractionary.

In March 1980, the government set out MTFS—a framework of yearly declining targets for the money supply and PSBR. This policy was intended to lock the state authorities into a project of severe financial discipline: 'If the targets were not met there would be automatic fiscal or monetary changes in government policy. The room for discretionary economic management, which was held to have been so destabilizing in the past, would be drastically reduced' (Gamble, 1994a: 109).

However, this strategy of depoliticized discipline required a degree of perseverance that Thatcher did not possess, despite popular opinion to the contrary. In 1980, the stagflation crisis reached its most critical stage and the British economy experienced the worst economic downturn since the interwar period. Faced with more than two million unemployed, record levels of bankruptcies, and a collapse in GDP, Thatcher reneged on the MTFS commitments by reducing interest rates—despite the fact that the money supply aggregates were far in excess of the proclaimed targets (Britton, 1994: 53). As Needham (2014: 162; emphasis in original) wryly observed, 'the lady *was* for turning'. The government consequently enacted a hybridized crisis governing strategy. Palliative assistance was extended to firms and homeowners, through a relaxation of interest rates that was intended to ease corporate and mortgage debt repayments, as well as depreciating sterling to the advantage of exporters (Tomlinson, 2007). Simultaneously, the government attempted to stick to its MTFS target commitments by balancing the loosening of monetary discipline with more expenditure cuts and tax increases, as well as by selling massive quantities of government debt to soak up liquidity in the banking system (Goodhart, 1995: 106–7) (examined in Chapter 5). In order to aid the anti-inflationary push, the government moved forward with restrictive trade union legislation with the 1980 Employment Act, which banned secondary picketing, attempted to disrupt the closed shop, and provided state aid for secret ballots (Dorey, 1995: 116). As such, by the March 1981 budget the Thatcher administration was operating a deeply contradictory governing strategy—pressing its feet on the brake and the accelerator at the same time.

This hybridized governing strategy continued throughout 1982 and most of 1983. Bank lending continued to grow, making a mockery of the government's MTFS targets; yet unemployment also climbed above three million (Dow, 2013: 290). The government thus continued to rely on fiscal tightening and massive government debt sales to combat monetary growth, while a less strict monetary policy was intended to keep the worst effects of the recession at bay—particularly in the run-up to the June 1983 general election. As this book demonstrates in Chapter 6, the state's struggle to manage this disciplining strategy was closely tied to the 1983 exemption of the LSE from a restrictive practices court case, which resulted in the 1986 Big Bang financial liberalization. Furthermore, additional restrictions on labour organizing were introduced with the 1982 Employment Act, which redefined trade disputes (Dorey, 1995: 126). Nevertheless, the worst of the stagflation crisis was over. By 1983, British profitability had begun to climb, and inflation fell below five per cent, the lowest since 1968 (Bank of England, 2018).

Nationally, the meek 1980s recovery was driven by the depth of the preceding recession that had seen the destruction of low-productivity enterprises and the devaluation of capital, the injection of competitive discipline into British business through privatization and stringent financial conditions, the comprehensive defeat of organized labour that slowed wage growth and re-established capitalists' dominion over the labour process, and credit expansion powered by the financial liberalizations studied in this book (Crafts, 1988; Crafts, 2012; Fuller, 2016). Globally, the profitability crisis had reached its trough and the world economy began to experience the seeds of a moderate upturn that would gather pace in the 1990s, after a contraction at the beginning of that decade. This growth was powered by several world-historical transformations: the cheapening and ration-alization of capital caused by the monetarist shock; the subjugation of the working class in the Global North through recession, deindustrialization, and labour market flexibilization, and the simultaneous expansion and disempowerment of the Global South working class through deagrarianization, debt crises, and struc-tural adjustment; the success of the US information technology industry and the reallocation of labour-intensive manufacturing from the US to Mexico, from Germany to Eastern Europe, and from Japan to Taiwan, South Korea, and ultimately China; and an extraordinary credit expansion fuelled by a gradual loosening of monetary policy and cumulative financial liberalizations (Schwartz, 2018; Brenner, 2006; McNally, 2011; Benanav, 2015). Yet this profitability recov-ery and moderate boom would run out of steam by the late 1990s, followed by the unprecedented financial collapse of 2008 and a return to grinding stagnation alongside the inflation not of consumer goods prices but of asset and credit bubbles.

* * *

The above stylized history of the governance of the stagflation crisis does not serve simply as a historical background against which the analysis of financial liberal-ization can be framed. Instead, the discrete regulatory changes that will be analysed in this book constituted elements of British policymakers' broader responses to the global profitability crisis and its national manifestations. Financial liberalizations during this period served as elements of strategies to manage both the impersonal domination of a capitalist system that had driven itself into deep crisis and the legitimacy imperatives arising from a population that was unwilling to sacrifice its needs in the name of national competitiveness.

While there has been a long-standing tradition of analysing British decline, which stretches back to the late nineteenth century, it is important to distinguish between the long decline of the British imperial economy and the more dramatic profitability crisis that erupted in the late 1960s. British stagflation, a national manifestation of the global profitability crisis, can be further divided into two distinct periods. The first, which lasted from 1967 to 1977, was characterized by a worsening trade performance and consequently by repeated currency crises. As a result, governments during this period tended to oscillate between two forms of crisis-governing strategy. Palliative measures designed to delay the accelerating crisis and preserve the government's legitimacy tended to worsen the balance of payments and spark sterling crises. Policymakers would consequently impose a programme of financial discipline to rescue the external position, and often attempt to mask these measures through some form of depoliticization device. This back and forth pattern can be clearly seen in Wilson's move from the ambitious 'National Plan' to the post-devaluation contractionary measures, the transformation of Heath's initially austere and unpopular 'Quiet Revolution' into the economically disastrous 'Dash for Growth', and the abandonment of Wilson's Social Contract in favour of spending cuts and tough incomes policy. The CCC liberalization (which will be examined in Chapter 4) was formulated and implemented during this phase of the stagflation crisis. This measure was intended to support the authorities' efforts to pursue a competitive restructuring of the British economy, following Wilson's 1967 sterling devaluation, without generating a damaging social backlash.

The second period, from 1977 to 1983, took on a different dynamic. The appreciation of the pound, provoked by North Sea oil and the IMF's seal of approval, insulated the British economy from currency crises; yet it brought problems of its own. The strong pound aided the government in its disciplinary battle against inflation, but threatened to plunge the British economy into a politically unacceptable recession. As such, the Thatcher government during this period sought to navigate this dilemma by implementing a hybridized crisis-governing strategy, which combined further disciplining measures with selective forms of palliation designed to assuage important constituencies. The other three financial liberalizations studied in this book took place during this latter phase of the crisis. The abolition of exchange controls, explored in Chapter 5, was motivated by a desire to gently lower the price of sterling so as to aid British exporters and thus provide palliative relief to the British economy. The Big Bang, studied in Chapter 6, was in part a result of the Thatcher government's efforts to rescue the ailing MTFS project—itself a strategy to impose painful economic discipline in a depoliticized manner. Finally, FSA, which Chapter 7 will examine, constituted an effort to tie a bow on the previous decade and a half of financial liberalization by creating a comprehensive system of financial governance that would shield British governments from the political fallout generated by future financial crises.

4

Competition and Credit Control

CCC, introduced in 1971, was among the first major financial liberalizations of the postwar period. This reform dismantled London's traditional banking cartels and scrapped most of the state's direct controls on the financial sector's ability to lend. In place of this old policy framework, CCC left a stripped down, marketized system of financial control. Bank lending was to be chiefly regulated by the Bank's official interest rate—Bank Rate—while in emergencies the authorities could further call upon banking institutions to place 'special deposits' at the Bank in order to reduce their lending capacity. Bank Rate itself was soon replaced by the partly marketized Minimum Lending Rate (MLR) in late 1972, which tied the rate at which the Bank loaned money to the financial sector to the going market rate for Treasury Bills. CCC also placed the traditional clearing banks on an equal competitive footing with the ascendant 'secondary' banks that had been capturing greater market share by offering more attractive interest rates than the clearing cartel. Following CCC, all banks—clearing or secondary—had to abide by a reserve asset ratio of 12.5 per cent. Finally, the state would be less eager to intervene in the market for government debt, allowing market forces to have greater sway over the prices of Treasury Bills and gilt-edged securities (Moran, 1984; Burnham, 2011; Needham, 2014). CCC, in short, represented a radical marketization of monetary policy and financial regulation, whereby the state retreated from direct controls over the banking sector associated with postwar social democracy and instead allowed credit to be chiefly allocated by the price mechanism.

By all accounts, this was a disaster. Bank lending to the private sector rose from £1.9 to £6.4 billion in a single year, with credit funnelled not into industry, which was suffering from declining profitability, but into an increasingly inflated property market. This property bubble finally burst in 1973–5 with the Secondary Banking Crisis, heralding an end to a quarter century of relative financial stability and requiring the authorities to launch a 'lifeboat' operation to rescue exposed banks (Wilson Committee, 1980: 6–7; Needham, 2014: 46). In the aftermath of the bursting of this credit bubble, the Heath government introduced a system of 'supplementary special deposits', known as the 'corset', which limited the growth of bank deposits in an attempt to reduce credit expansion (Reid, 1982: 85). As Michael Moran (1984: 73) argues, this represented a 'partial return to control' of the financial sector 'by administrative decree', but many of the changes in the British financial sector sparked by CCC were 'irreversible'.

Governing Financialization: The Tangled Politics of Financial Liberalization in Britain. Jack Copley, Oxford University Press.
© Jack Copley 2022. DOI: 10.1093/oso/9780192897015.003.0004

In the decades following this episode, this pattern of inflation and bursting of asset bubbles, supercharged by a liberalized financial sector, would become very familiar. CCC, as such, was a crucial step in the construction of Britain's highly financialized economy—compounding a process that had been set in motion by the 1957 creation of London's Eurodollar market. Yet contrary to the claims of much of the financialization literature, this radical policy was neither a consequence of the City's unique access to the levers of political power nor an automatic reaction to economic crisis. Instead, this chapter will demonstrate that this financial liberalization resulted from the British state's tortured attempts to manage the controversial politics of governing the British economy during the onset of the global profitability crisis. Rather than constituting an intentional first step in a larger scheme to financialize the British economy, CCC was designed to provide relief to policymakers as they sought to navigate between the faceless domination of world value relations and the immediate demands of domestic constituencies in the context of the dissipating postwar boom.

British monetary governance in the postwar era was characterized by a diverse array of formal and informal state controls over a highly cartelized and oligopolistic banking system. From the 1960s, however, this system began to be eroded by the rise of new banking institutions that evaded both the City's cartels and the state's directions. It was in the context of this fraying governance model that the British state sought to impose a tough monetary tightening following the 1967 devaluation of sterling. The aim of this monetary stringency was to discipline the British economy in line with global competitiveness standards by implementing a painful monetary squeeze alongside a range of austerity measures. However, as stagflation began to gather pace, this disciplining strategy ran aground. With companies facing falling profit rates, the credit restriction threatened their ability to fund investment for export and thus risked jeopardizing the balance of payments recovery. In response to this dilemma, the state's strategy began to shift from a strictly disciplinary project to a hybrid discipline–palliation strategy, whereby the authorities sought to limit credit to persons for the consumption of imports while extending credit to exporting companies.

Yet this strategy began to put unbearable strain on the increasingly antiquated monetary governance system. The state's instruments of credit control proved ill-suited for simultaneously reducing credit for consumption and boosting credit for companies, while they generated growing political backlash against the state institutions attempting to wield them. The functional shortcomings and rapid politicization of the existing monetary controls led the government, Treasury, and Bank to consider alternatives; yet it was the Bank in particular that produced the uniquely hands-off CCC proposals, driven in part by a desire to bolster its own institutional autonomy. While the government and Treasury were anxious about various aspects of CCC, they were attracted by the possibility of enforcing monetary discipline in a more depoliticized manner. A combination of persuasion and political manoeuvring by the Bank ensured the proposals' transformation into policy. Thus, as the world profitability crisis was beginning to rear its head, CCC emerged as an ultimately flawed strategy to discipline British monetary relations in an arm's-length, depoliticized fashion, so as to align Britain's economy with the impersonal dictates of the global law of value without generating destabilizing political backlash.

The City in Flux

Britain's postwar political economy relied on an uneasy compromise between an oligopolistic, cartelized banking sector and a state oriented towards meeting social democratic goals (A. Davies, 2017: 76). The UK banking sector was run according to 'officially sanctioned "cartel" agreements' among the biggest deposit banks, known as clearing banks, who agreed upon a set interest rate on their deposits and loans (Haache and Taylor, 2013: 5). The money market was also characterized by oligopolistic arrangements, with financial institutions called discount houses acting as privileged intermediaries between the Bank and the private banking system, providing liquidity to the financial system. In turn, the clearing bank and discount house cartels were linked together by their own rigid agreements, whereby the former would lend money to the latter at an agreed rate (Needham, 2014: 31). In stark contrast to today, banking was widely understood as 'an activity where intense competition would endanger prudent judgement' (Moran, 1984: 36).

This traditional, uncompetitive banking system was useful for the British state, as monetary policy decisions could be transferred via the cartels to the rest of the British economy through a combination of formal controls and 'moral suasion'. For part of the postwar period, until CCC, the state authorities utilized a combination of six key instruments to implement monetary policy: liquidity ratios, which forced banks to hold a certain percentage of their deposit liabilities in liquid assets; hire purchase terms controls, which limited the purchase of consumer goods by instalment; open market operations, which meant the government sold or bought gilt-edged securities to or from the non-bank sector in order to influence the level of bank liquidity; Bank Rate, the rate at which the Bank lends money to financial institutions; special deposits, which were deposits that banks would be requested to hold at the Bank in order to reduce their liquid assets and thus their lending capacity; and lending ceilings, a combination of formal and informal requests for banks to keep their total lending below a certain level (see Needham, 2014: 14–18). With this panoply of policy instruments, the state sought to regulate the creation of credit within Britain's rigidified banking system in accordance with its macroeconomic objectives.

However, this monetary policy mechanism became less effective with the rise of the 'fringe' or 'secondary' banking sector, which began in the 1950s and accelerated in the 1960s. Parallel to the clearing bank and discount house cartels, a new money market emerged, with various institutions attracting deposits by offering higher interest rates than the clearing cartel, and in turn lending these funds out to borrowers who could afford higher rates (Reid, 1982: 24–5). A wide variety of financial institutions took part in this secondary banking sector, with some taking large, wholesale deposits (accepting houses, overseas banks, foreign banks) and others specializing in consumer banking taking retail deposits (building societies, finance banks, savings banks) (Gola and Roselli, 2009: 6–7). While this banking activity was conducted with sterling, these loans were not secured by the Bank as lender of last resort, nor were they subject to the same credit limits as the cartel banks (Reid, 1982: 25). During this same period, huge volumes of US dollar deposits, known as Eurodollars, began to accumulate in banks located in London in an attempt to escape US regulations, as discussed in Chapter 3 (Strange, 1994). British banks welcomed the opportunity to conduct their business in dollars, given the state limits on the use of sterling and the fact that decolonization had resulted in a loss of market share for these banks in countries like India (Green, 2020: 110). The Eurodollar market operated in a 'non-regulatory vacuum', yet officials within the Bank aided in the development of this market as a way to bolster the City's status as a global financial centre, despite the detrimental effect of these unrestricted financial flows on the Bretton Woods order (Burn, 1999: 236). One result of the creation of the Eurodollar market was the influx of US banks into London during the 1960s, creating deep interdependencies between the British and US financial systems (Green, 2020: 124). Outside of the UK's cosy banking cartels, then, a highly competitive financial market had emerged. This fringe banking system began to sap deposits from traditional banks by offering higher interest rates, with the clearing banks' share of total deposits falling by half between 1951 and 1967 (Moran, 1984: 43). In response, clearing banks manoeuvred to evade the cartel restrictions by setting up subsidiaries that operated in the secondary markets.

As credit creation began to balloon outside of the traditional cartels, the state's methods of control became less effective. Moran (1984) argues that the Bank had long sought to govern the City in an informal manner, regulating the creation of credit through personal relationships with the banking oligopoly. To this end, the Bank resisted, with varying degrees of success, attempts by governments in the postwar period to harness credit control for the purposes of demand management through formal restrictions. However, as the scale, diversity, and international character of British banking increased, the 'social cohesion' of the City's cartelistic networks, 'which had allowed the Bank to exercise delicate control by private, personal communications', was eroded (ibid.: 49). The clearing banks, which were the chief vessels through which monetary control was exercised, were in danger of being eclipsed by new competitors. While this changing financial environment represented a gradual wearing away of the state's monetary policy transmission mechanism, this became a matter of emergency as the state sought to implement a severe credit squeeze following the 1967 sterling devaluation.

The Dilemmas of Monetary Discipline

As discussed in the previous chapter, the Wilson government devalued sterling in 1967 in response to repeated currency crises provoked by stubborn balance of payments deficits and deteriorating world economic conditions—respectively, national and global manifestations of the nascent profitability crisis. In addition to devaluation, which would help British exports, Wilson attempted to boost Britain's economic competitiveness on the world market through a steep domestic contraction. This was intended to rescue Britain's balance of payments position and ward off speculative attacks on sterling. Monetary tightening was the jewel in the crown of this disciplining project, and lending ceilings were the most import-ant element of the monetary policy toolkit. This focus on credit creation was compounded by the fact that the government secured IMF loans in 1967 and 1969, and an important condition of the latter loan was adherence to a target for a monetary aggregate called Domestic Credit Expansion (DCE) (Clift and Tomlinson, 2012). The IMF's influence during these years spurred a growing interest among Treasury and particularly Bank officials in targeting monetary aggregates, leading to the creation of the Bank's Money Supply Group in 1968 (Needham, 2014: 25). Yet rather than seeking to effect a general credit squeeze, the Treasury and Bank sought to reduce bank lending to persons, in order to weaken consumption of imports, while maintaining bank lending to exporting companies (Aveyard, Corthorn, and O'Connell, 2018). The ultimate aim of this strategy to shift credit resources from persons to export companies was to create a balance of payments surplus and ensure the competitive viability of the British economy on the world market.

This strategy immediately ran into several intractable problems that brought the entire system of monetary control into question and set the stage for CCC. The lending ceilings were too blunt an instrument to effectively repress personal borrowing *and* allow industrial exporters to expand their borrowing. The state thus faced a perpetual dilemma as to whether to maintain the credit squeeze in order to discipline stubbornly high consumer lending or relax monetary policy in order to provide a palliative response to a company sector that was facing falling profit rates. In addition, because this monetary tightening was chiefly pursued through restricting the lending of the clearing banks, it further exacerbated their eclipse by the fringe banking sector, whose lending was far more difficult to restrain. This led to the rapid politicization of the lending ceilings, as banks, industrial companies, sections of the media, and various politicians began to protest this uneven credit squeeze. Ultimately, the existing monetary toolkit could not politically bear the weight of the disciplining strategy that it was tasked with enforcing, leading the government, Treasury, and Bank to seek an alternative system of monetary control.

Personal Borrowing

Wilson's post-devaluation budget exerted a powerful downward pressure on British living standards. To resist this, people increased their borrowing from banks. Lending to persons continued to rise for a full nine months after the monetary tightening that accompanied devaluation.[1] As a result, in the second half of 1968 total consumer spending was exceeding its 1967 level, in spite of the Budget's goal to restrict it by two per cent. This surprised Chancellor Jenkins, who told the Bank Governor:

> It could not be argued that the Budget had been insufficiently harsh in respect of personal consumption, yet it was clear that people were very resistant to lowering their standard of living. There was little reason to believe that they would not take countervailing action to maintain their standard of living... [I]f additional measures were needed before the Budget he would be inclined to move on monetary policy, for example by lowering the ceiling for bank advances.[2]

Thus, in November 1968 the credit ceiling was reduced further to 98 per cent of its 1967 level, with credit for exports and shipbuilding excluded. In addition, stricter hire purchase controls acted to shrink demand for consumer credit. The explicit goal of this approach was to transfer credit resources away from persons and towards export companies. As Treasury economist Arnold Lovell argued in November 1968: 'We do not want to inhibit industrial expansion or activity I would have thought... we do want to curb the growth in consumer demand, in the hope that this will encourage the shift of resources into exports'.[3] This strategy was explicitly mentioned in the House of Commons by the President of the Board of Trade, Anthony Crosland, who explained that people had to accept a drop in their consumption 'in the interests of achieving our over-riding national objective, which is to increase our exports, import-saving production and capital investments' (Aveyard, Corthorn, and O'Connell, 2018: 103).

Yet it was extremely difficult to enforce this consumer credit restriction. The clearing banks continually struggled to bypass the ceiling, out of fear of losing further depositors to the secondary banks. In 1966 all major banks had begun

---

[1] TNA T 326/961, Bank lending, 22 November 1968.
[2] TNA T 326/961, Dowler to Hawtin, 25 October 1968.
[3] TNA T 326/961, Lovell to Armstrong, 14 November 1968.

issuing credit cards, and by 1969 the banks were consistently breaching the lending ceiling (ibid.: 104–7). The Chancellor met with the clearing bank chairmen in February 1969 and expressed how 'disappointing' and 'disturbing' he found the rate of bank lending.[4] He 'reiterated his absolute determination to carry through the Government's economic strategy...Weakness in the credit field must not be allowed to undermine the strategy'.[5] Yet the authorities recognized the dilemma faced by the clearing banks: they could either violate the lending ceilings or risk ceding market share to the more competitive secondary banks. Treasury official Michael Posner acknowledged in October 1969 the frustration of attempting to effect a credit squeeze when so little influence could be exerted over the fringe banks: 'we must continue to be very concerned about the very high liquidity of the non-clearing banks...I think that we must certainly envisage some method of robbing these banks of their power to lend'.[6] The attempt to keep personal lending under control continued to be an uphill battle. By April 1971, Barclays had announced the launch of a new personal loans scheme that would extend credit 'from £100 to £1,000, to anyone over 18, whether a customer of Barclays or not, who is credit-worthy and in regular employment'.[7] Though these schemes were 'embarrassing', they did not represent a 'serious immediate threat to our credit control'. However, these developments were a worrying indication of what was to come: 'It is clear that the banks see the consumer loan market as the major area for expansion over the years ahead and are preparing themselves for a major assault on that market'.[8]

In addition to wielding monetary policy to reduce lending for personal consumption, the state also intended to use the credit squeeze to discourage companies from making inflationary wage settlements. Industrial conflict intensified from the mid 1960s, with the number of days lost to strikes rising from 2.8 million in 1967 to 10.9 million in 1970 when the Conservatives arrived in power (Whittingham and Towers, 1977: 77). From the Treasury's perspective, this strife meant that any perceived relaxation of monetary policy could be interpreted by the unions as the beginning of another boom period, fuelling bolder pay demands. Further, if monetary relaxation boosted demand when industrial output was crippled by strikes, the effect on the balance of payments would be damaging. This was a particular concern with regards to the British auto industry: 'There was a distinct chance of industrial unrest and if this transpired it would be dangerous to stimulate demand for cars since the effect would be to increase imports'.[9]

Yet the aim of reducing companies' ability to make wage concessions to trade unions came into direct conflict with the need to relieve companies' growing

---

[4] TNA T 326/961, Note of a meeting, 28 February 1969.   [5] Ibid.
[6] TNA T 326/966, Posner to Hudson, 28 October 1969.
[7] TNA T 326/1352, Note for the record, 15 April 1971.
[8] TNA T 326/1352, Cassell to Ryrie, 16 April 1971.
[9] TNA T 326/1109, Note of a meeting in the Chancellor's room, 16 January 1970.

financial difficulties in order to boost exports. Treasury official Wass wrote in June 1971 that credit relaxation would 'enable the [car] industry to sustain their medium term investment plans, and so establish their competitive position vis-a-vis the Common Market producers', and 'if other things were equal, we would I am sure want to support the case for some relaxation on industrial grounds'.[10] Yet this would convey the wrong signal to car manufacturers in terms of pay settlements:

> Unfortunately other things are not equal. The industry has undoubtedly been the maverick of employers in the private sector so far as incomes restraint is concerned. It has totally disregarded the Government's exhortations to exercise moderation: and although Fords did stand up to strong union pressure for several weeks, in the event they climbed down and conceded a two-year inflationary pay award.[11]

As such, if any monetary relaxation took place, 'the industry will I am sure feel that it has nothing to fear from the Government and that much of the talk about punishment for those who transgress in the field of pay negotiations is without substance'.[12]

In attempting to address the balance of payments problems through monetary policy, the authorities began to understand the scale of the challenge they faced. Personal borrowing was proving resistant to credit restriction, while any suggestion by the authorities of future monetary relaxation entailed the danger of encouraging companies to grant their workers inflationary pay rises that would further imperil the balance of payments recovery. These factors all suggested that an even stricter monetary stance was appropriate. Yet, as will be examined next, this monetary tightening risked damaging the balance of payments in another way: by starving cash-strapped industrial exporters of much needed credit.

Company Liquidity

As suggested above, the state's attempt to restructure the British economy in line with global competitivity standards at a moment of growing world crisis, through the imposition of a tough credit restriction, began to run up against the problem of the worsening financial position of exporting companies. Falling profit rates had by the late 1960s led to a critical drying up of company liquidity. As such, it became increasingly difficult for many companies to fund existing working capital, let alone commit capital to future investments. This was exacerbated by

---

[10] TNA T 326/1263, Wass to Henley, 10 June 1971.   [11] Ibid.   [12] Ibid.

the policy of lending ceilings, which strangled the flow of bank credit that had made up for the decline in company profits.

There was increasing evidence in 1969 that low company liquidity was beginning to threaten the recovery in the balance of payments. Official statistics revealed that London clearing bank lending increased by £563 million from November 1967 to mid September 1969, £537 million of which was directed to manufacturing industry.[13] At an informal dinner in the City in October, merchant bankers warned Treasury officials that 'companies were beginning to feel the pinch': 'A number of companies had been counting on certain rates of profit in order to enable them to meet their obligations... and the profit record was not coming up to expectations'.[14] In a meeting on 18 December, the Bank Governor Leslie O'Brien argued that some monetary easing was now appropriate, although only 'without giving the impression of any general relaxation'.[15] These pressures intensified in 1970. In January, O'Brien informed Jenkins:

> our monetary forecasts project an extremely tight financial position for companies, especially in this current quarter, but also beyond if present policies continue unchanged. So far it appears that companies have coped with the squeeze on them by running down their liquid resources, taking trade credit wherever possible, repatriating funds from abroad and economising on stocks... The question is whether, nevertheless, companies will be forced by the financial stringency to prune their investment plans unless steps are taken to enable them to acquire extra finance from the banks, from the capital market or from the Government.[16]

Statistical analyses from February to May 1970 showed that the majority of bank advances had been to manufacturing industry, particularly engineering, followed by construction and mining. Indeed, when the Chancellor enquired about the causes of the rise in bank lending at a meeting on 27 July, the Bank Governor replied that one crucial factor was the 'difficult liquidity position of the company sector'.[17] Financial forecasting concluded that corporate liquidity was 'exceptionally tight by past standards', such that it was feared companies would try to extend their borrowing at home and abroad or 'be tempted to cut back or postpone some of their investment'.[18]

A contradiction emerged in the Treasury's management of monetary policy. On the one hand, the expansion of the money supply, which had gained new importance

---

[13] TNA T 326/963, Lovell to Neale, 16 October 1969.
[14] TNA T 326/963, Armstrong to Allen, 31 October 1969.
[15] TNA T 326/963, Record of a meeting, 19 December 1969.
[16] TNA T 326/1109, O'Brien to Jenkins, 9 January 1970.
[17] TNA T 326/1352, Note for the record, 27 July 1970.
[18] TNA T 326/1352, Painter to Figgures, 7 August 1970.

since the IMF's intervention, suggested that significant tightening was necessary. Reducing personal loans and deterring inflationary pay settlements would dampen the demand for imports. On the other hand, the performance of the company sector pointed in the opposite direction. If falling profitability was undermining companies' investment plans, then Britain could not export its way out of its balance of payments problems unless companies could secure adequate credit. Second Permanent Secretary Frank Figgures was informed by Treasury official R. J. Painter in August 1970 that

> the forecast financial position of companies still looked very tight, and this ... throws up the question whether continuation of present policies would cause companies to cut back their investment plans. At the same time we have to recognise that action of any kind which facilitated a larger increase in the money supply could tend to affect the reserves adversely.[19]

As the forces of stagflation gathered pace, the Bank Governor admitted to the new Chancellor in July 1970 that the 'economic indicators presented a confused picture'.[20] 'Output had been stagnant and unemployment had risen', while simultaneously 'there had been a weakening in the current account of the balance of payments and wage inflation had not been brought under control'.[21] This accelerating global crisis, which was felt particularly acutely in Britain due to its relative lack of competitiveness, began to render the instruments of postwar demand management increasingly anachronistic: the worsening economic slump indicated that credit restrictions should be relaxed, while the state of personal borrowing, wage inflation, and the current account suggested a tightening. The system of lending ceilings proved itself incapable of reconciling this paradox. As the Prime Minister's Principal Private Secretary and former Radcliffe Committee secretary Robert Armstrong explained, 'there is no future in retaining the ceiling but exempting "credit for investment" from it. This is simply unworkable: the banks cannot identify credit to particular firms by purpose to the extent that this would indicate'.[22] Indeed, even if the credit ceiling could discriminate between borrowers in this manner, the Treasury's Permanent Secretary Douglas Allen claimed that 'it could not be altered frequently, and it was difficult to enforce effectively'.[23]

The attempt by both the Wilson and Heath governments to render the British economy viable on the world market—in the context of a global profitability crisis that was gathering pace—was threatened by the contradictory state of domestic credit growth. While the increase in personal borrowing suggested the need for disciplinary credit tightening in order to reduce imports, the dire state of

---

[19] Ibid.   [20] TNA T 326/1352, Note for the record, 27 July 1970.   [21] Ibid.
[22] TNA T 326/1109, Armstrong to Figgures, 8 January 1970.
[23] TNA T 326/966, Minutes of a meeting, 29 October 1969.

corporate liquidity suggested that palliative credit should be extended to companies in order to boost exports. This contradiction was pulling the existing system of credit controls in opposing directions, and it became clear that the monetary tools at the state's disposal were not flexible enough to effectively achieve both goals simultaneously. Yet in addition to the functional shortcomings of these controls, they were also becoming increasingly politicized, endangering the legitimacy of the state institutions tasked with implementing them.

The Politicization of Discipline

Lending ceilings, which had been employed in 1957–8 and 1961–2 before being implemented again in 1967, were initially considered a depoliticized avenue through which to discipline credit expansion. Two institutional layers acted to separate the government from direct borrowers: the clearing banks and the Bank. This allowed the government and Treasury to conduct monetary policy at arm's length. As Painter commented:

> The whole apparatus of 'control' is a voluntary arrangement, operated as the City seem to prefer through the Bank of England in the driving seat. As long as the business carries on without too much controversy, there are advantages to Westminster and Whitehall in it being conducted at this remove.[24]

Yet as this system of credit control came under greater pressure to enforce the state's disciplining measures, controversy began to come frequently, in large doses, and from a range of sources.

In the context of the incipient stagflation crisis, the Wilson government's extended and painful credit squeeze began to provoke increasing political contestation. In May 1968 in the House of Commons, Chancellor Jenkins was questioned repeatedly by Conservative MPs about the relationship between the monetary tightening and 'the worst consecutive period of heavy unemployment which we have known since the 1930s'.[25] Jenkins was publicly taken to task again in 1970, as Conservative MP Kenneth Baker asked why the credit squeeze could not be eased: 'Is there not ample evidence that the economy needs reflating?'[26] Further pressed on whether the construction industry could be exempted from the lending ceilings due to the high number of unemployed building workers, Jenkins responded that if every struggling sector was given exemption, the general economic strategy would come apart: 'Once one has already made a great number of

[24] TNA T 326/1352, Painter to Armstrong, 18 May 1970.
[25] TNA T 326/791, House of Commons, 24 May 1968.
[26] TNA T 326/1109, House of Commons, 17 February 1970.

holes in any piece of cloth there is not much of the cloth left'.[27] Even when monetary policy was somewhat relaxed in 1971 by Heath, the *Daily Express* seized upon the credit easing's pro-company bias, running the subheading: 'Not you! ... [M]an-in-the-street borrowers can't expect to get anything extra from the new deal' (McKelvie, 1971).

Despite the aim of monetary policy being to shift resources from persons to industry, the Treasury came under sustained pressure from the CBI to go further. The CBI stated in 1969 that 'a relaxation of the pressure on company liquidity is now called for', which should be achieved by shifting emphasis away from tax policy towards monetary policy.[28] In January 1970, during preparations for a meeting between the CBI and the Treasury, a brief was circulated which stated that the 'suggestions that we have put forward [to the Treasury] over the last few months for easing the pressure of company liquidity' include '[r]elaxation of the restrictions on bank lending'.[29] The CBI believed it important to 'repeat our arguments' to the Treasury regarding credit liberalization because ten per cent of manufacturing firms were expected to reduce their output due to a 'shortage of credit or finance'.[30] Such requests were likely made through official channels and during 'regular CBI/Treasury Tea Parties'.[31]

The state's relationships with the clearing banks also began to fray. At a meeting between Bank officials and clearing bank representatives in early 1969, the clearing banks complained that they were being forced to implement the government's painful and unpopular disciplining strategy: 'Managers were tending to lose heart and the public image of the banks was getting worse and worse ... The banks wondered whether H.M.Goverment [sic] fully understood their difficulties. They (the banks) feared that they would have to take the blame for the consequences of credit restriction.'[32] In addition, the clearing banks stated that they 'were increasingly perturbed at the loss of new style business to outside competitors' that 'were not subject to ceilings'.[33] The clearers were not only relied upon to enforce the credit squeeze, but were being usurped by competitors in the process. Furthermore, it was not entirely clear whether the state even had the power to enforce the government's lending directives. In 1969, a Bank solicitor informed Lovell that attempts to limit bank lending through restrictions on overdrafts and special deposits may not be legally enforceable.[34] Fear grew within the Bank that the clearers, in their frustration, could mount a legal challenge to the Bank's authority granted to it under the 1946 Bank of England Act (Needham, 2014: 30). Such overt conflict threatened to undermine the Bank's regulatory authority

[27]   Ibid.   [28]   MRC MSS.200/C/3/ECO/2/29, CBI staff comment, 4 November 1969.
[29]   MRC MSS.200/C/3/ECO/2/29, Brief for CBI/Treasury meeting, 19 January 1970.   [30]   Ibid.
[31]   MRC MSS.200/C/3/DG2/22, Note of a meeting, 25 November 1971.
[32]   TNA T 326/962, Note for the record, 1 April 1969.
[33]   TNA T 326/962, Note for the record, 1 April 1969.
[34]   TNA T 326/963, Brooke to Lovell, 10 September 1969.

over the City, which relied on informal customs, personal relationships, and cooperation. As such, in pursuing balance of payments objectives through the enforcement of lending ceilings, the authorities risked sparking a very public contest with the City, which they could not be sure they would win.

This growing backlash against the post-devaluation credit restriction was compounded by a long-term trend in British politics towards the advocacy of greater banking competition. As Aled Davies (2017) shows, pressure grew across the political spectrum in the 1960s for the dismantling of the City's cartelistic, oligopolistic arrangements. Within the Labour Party during this period, 'City financiers re-emerged as the villains who, through constant speculation against sterling, were destroying the government's grand plans for economic moderniza-tion and social equity' (ibid.: 88). This view gelled, in an uneasy manner, with the Conservatives' support for the free, competitive operation of the price mechanism. In 1966, the Department of Economic Affairs tasked the NBPI with producing a report into the clearing banks' activities. The 1967 report advocated the expan-sion, diversification, and increased transparency of the clearing banks, as well as their abandonment of the cartel (Capie, 2010: 442). *The Economist* commented on the 'supreme irony in the prospect of the gentle oligopolies of Lombard Street finally being propelled into all this capitalistic rough stuff by a socialist govern-ment' (A. Davies, 2017: 91). The NBPI's findings were reinforced in 1971 by the report of the Crowther Committee, which went further in emphasizing that credit should be allocated according to the competitive principles of the market (Capie, 2010: 442). As support grew across the partisan divide for ending the City's uncompetitive practices, the state came under increasing pressure to discover a different method of monetary control that relied less on the banking cartels.

If the post-devaluation system of credit controls ever constituted a depoliticized mechanism for imposing discipline upon the British economy, this was no longer the case by the early 1970s. Not only were credit controls being tugged in opposing directions by the contradictory forces of buoyant personal borrowing and dwin-dling company liquidity, but they had also become deeply politicized. As the state's disciplining strategy came under greater scrutiny, provoking a backlash from industry, the banks, and both major political parties, it became clear that a radical alternative was needed.

The Search for a New Approach

CCC was the Bank's brainchild. It emerged from debates that had taken place within the Bank's Money Supply Group following the 1967 IMF intervention. A key objective for Bank officials was to rescue the vessel—the clearing banks—through which they conducted their peculiarly British form of financial regulation and monetary policy. This would be achieved by levelling the competitive playing field between the clearers and the fringe banks, through the scrapping of lending ceilings, abolition of the clearing cartel, and introduction of a standard reserve asset ratio that would apply to all banking institutions. Despite its name, the Bank understood CCC as a way to consolidate the clearing banks' dominance, rather than introduce more competition (Needham, 2014). Yet CCC cannot be explained by reference to the Bank's preferences alone. By the early 1970s, the Treasury and government had 'lost faith in ceilings' but were 'uncertain about where to go next' (Moran, 1984: 52). Relying on lending ceilings to both discipline personal borrowers and extend palliative credit to exporting companies had proven functionally difficult and politically painful. CCC appeared to offer an imperfect solution to these problems.

In spite of the supposedly radical character of the Bank's CCC proposals, Chancellor Jenkins had flirted with the 'the abandonment of the rigid 98% [lending] ceiling', 'the break-up of the cartel', and the tolerance of 'higher interest rates' as early as spring 1969.[35] His Treasury officials, however, concluded 'with a good deal of reluctance' that 'so long as we are aiming at as severe a degree of restraint as we are at present trying to achieve and maintain', there was no 'more effective method than the ceiling in sight'.[36] While Posner 'sadly' agreed, he urged that the authorities continue to search for a better system of control: 'Ratios of some sort, or special deposits, or *something*, will eventually be deployed and worked, whoever may be the personalities in Westminster, Whitehall and the City'.[37] Such a Treasury–Bank search party was set up in the autumn of 1969 under the title of the Working Group on Control of Bank Credit, which became the Group on Monetary Policy in 1970 (Aveyard, Corthorn, and O'Connell, 2018: 107). After ruling out bolder changes, the group advised the Chancellor in March 1970 to scrap lending ceilings while maintaining guidance to the clearing banks on the preferred rate of bank lending (Needham, 2014: 32–3). Special deposits were to be retained as a fine for possible violations of the authorities' requests. The Chancellor acquiesced.

A greater reliance upon changes in Bank Rate to control credit creation had up until this point troubled both the Treasury and the Bank, and acted as an impediment to more strident reforms. This was due to fears that attempts to rein in bank lending with frequent interest rate changes would destabilize markets for the state's gilt-edged bonds, thus endangering Britain's ability to fund the National Debt (Dutta, 2017: 10). Yet during the summer of 1970 opinion began to change within the Bank, following discussions with the US Federal Reserve. As Needham (2014: 35) argues, growing agreement that the impact of Bank Rate changes upon the saleability of gilts had been exaggerated contributed to the

[35] TNA T 326/962, Note of a meeting, 27 March 1969.
[36] TNA T 326/962, Armstrong to Neale, 2 June 1969.
[37] TNA T 326/962, Posner to Neale, 9 June 1969; emphasis in original.

Bank's belief that 'the final obstacle to managing the money supply had been overcome'.

This theoretical transformation within the Bank was compounded by its growing political frustration with the government. Following Heath's election victory in June 1970, on a political platform that foregrounded the need for greater economic competition, the Bank expected to find a receptive audience for their new ideas about controlling the money supply. Yet this soon turned out to be false hope. When the Governor implored Chancellor Barber in October to raise Bank Rate in response to a concerning increase in bank lending and inflation, he was rebuffed due to the negative impact this tightening would have on growth (Needham (2014: 37–9). Spurred by a desire to circumvent these political roadblocks, the Bank began with new urgency to put together the proposals for monetary reform that would end up as CCC. As Burnham (2007: 413) argues, this attempt to depoliticize economic discipline by sidestepping government should be understood as part of a long-standing desire by the Bank to 'shore up its traditional role that had been questioned repeatedly since 1945'. Indeed, Bank official Kit McMahon had claimed that one of the reasons the Bank had adopted the IMF's DCE targets after devaluation was to place an external constraint on government (Capie, 2010: 455).

The Bank revealed CCC to the Treasury in January 1971. The Treasury immediately recognized that the new proposals offered a way to govern credit creation in a more depoliticized manner, shielding the authorities from the painful backlash to their disciplining project. As Posner observed, 'several of us were attracted by the notion that we could escape from the ceilings and run an "arms-length" [sic] control of the banking system...the scheme suggested would (if it worked) serve our original purpose, and I think the Finance Group economists all rather admire it'.[38] In addition to the depoliticized nature of CCC, it chimed with the competition rhetoric of the new Conservative government. Chancellor Barber admitted that 'he was attracted by the approach of abandoning methods of credit control which restricted competition'.[39] The Minister of State too 'found the proposals heartening, and in accordance with the Conservative approach'.[40]

However, the Treasury had serious concerns that delayed the progress of CCC. There remained anxieties among certain Treasury officials that the new system of frequent interest rate changes could 'have an undesirable effect on the marketability of Government debt'.[41] Yet two bigger fears predominated. Firstly, while CCC could serve as an effective tool to impose monetary discipline in a depoliticized fashion, it was less adept at extending palliative credit to the export sector. In this sense, it failed to solve one of the main problems of the lending

---

[38] TNA T 326/1261, Posner to Cowdy, 18 February 1971.
[39] TNA T 326/1261, Note of a meeting, 3 March 1971.   [40] Ibid.
[41] TNA T 326/1261, Minutes of a meeting, 26 March 1971.

ceilings, that is, their inability to properly discriminate between personal and company borrowing. CCC 'would be more flexible than ceiling controls, but it would not be possible to operate it selectively by applying different rules to different kinds of lending'.[42] As Neale explained, the new system could be operated to reduce 'the total increase in the money supply', 'but at the cost of larger movements in interest rates which might have a further dampening effect on investment intentions'.[43] Furthermore, it was suggested that '[c]onsumer credit demand was less sensitive to changes in interest rates than industrial investment demand', and thus 'there was a danger that reliance on high interest rates to control total credit would result in industry bearing the brunt'.[44] Andrew Britton, the Treasury's Senior Economic Adviser, explained the dilemma in March: 'The present forecasts show a company sector financial position which is quite possibly critical in the short run and which is certainly not sustainable in the medium term. *The* policy problem is to help companies without an excessive growth of money supply.'[45] In June, Home Finance Adviser Frank Cassell was tasked with discovering a compromise between CCC and the existing export credit scheme, but concluded that the 'blunt fact is we think they do not tie in together at all well'.[46] These directional controls on lending clashed with CCC's philosophy of allowing banks to arrange their portfolios however they pleased. CCC had the potential serve as an effective tool of depoliticized discipline, but the palliation strategy would have to be abandoned.

Secondly, Treasury officials were concerned that a credit boom could occur during the transition period between the lending ceilings and CCC. As Allen explained to Chancellor Barber, 'although the system might be satisfactory in the long term, there was reason to be cautious about the transition'.[47] Articulating the same sentiment, Donald MacDougall pointed out that if CCC was implemented 'at that time when the balance of payments was weakening and the demand for loans increasing', '[a]ny easing of monetary policy which resulted from the introduction of the scheme might well be disastrous'.[48] If the state authorities were to let go of the reins of monetary control, even for a short period, the long, arduous recovery in British world competitiveness since 1967 could be jeopardized. For these reasons, the CCC proposals made slow passage through the Treasury: in March, prior to his Budget speech, Barber stated that he 'saw no need, from a political point of view, to move at present in the direction suggested' by the Bank.[49]

[42] TNA T 326/1384, Note of a meeting, 25 June 1971.
[43] TNA T 326/1261, Neal to Figgures, 9 March 1971.
[44] TNA T 326/1384, Note of a meeting, 25 June 1971.
[45] TNA T 326/1261, Britton to Posner, 5 March 1971; emphasis in original.
[46] TNA T 326/1263, Cassell to Henley, 4 June 1971.
[47] TNA T 326/1261, Note of a meeting, 3 March 1971.
[48] TNA T 326/1261, Minutes of a meeting, 22 February 1971.
[49] TNA T 326/1261, Note of a meeting, 3 March 1971.

Yet the Treasury's worries over the new system were ultimately eased by a combination of Bank persuasion, manoeuvring, and concessions, leading Whitehall and Downing Street to accept the CCC proposals and launch them on 16 September 1971. Regarding the inability of CCC to both discipline personal borrowers and extend palliative credit to exporting companies, the Bank insisted that while rising interest rates would make credit more expensive, this was preferable to credit being absolutely capped by lending ceilings. In March, Figgures was reminded by Bank Executive Director John Fforde that 'under the present arrangement some companies were denied credit at any price. The proposed scheme would help the financial position of these businesses'.[50] Days later, Bank Governor O'Brien wrote to Barber that the shift away from the 'physical rationing of credit' would mean that 'some potential borrowers will be able to get funds, at a price, to which they previously had no access at all'.[51] These arguments were reinforced by the industrial lobby's representations to the Treasury. The CBI had argued as early as 1969 that 'more reliance should be placed on interest rates than restricting the availability of credit'.[52] In 1970, the President of the CBI insisted that 'the availability of finance was a more serious problem than its cost. These considerations suggest to me than an attack on the credit ceiling, in which we were associated with the Clearing Banks, would be preferable to a request to them to revert to their earlier interest rate structure'.[53] The CBI explicitly expressed their approval of the Bank's plans in an Economic Committee Meeting in July 1971: 'the analysis and proposals set out in "Competition and Credit Control" are in line with the views of the Committee... notably the intended change in emphasis from quantitative limits to interest rate policy'.[54] Indeed, as the CBI admitted in 1974, they 'had welcomed the liberalisation of monetary policy late in 1971 as providing a much needed stimulus to industry and to the economy as a whole'.[55]

Further, the Treasury's worries about a lending boom during the transition period were allayed by the Bank agreeing to undertake a 'large quasi "open-market operation"', whereby the authorities would sell £750 million in gilts to the banks in order to soak up liquidity and limit their ability to lend (Needham, 2014: 42). Yet despite this initial move, it was acknowledged that adequate control over credit creation would require the authorities to be willing to raise interest rates. As Figgures commented on CCC: 'if the authorities were willing to turn the necessary taps, the system could be effective'.[56] The problem, accepted by both Treasury and

---

[50] TNA T 326/1261, Minutes of a meeting, 10 March, 1971.
[51] TNA T 326/1261, O'Brien to Barber, 12 March 1971.
[52] MRC MSS.200/C/3/ECO/2/29, CBI staff comment, 4 November 1969.
[53] MRC MSS.200/C/3/ECO/2/29, Anderson to Plumb, 19 May 1970.
[54] MRC MSS.200/C/3/ECO/2/29, Economic Committee meeting, 5 July 1971.
[55] MRC MSS.200/C/3/ECO/2/7, Report, 19 September 1974.
[56] TNA T 326/1261, Note of a meeting, 3 March 1971.

Bank officials, was that alterations in Bank Rate were politically difficult, because they were understood as announcements to the public and the markets of a fundamental change in economic prospects (Burnham, 2011: 466). In January 1971, the Group on Monetary Policy had reported that 'increases in Bank Rate have come to be regarded, not as a signal of the Authorities' views about the appropriate level for interest rates, but rather as signals of economic crisis'.[57] In a monetary policy regime that relied chiefly on interest rates to control credit, this political sensitivity could be a major obstacle to discipline. As such, the Treasury and Bank began discussions in autumn 1971 to 'diffuse' Bank Rate. As Fforde commented, 'there would be problems for the Bank in operating the new approach if there was political nervousness about Bank Rate changes'.[58] This could be overcome, the Bank suggested in November, by flexibilizing and partly marketizing Bank Rate, such that it would be 'following movements in market interest rates rather than leading them'.[59] The Treasury 'stressed that they were generally in favour of the Bank's proposals', which would 'reduce the political problems about changes in Bank Rate'.[60] This draft proposal would later be developed into the MLR system that was implemented in 1972.

*   *   *

The 1971 CCC reforms appear, with the benefit of hindsight, as a crucial first step in the construction of Britain's financialized political economy. This policy favoured the most established interests in the City—the clearing banks—by placing them on equal footing with their new competitors, and was justified with a form of free market, pro-competition rhetoric that would become all too familiar from the 1980s onwards. Yet the state's motivations for implementing this landmark liberalization cannot be explained by appeal to a political blueprint to create a financialized economic model, the role of City lobbying, nor the influence of neoliberal ideas. Rather, CCC emerged from a contested period of economic governance, 1967 to 1971, during which the state attempted, with varying degrees of success, to discipline British social relations according to the invisible domination of world value imperatives at a moment of accelerating global crisis, while struggling to manage the painful political repercussions. It was hoped that CCC would offer policymakers an escape—a technology of governance that would allow the authorities to more rationally manage credit creation in accordance with changing global market conditions without being dragged into messy political disputes. In fact, this reform led to the highly politicized disaster that was the 1973–5 Secondary Banking Crisis.

CCC, it is true, was chiefly formulated by the Bank. It emerged in part due to the growing influence of monetarist thinking, but more importantly it reflected

---

[57] TNA T 338/39, Report of the Group on Monetary Policy, 20 January 1971.
[58] TNA T 326/1702, Note of a meeting, 18 November 1971.   [59] Ibid.   [60] Ibid.

the Bank's desire to re-establish its traditional, politically insulated forms of control over the City in a context of growing competition within the banking sector. However, the Bank's proposals found a receptive audience in the Treasury and government—both of which were increasingly frustrated with the inability of the existing system of lending ceilings to adequately support the balance of payments recovery in the years following the 1967 devaluation. In order to reduce imports and boost exports, the state authorities sought to wield the existing monetary toolkit to both discipline personal borrowers in a depoliticized manner and extend palliative credit to exporting firms. This became more difficult as the forces of stagflation gathered steam and the state's monetary tightening came under greater scrutiny from various sectors of society, resulting in the postwar instruments of monetary control becomingly politically too hot to handle. In this context, the Treasury and government were attracted by CCC's depoliticized nature. Yet they were concerned about the inability of this new system to both impose credit stringency on persons and provide credit leniency to companies, and were worried that a credit boom could occur during the transition away from the lending ceilings. These anxieties, however, were assuaged by the Bank, who both insisted that CCC would allow companies to access *more* credit, albeit at a higher price, and made concessions that would allow the authorities to soak up bank liquidity in the transition period. In addition, the Bank and Treasury began to discuss a scheme that would let Bank Rate rise with fewer political difficulties, hopefully transforming CCC into a truly effective system for imposing depoliticized discipline on domestic money relations in a context of global crisis.

5

Abolition of Exchange Controls

The day that Thatcher abolished the last of Britain's exchange controls, the *New York Times* reported on the cheerful mood in the City. Nicholas Goodison, the head of the LSE, welcomed the move because it dismantled a system of regulations that had 'done a lot of harm to London as one of the leading financial centers' (Collins, 1979). Within the political economy literature too, this liberalization has acquired a special status as one of the 'crucial turning points' in the propulsion of the City to its global status and in the broader inauguration of a financialized international order (Best, 2005: 126).

Exchange controls constituted a system of limits on the use of UK funds for overseas investment and rules for the repatriation of profits earned overseas (Shepherd, Silberston, and Strange, 1985: 156). They did not directly restrict overseas investment, but rather affected the currency with which these investments were financed. The overarching goal of this system was, in the words of former Treasury Under Secretary Britton, to 'conserve the UK's holdings of gold and foreign currency' and as such 'assist the balance of payments'.[1] These controls came into being in 1939 for emergency use during the war and were given a statutory basis with the 1947 Exchange Control Act (Cairncross and Sinclair, 1982: 403).

While Britain's exchange controls liberalization has generally been accompanied by words like 'overnight', 'unexpected', and 'radical' (IMF, 1992: 7; Jenkins, 2006: 58; Johnson, 1991: 37), exchange controls were actually removed in four stages by the Callaghan and Thatcher governments: October 1977, January 1978, July 1979, and October 1979. The cumulative effect of these liberalizations was to increase the horizon of capital accumulation beyond the national stage and facilitate an enormous shift of investment from industrial to financial assets. Perhaps more than CCC, this deregulation had enormous implications for the financialization of both the British and world economies. In the first half of 1980, insurance companies and pension funds channelled four times as much investment into overseas equities as they had in the first half of 1979 (Coakley and Harris, 1992: 44). Indeed, the yearly flow of investment overseas increased from £1 billion in 1979 to £18 billion in 1985 (Bellringer and Michie, 2014: 119). Furthermore, this deregulation accelerated the transformation of British investment

---

[1] TNA T 381/145, Paper by Britton, May 1978.

Governing Financialization: The Tangled Politics of Financial Liberalization in Britain. Jack Copley, Oxford University Press.
© Jack Copley 2022. DOI: 10.1093/oso/9780192897015.003.0005

holdings away from long-term industrial assets. Overseas direct investment in assets other than oil, banking, and insurance rose by around 50 per cent between 1978 and 1981, while overseas portfolio investment rose by roughly 142 per cent (Shepherd, Silberston, and Strange, 1985: 7).

In order to understand the decision to scrap exchange controls, the political economy literature has chiefly relied on two explanations: the Thatcher administration's neoliberal ideology and commitment to boosting the City's global competitiveness. As Helleiner (1994: 150) wrote in his landmark book *States and the Reemergence of Global Finance*, the 'key explanation' for this liberalization 'was the neoliberal orientation of the new Thatcher government, which perceived exchange controls as preserving outdated Keynesian strategies'. This was bolstered by the fact that 'the Bank of England saw the abolition of exchange controls as a way of attracting more financial business to London' (ibid.: 151)—a point that Jeremy Green (2016: 447) has reiterated. Indeed, Randall Germain (1997: 147) captured the scholarly consensus well when he summarized the causes of exchange control abolition as 'the ideological predispositions of the newly elected Thatcher government and the clear desire to maintain London's position at the center of the Eurocurrency market and European finance'. This closely reflects the broader claims about the politics of financialization advanced by the interest-based and ideational approach.

This chapter will demonstrate that these explanations do not capture the full story. Exchange control abolition was not chiefly driven by a pro-City bias nor by neoliberal fanaticism, as interest-based and ideational explanations claim. Further, it was not simply motivated by the need to allow capitalists to escape British territory for more profitable climes, as the functionalist approach insists. Instead, this liberalization constituted a pragmatic political strategy to allow the British state to reconcile the contradictions arising from the crisis of capitalist society itself. In the context of an appreciating pound, following the 1976 IMF bailout and rising revenues from North Sea oil, the British state was confronted with a dilemma: the strong pound acted as an automatic disciplining mechanism that aided in combating inflation, yet it simultaneously pushed the competitiveness of the struggling industrial export sector to dangerous lows and thus risked provoking a politically unacceptable recession. In an attempt to navigate this contradiction, churned up by the global profitability crisis, both the Callaghan and Thatcher governments sought to achieve a managed depreciation of sterling by relaxing exchange controls and encouraging an investment outflow. This, it was hoped, would allow them to walk a fine line between disciplining British society in accordance with the dictates of global value relations in a moment of deep world crisis and maintaining domestic political legitimacy by delaying the worst effects of the slump.

However, two obstacles stood in the way of this timid palliation strategy. Firstly, the trade union movement was opposed to exchange control liberalization.

Secondly, in a context of floating exchange rates, any attempt to manufacture a currency depreciation could spook currency markets and provoke a sterling crisis. This chapter will demonstrate that these hurdles ultimately impeded the Callaghan administration from pursuing full exchange control liberalization. After reneging on the Social Contract, imposing a harsh incomes policy on the trade unions, and becoming a minority government, Callaghan lacked the political leeway to directly confront the unions on the issue of exchange controls. Furthermore, no strategy had been devised which would allow a devaluation to be effected via exchange control deregulation without spooking global financial markets. The Thatcher government, on the other hand, faced a weakened union movement following the Winter of Discontent, and managed to construct a rhetorical strategy that attempted to placate global currency markets by empha-sizing that exchange control abolition was a credible policy driven by laissez-faire ideology. This provided the Thatcher administration with the confidence to abolish exchange controls completely in October 1979 and thus attempt to provide palliative relief to the British economy in the depths of the global profitability crisis.

The Sterling Dilemma

The 1971 CCC liberalization took place in the early years of the profitability crisis, as the twin dynamics of stagflation began to become apparent to the perplexed state authorities. The dismantling of exchange controls, between 1977 and 1979, was undertaken near the height of this crisis. The IMF's seal of approval and the flow of North Sea oil had by autumn 1976 begun to drive up the price of sterling, which simultaneously insulated the pound from speculative crises and acted as a form of automatic disciplining mechanism upon the British economy. The strong pound helped to combat inflation, by both decreasing the price of imports and punishing exporting firms such that they were discouraged from paying large wage settlements to their workers. Yet it did so at the cost of plunging the economy into a politically unacceptable recession. According to the CBI's calcu-lations, British non-oil industrial and commercial companies' rate of profit had fallen to four per cent in 1977, down from 8.6 per cent in 1971, while earnings were increasing much slower than the rate of inflation (Britton, 1994: 251).[2] Governments during this second phase of the profitability crisis in Britain (1977–83), were torn over whether to support the strong pound's disciplining effects, or act to depreciate sterling as a palliative strategy to delay economic pain and protect governing legitimacy.

---

[2] MRC MSS.200/C/3/DG2/23, *Trade and Industry*, 22 September 1978.

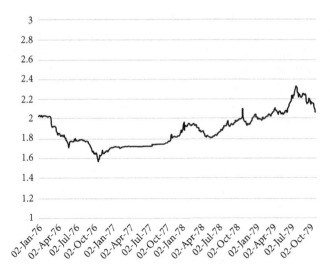

Figure 5.1. The sterling exchange rate (spot exchange rate, US dollars into sterling), 1976–79 (Bank of England, 2020).

As Treasury Under Secretary Peter Middleton explained, with Britain stuck in a low growth, high inflation trap, the 'policy dilemma is whether in these circumstances there are any measures which could be taken which simultaneously increase output and reduce inflation'.[3] Yet such a magic bullet was not forthcoming: 'it is felt that the possible benefits of policies explicitly intended to bring inflation down are outweighed by the possible adverse reaction to...its contractionary effects on output and prices', while the 'inflationary monetary consequences of a more expansionary fiscal policy, preclude [the government] from going for more growth. The position is an awkward sort of stalemate'.[4] Exchange control liberalization was employed by both the Callaghan and Thatcher governments to navigate this impasse. By relaxing these controls, the authorities could encourage an outflow of investment that would reduce the price of sterling (see Figure 5.1). This would boost the competitiveness of British exports and ease the worst effects of economic stagnation. This subtle palliative measure was preferable to direct forms of economic stimulus, such as overt currency devaluation or fiscal stimulus, which would threaten to drastically exacerbate inflation.

However, there were two important obstacles that had to be overcome before this strategy could be pursued: it was not at all clear how exchange control relaxation could be sold to an opposed trade union movement, nor how an orderly depreciation of sterling could be brought about in the context of volatile floating exchange rates. The first problem arose from the fact that the TUC favoured a

---

[3] TNA T 388/152, Middleton to Hancock, 15 June 1978.   [4] Ibid.

strong pound, because of its downward pressure on the cost of living, and supported the extension of exchange controls as part of a proactive industrial strategy. As the unions were bearing the brunt of Callaghan's anti-inflation incomes policy, Labour policymakers were wary of further incensing them. The second problem was a direct result of the move to floating exchange rates in 1973. The onset of this currency regime entailed an increase in speculative activity and a consequent rise in exchange rate volatility. As a result, governments struggled to reconcile their political and economic objectives with the 'imperatives of exchange rate stabilization' (Eichengreen, 2008: 141). This was amplified in the case of Britain by the massive overseas holdings of sterling, the liquidation of which could result in a sterling crisis. As former Treasury Permanent Secretary Wass (2008: 336–8) observed, an immediate 'step-change in a floating environment would have been a policy without precedent' and one which threatened to 'shatter' confidence in sterling altogether. Yet the alternative—a gradual depreciation—was also 'without precedent', 'uncertain and indeed potentially dangerous' (ibid.: 336). Thus, any attempt to manipulate the price of sterling required extremely careful public presentation, so as to avoid provoking speculative attacks against the pound. In order to boost the competitiveness of UK exporters through exchange control relaxation, then, politicians required an appropriate strategy that would both disarm the unions' opposition and avoid spooking global financial markets. This chapter will argue that the Callaghan and Thatcher governments' different degrees of success in developing such a strategy is what best explains the dynamics of exchange control liberalization in the years 1977–79.

The Callaghan Administration

On 26 October 1977, Labour Chancellor Healey announced the relaxation of exchange controls affecting inward direct investment, travel, cash gifts, and emigration. Then, on 1 January 1978, the government relaxed controls on outward direct and portfolio investment in the EEC, by abolishing the rule whereby British investors had to surrender 25 per cent of proceeds from foreign currency sales to the Bank for conversion into sterling.

The pressure that motivated a Labour government to enact the most significant dismantling of exchange controls in nearly forty years was not immediately apparent. At first glance, it appeared that in 1977 Healey could 'boast that he was one of the few post-war Chancellors to preside over a growing economy, falling inflation, falling unemployment, and a balance of payments surplus' (Needham, 2014: 109). Yet in private discussions government officials displayed an awareness of the underlying problems veiled by the IMF's endorsement and North Sea oil. An inward surge of capital was causing sterling to appreciate steeply, thus aiding the government's attack on inflation but exacerbating the dire circumstances faced by non-oil exporters. It was against this background that the dismantling of exchange controls became a topic of interest, as it could create an outflow of investment that would weaken sterling's appreciation.

On 19 October, Healey circulated a proposal that outlined various possible exchange control relaxations. His motivations for proposing the consideration of these changes, he explained, were threefold. Firstly, exchange controls had been used to support Britain's weak balance of payments performance in the postwar era, yet this was increasingly difficult to justify during a period of sustained current account surplus. Secondly, the government should give some indication to the EEC that it took seriously the EEC's stance on free capital mobility. Thirdly, and more immediately, there was a need to offset inflows of capital that were destabilizing the exchange rate and money supply.[5] The responses Healey received from various government departments generally focused on his third concern as the most important. Labour's Roy Hattersley, Secretary of State for Prices and Consumer Protection, urged Healey against taking the measures (unsurprisingly considering his remit). Hattersley argued:

> For exporting industries, a policy of depreciation would represent the abandon-ment by Government of an important sanction in our fight against inflation. Firms in these industries would be free to enter into excessive wage settlements, secure in the knowledge that the Government would mitigate their effects on profitability by allowing the exchange rate to slide.[6]

However, Hattersley was in the minority. The Department of Trade (DoT), Department of Industry (DoI), and the Bank all clearly favoured some depreci-ation of the exchange rate in order to ease the pressure on exports. DoT official Hans Liesner wrote to his Secretary of State, Edmund Dell, that the 'the UK's long-run trade and hence industrial performance will be threatened by a worsening of competitiveness, and that exchange rate policy should be con-ducted accordingly... [This] is where the exchange control relaxations should help'.[7] In turn, Dell emphasized the severity of the problem to Callaghan, Healey, and Bank Governor Gordon Richardson at a meeting the following week. He argued that further sterling appreciation 'would be deleterious to investment, to employ-ment, and to the industrial strategy', and thus recommended a close examin-ation of exchange control relaxation, which would allow 'money to flow out of the country as freely as it could now flow in'.[8]

---

[5] TNA FV 89/2, Healey to Callaghan, 19 October 1977.
[6] TNA FV 89/2, Hattersley to Healey, 19 October 1977.
[7] TNA FV 89/2, Liesner to Secretary of State, 20 October 1977.
[8] TNA PREM 16/2108, Note of a meeting, 28 October 1977.

Similarly, the DoI informed Callaghan that it 'very much welcome[d]' Healey's proposed deregulation, on the grounds that 'there is scope for certain selective relaxations of controls on outward investment that could benefit UK industry directly in the medium term'.[9] Such a relaxation would keep the exchange rate competitive, allow companies to invest abroad in raw material exploitation, and permit them to build up overseas investments that would benefit future exports.[10] The Secretary of State for Industry, Eric Varley, further emphasized the gravity of the situation at the meeting with Callaghan, Healey, and Richardson, when he explained that while he understood the counter-inflationary benefits of the strong pound, 'the effects on manufacturing industry could not be ignored':

> Some of our industry was barely competitive at the present exchange rate. The textile and clothing sectors, for example, employing 850,000 people, would be severely hit, with serious political consequences... The prospect for export-led growth, on which the industrial strategy rested, could be greatly reduced by too rapid an appreciation of the exchange rate.[11]

Sir Kenneth Berrill, head of the Central Policy Staff Review of the Cabinet Office, echoed this sentiment to Callaghan in November, when he insisted that the 'United Kingdom's high exchange rate reduces our export prospects in this gloomier market. Domestically, there is no sign of a great revival in United Kingdom industrial investment which the IMF team told us would come if we took the measures they advocated'.[12]

The Bank too positioned itself against the existing controls. The Bank had been traditionally hostile towards exchange controls, yet this sentiment intensified following the abandonment of fixed exchange rates (Dow, 2013: 143). By the middle of 1977, Bank adviser Charles Goodhart was advocating the greatest relaxation possible, while Executive Director McMahon and First Deputy Chief of Exchange Control Douglas Dawkins also favoured relaxation but were more concerned about the timing (Capie, 2010: 766–7).

There was significant lobbying from British business in favour of exchange control relaxation, yet there is as much evidence of pressure from domestic industry as from the financial sector, in marked contrast to the assumptions of much of the financialization literature. Since the late 1960s, the City had been campaigning for the relaxation of exchange controls through the Committee on Invisible Exports, which was made up of prominent City businessmen (A. Davies, 2017: 156–77). In July 1977, Treasury Permanent Secretary Leo Pliatzky went for dinner with LSE Chairman Goodison. Goodison thought that a relaxation of

---

[9] TNA FV 89/2, Varley to Callaghan, 24 October 1977.   [10] Ibid.
[11] TNA PREM 16/2108, Note of a meeting, 28 October 1977.
[12] TNA PREM 16/2108, Berrill to Callaghan, 18 November 1977.

exchange controls could help the City become the centre of securities in Europe, but feared (quite melodramatically) that 'Treasury people at Ministerial and official level' were 'uninterested in anything except the manufacturing sector'.[13] Yet he did not call for an immediate abolition of all exchange controls, instead claiming that he would be satisfied to see some relaxation within a timeframe of three years. Certain state officials vocally supported exchange control liberaliza-tion due to the advantages for the City and Britain's invisible earnings. The Treasury's Deputy Secretary, F. Russell Barratt, circulated a paper in May 1977 that claimed that it was 'very much in the national interest that the general capacity of the City to engage profitably in international financial business should be sustained and enhanced', which was in turn dependent on the ability to operate freely in foreign currencies.[14] This sentiment was echoed by the DoT's Dell, who, as sponsoring minister for the Stock Exchange and insurance industry, 'welcome[d] the prospect of further strengthening of the overseas position of UK insurance companies and of the relaxation on overseas portfolio investment respectively'.[15]

British industry launched an equally systematic campaign against exchange controls from at least the early 1970s—with the CBI informing Heath's Financial Secretary Patrick Jenkin in 1971 that 'the CBI has long urged the Treasury to ease and then remove exchange controls on outward investment as soon as the balance of payments permits'.[16] As industry's rate of return continued to fall, compounded by the oil shocks and the appreciation of sterling, the CBI's pressure on the government intensified. Through its Overseas Investment Committee, the CBI launched a renewed campaign in 1976 to convince the government of the benign effects of overseas investment, so as to hasten the removal of exchange controls. This included commissioning the Metra Consulting Group to produce a favourable report on overseas investment, as well as lobbying the government through the NEDC and directly through meetings with the Treasury.[17]

The creation of a consensus within the Callaghan government and the Bank in favour of some degree of exchange control liberalization was primarily the result of political concerns over the dangerously low competitiveness of British indus-trial exports in a moment of deep crisis. The relaxation of exchange controls was pursued in a context in which the government was under pressure to comply with EEC guidelines on capital controls, the positive balance of payments outlook appeared to render such controls anachronistic, and British industry and finance

[13] TNA PJ 1/92, Pliatzky to Wass, 6 July 1977.
[14] TNA T 388/154, Barratt to Payton, 27 May 1977.
[15] TNA FV 89/2, Dell to Callaghan, 21 October 1977.
[16] MRC MSS.200/C/3/DG2/22, Anderson to Jenkin, 23 September 1971.
[17] MRC MSS.200/C/3/ECO/11/24, Memorandum, 1 February 1978; MRC MSS.200/c/3/ECO/11/25, Minutes of meeting at National Economic Development Office, 6 July 1977; MRC MSS.200/C/3/ECO/11/26, Memorandum, 11 October 1977.

continued to lobby for controls to be loosened. However, the overwhelming motivation for this financial liberalization was to provide a palliative response to exporters' woes by depreciating sterling. The next section will examine why, despite the legitimacy concerns over the pressures of the strong pound, the Callaghan administration did not go further in liberalizing exchange controls.

Market Uncertainty and Union Militancy

There is no single reason why the Callaghan government did not completely abolish exchange controls. One important factor was that the deregulation of controls on investment was counter-intuitive to a Labour government that had come to power promising an interventionist industrial strategy. Indeed, Healey explained to Callaghan that he did not intend to go too far with exchange control relaxation because it was 'much more consistent with the industrial strategy to find ways' to use the benefits of North Sea oil 'more directly to build up the UK industrial base'.[18] The rise of the AES on the left wing of the Labour Party, which advocated for exchange controls as part of a broader turn to economic planning, also made it difficult to move towards full liberalization. Yet of greater importance were two more immediate problems: the difficulties of managing currency depreciation and the political constraints upon the Chancellor and Treasury ministers exerted by their fractious relations with the trade unions. The Callaghan administration was unable to craft a strategy to assuage financial markets through declarative signals, nor disarm the labour movement, resulting in the moderate exchange control liberalizations of 1977–78.

In May 1977, when talks about exchange control relaxation began in earnest, the Bank was split on the issue of the best way to devalue sterling. Bank adviser McMahon thought a step change was the least risky option, while officials David Holland and John Sangster preferred to move gradually.[19] The Treasury was also divided, with some pushing for an overnight devaluation and others, most notably Treasury Under Secretary Peter Middleton, arguing that a gradual depreciation would be least damaging.[20] This disagreement was symptomatic of an institutional unfamiliarity with exchange rate policy in the context of floating rates. By October, on the eve of Healey's first exchange control relaxation, Treasury Permanent Secretary Wass admitted that there was still 'no effective means for bringing the rate down in the current situation. A step devaluation, always difficult in a floating-rate regime, would in the current circumstances lead to a chaotic market'.[21] Yet a gradual 'engineered slide would require a change in market

---

[18] TNA FV 89/2, Healey to Callaghan, 19 October 1977.
[19] TNA T 388/154, Note of a meeting, 1 June 1977.   [20] Ibid.
[21] TNA FV 89/2, Note of a meeting, 25 October 1977.

sentiment' with regards to sterling that was similarly difficult to manufacture.[22] After meeting Treasury officials in October to discuss exchange control relaxations, Graham Mason, the CBI's Deputy Overseas Director, explained: 'I can characterise the attitude of the Treasury officials as exceedingly cautious...They were clearly not confident that the large inflow of currency into our reserves of late is here to stay'.[23] This deep uncertainty as to the side effects of sterling depreciation contributed to the general apprehension among the Callaghan administration towards exchange control relaxations, as these relaxations were designed precisely to exert a downward pressure on the pound.

The government was also impeded by its tense relations with the unions. As discussed in Chapter 3, Labour had come to power in 1974 promising a Social Contract, in which the unions would voluntarily moderate their wage demands in return for greater welfare provisions and a favourable industrial policy, creating a 'self-reinforcing spiral of disinflation' (Britton, 1994: 19). While Phases I and II of the government's incomes policy were quite successful in balancing strict wage restraint with social expenditure, this compromise came under increasing strain due to the public spending cuts necessitated by the IMF bailout. This marked the unofficial end of the Social Contract, engendering a 'strong undertow of tension and resentment' within the union movement (Thorpe, 1999: 144). Phase III began in August 1977 without formal TUC backing, as union leaders struggled to impose the government's requests on their increasingly dissatisfied membership—a membership that voted overwhelmingly for an immediate return to free collective bargaining at the 1977 TUC conference (ibid.: 144–5). As Jack Jones, head of the Transport and General Workers' Union, argued in May 1977, for the unions to gain grassroots backing for the government's incomes policy, the government needed to present an 'an alternative economic policy', which—importantly for our purposes—would include 'import deposits or controls' (Coates, 1980: 73).

Thus, an extensive relaxation of exchange controls, during a period in which the government was attempting to impose Phase III of its incomes policy on a disillusioned union movement, appeared politically very risky. Not only were important union officials like Jones calling for greater import controls, but the TUC was in fact lobbying the government in 1977 for the creation of a new 'tripartite' agency that would 'examine all applications for outward investment' on a case-by-case basis.[24] 'The exchange control system', the TUC argued, 'should be supplemented to consider these wider questions' of domestic job creation.[25] To entirely disregard the TUC's concerns by abolishing controls ran the risk of undermining union acquiescence to the government's already embattled incomes

---

[22] Ibid.   [23] MRC MSS.200/C/3/ECO/11/26, Memorandum, 11 October 1977.

[24] MRC MSS.292D/462/3, TUC comment on NEDC paper, 1 July 1977.

[25] MRC MSS.292D/462/3, TUC comment on NEDC paper, 1 July 1977; MRC MSS.292D/40.2LPMR/2, Report of TUC–Labour Party Liaison Committee Meeting, 25 April 1978.

policy. As Barratt argued in a meeting with Treasury and Bank representatives in May 1977, 'the need to move gently in such a politically sensitive area...had deterred the Treasury from putting forward definite proposals for relaxation at this stage'.[26] Indeed, Joel Barnett, Chief Secretary to the Treasury, explained to Callaghan's Principal Private Secretary, Kenneth Stowe, in September 1977 that 'political considerations apart...[a] small relaxation would be a sensible proposal. But we cannot ignore political considerations, and in my judgement the inevitable (if ill-informed) outcry there would be is not worth provoking for a comparatively modest relaxation'.[27] Thus, when Healey finally announced his exchange control proposal in October, he acknowledged that the more radical measures like abolishing the 25 per cent surrender rule 'might cause some political difficulty, especially with the TUC'.[28] Callaghan echoed this concern, insisting on delaying any extensive relaxations 'until there has been the discussion in the TUC/Labour Party Liaison Committee'.[29]

Furthermore, despite essentially constituting a reflationary measure, due to its stimulating effect on exporting industries, dismantling exchange controls could potentially have the doubly negative effect of alienating the TUC *and* the general electorate by exacerbating inflation. As Hattersley emphasized to Healey in December 1977: 'Our economic progress and our political success will in very large part be judged on our success or otherwise in avoiding a return to inflation at or above 10 per cent. The Conservatives are already making it clear that they do not believe that we shall succeed.'[30] In addition, the high pound automatically reduced inflation without the need for direct government intervention, which had significant political advantages. It was, in this sense, a quasi-automatic depoliticized disciplining mechanism. Healey explained to an audience that included Callaghan and Richardson in November 1977 that the alternative to a strong pound 'would be a very restrictive fiscal and monetary regime which would probably be just as damaging'.[31]

There undoubtedly existed a consensus in favour of a significant degree of exchange control relaxation, primarily to check sterling's appreciation and consequently avert disaster for British exporters—thus constituting a palliative strategy to protect governing legitimacy by postponing the effects of the global crisis. Yet there was also considerable apprehension within the Treasury as to the external economic and domestic political consequences. Labour, weakened by their minority status and their clashes with the unions over incomes policy, lacked

[26] TNA T 388/154, Note of a meeting, 1 June 1977.
[27] TNA T 364/211, Smith to Stowe, 30 September 1977.
[28] TNA FV 89/2, Healey to Callaghan, 19 October 1977.
[29] TNA FV 89/2, Owen to Callaghan, 24 October 1977; TNA PJ 1/92, Stowe to Battishill, 26 October 1977.
[30] TNA FV 89/2, Hattersley to Healey, 20 December 1977.
[31] TNA PREM 16/2108, Note of a meeting, 28 October 1977.

a strategy that could both convince markets that exchange control abolition was *not* a cynical strategy to boost exports and disarm the opposed trade union movement. This interplay of pressures for and against the dismantling of exchange controls resulted in the moderate relaxations of October 1977 and January 1978.

The Thatcher Administration

On 12 July 1979, Conservative Chancellor Howe announced extensive relaxations of exchange controls on outward direct investment and minor relaxations on outward portfolio investment. The remaining controls were completely abolished on 23 October. This bold move was not simply foisted upon the civil service and Bank by a clique of ideologues, as much of the existing literature on exchange control abolition suggests. Instead, the Conservatives' proposals—which were no doubt motivated by a radical political vision—found a receptive and prepared audience in the Treasury, Bank, and various government departments. Much like the Callaghan administration, the Thatcher government's desire to dismantle exchange controls was driven chiefly by the political necessity to ease the pressure on British exporters, and thus provide palliative relief to the British economy, by putting downward pressure on the pound.

In spite of the Callaghan administration's inability to implement further measures on exchange controls following the Winter of Discontent, preparations for further relaxations carried on in Whitehall. In early March 1979, the Cabinet's Official Committee on External Economic Affairs advised 'supporting the idea of a gradual relaxation of exchange control for outward investment'.[32] The 'line' that they were taking was that 'despite our common concern about inflation, we are beginning to be worried about the effect of the continued strength of sterling on manufacturing industry competitiveness and that some relaxation may help to ease the rate down a little'.[33] In April, some members of the Overseas Trade Board expressed similar concerns, arguing that 'the present rate imposed a severe strain on some export activity' due to the poor state of domestic profitability, which could be alleviated by some exchange control relaxations.[34] A week before the May general election, Treasury Under Secretary David Hancock, anticipating further exchange control measures in the case of a Conservative win, drafted a proposal of relaxations 'for a Conservative Chancellor only'.[35]

Once in office, Financial Secretary Nigel Lawson—driven by a deep-seated ideological opposition to exchange controls—set up a team, led by Hancock and

---

[32] TNA PJ 1/92, Coates to Lanchin, 1 March 1979.   [33] Ibid.
[34] TNA PJ 1/92, Wilks to Pliatzky, 5 April 1979.
[35] TNA T 388/202, Hancock to Sallow-Smith, 26 April 1979.

Dawkins, the Bank's Chief of Exchange Controls, to investigate the possibility of further relaxations (Capie, 2010: 769). This team in turn set about consulting the relevant departments. As in the Callaghan years, there was some division as to which policy goal should be prioritized: reducing inflation or rescuing export competitiveness. As Hancock succinctly explained, officials would of course prefer to increase competitiveness by reducing inflation below that of Britain's competitors, yet in current circumstances this was wishful thinking:

> Like the Irishman, we would prefer not to start from where we find ourselves. The controversial question is what we should do given our present situation. In particular, given that we significantly lost competitiveness over the past winter, is it better: (i) to pursue policies which help to get our rate of inflation down and thus keep the rate high; or (ii) to encourage the nominal exchange rate to fall (if we can) in the hope that this will increase output in the short term and thus possibly mitigate the damage that is being done to our industrial base.[36]

Wass believed that the balance of opinion might lean towards focusing on the former goal, especially among radical Conservative politicians: '[i]t may well be the case also that Ministers are rather pleased about the exchange rate, partly because of the beneficial price effects it will have and partly because, by reducing corporate profit margins, it will put increasing pressure on private employers to bargain toughly in the next pay round'.[37] This line of reasoning was adopted by P. V. Dixon of the Treasury's Industrial Economic Division. Industry, he explained, was 'caught between the upper millstone of monetary policies/ exchange rate and the lower millstone of wage costs'.[38] This was something to be encouraged, not alleviated: 'Industry has to realise that the climate for profits is potentially very unpropitious; firms will go bust if there is not a very substantial deceleration of wage costs'.[39] For this reason, Dixon urged Lawson not 'to move too quickly to industry's rescue' regarding exchange controls.[40] He wrote that the 'way industrialists are talking about pay does not suggest that they are yet seeing their financial position as the constraint which will cause the rate of pay settlements to decelerate sharply. The Budget cannot succeed unless this is perceived'.[41] The ultimate goal of this approach, as outlined in a DoT paper in July, was to facilitate a 'deterioration in the prospects for the traded goods and services sector, both in terms of output and profitability' so as 'to stiffen employer resistance to pay claims, and once again to moderate wage demands'.[42]

---

[36] TNA T 388/203, Hancock to Butler, 23 May 1979. Hancock's choice of language presumably reflected his views on the Northern Ireland conflict that was smouldering at the time.
[37] TNA T 388/154, Wass to Couzens, 19 July 1979.
[38] TNA T 381/145, Dixon to Airey, 31 May 1979.   [39] Ibid.
[40] TNA T 381/143, Dixon to Lawson, 29 June 1979.   [41] Ibid.
[42] TNA PJ 1/95, Department of Trade paper, 31 July 1979.

However, the majority of opinion within the government viewed this disciplining strategy as too risky, which casts doubt on accounts that emphasize the Thatcher government's disregard for the fate of domestic industry (Coakley and Harris, 1992; Talani, 2012). British industry's profits had fallen by 13.5 per cent in the first three months of 1979, which became a central concern for the Treasury (Riddell, 1979a). When Howe arrived in office in May, Bank Governor Richardson advised him that the government should respond to the overvaluation of sterling with 'significant relaxation of exchange control'.[43] At a CBI–Treasury meeting the same month, the CBI recommended 'measures aimed at restoring competitiveness and adequate levels of profitability', which included the 'abolition of exchange controls'.[44] The nature of the dilemma was captured best by Treasury official G. M. Gill, who explained to Hancock in late June that 'we may well be moving into an area now where the benefits to inflation from a higher rate may be obtained at too great a cost in terms of output and the current account of the balance of payments'.[45] There was a great difference, Gill argued, between an 'organically' high rate based on a strong economic performance, and a high rate 'imposed on industries which were inherently weak'.[46] Britain faced an inorganically strong pound, such that 'too fast a rise in the rate will cause immediate damage to the viability of these industries before the counter-inflation benefits have had time to come through'.[47] He encouraged Lawson to proceed with exchange control relaxation.

The DoT and DoI also positioned themselves against exchange controls. The Under Secretary for the DoT explained in early May that 'we have been losing competitiveness and there is nothing much in prospect to suggest a rapid change in trend is likely...Despite the inflationary disadvantages I think from the Department's point of view there is a strong case for supporting *some* relaxation'.[48] A similar message was put in starker language in July, when a Trade official informed Treasury Minister of State Peter Rees that 'with shipping in worldwide recession...the profits of UK shipping companies [are] decreasing or non-existent', further necessitating the 'commercial flexibility' that would accompany exchange control relaxations.[49] Hancock was also contacted by a top DoI official in early May, who urged the Treasury to address the 'serious and general lack of competitiveness...in British industry'.[50] The kind of monetarist penance advocated by some in the Thatcher administration, he wrote, was wrong-headed: 'I do not believe that the adjustment that is necessary in our economy will come

---

[43] BOE G3 F1, Richardson to Howe, 4 May 1979, https://www.margaretthatcher.org/document/113156.

[44] TNA PREM 19/29, Record of a meeting, 29 May 1979.

[45] TNA T 388/204, Gill to Hancock, 25 June 1979.   [46] Ibid.   [47] Ibid.

[48] TNA PJ 1/93, Lanchin to Gray, 8 May 1979; emphasis in original.

[49] TNA PJ 1/94, Darrell to Rees, 29 June 1979.

[50] TNA PJ1/93, Lippett to Hancock, 3 May 1979.

about through an overvalued pound, Germany and Japan did *not* attain their virtuous circles in that fashion'.[51]

A different argument, albeit with the same policy prescription, was put directly to Howe by Secretary of State for Industry Keith Joseph on 1 June. Joseph argued that 'restrictions on portfolio investment overseas reduce the return on investment in the UK, since by restricting international capital movements we reduce the pressure on British management to increase profitability'.[52] Exposing British capital to global competition via exchange control relaxation could reinforce the need for companies to economize on labour costs and counteract the inflationary effects of exchange control abolition. Finally, the Foreign and Commonwealth Office (FCO) too made their position clear. At a May meeting with officials from the Treasury (including Hancock), Bank (Dawkins), DoT, and DoI, the FCO representative, M. D. Butler, explained with great clarity that there was a 'case for relaxing exchange controls completely over the next three years, in order to stimulate large outflows to balance the large increments to the balance of payments from North Sea oil, and thus to keep the exchange rate competitive'.[53]

Summarizing the various discussions taking place on this topic, Hancock wrote to Lawson in June that, while depreciating sterling through exchange control relaxation could damage the fight against inflation, it was likely a less inflationary strategy for effecting a competitive depreciation than direct intervention to lower the exchange rate.[54] Indeed, Needham (2014: 142) argues that given the government's determination to hit their money supply targets, with the overarching aim of reducing inflation, liberalization of exchange controls was the only instrument available to reduce the upward pressure on sterling. As the DoT echoed, 'inducing additional capital outflows' through exchange control relaxation 'should reduce the exchange rate without any direct adverse consequences for monetary management'.[55] Nevertheless, Lawson explained to Howe that once exchange controls were fully abolished, any attempts to impose direct controls on the banking system to regulate the money supply—such as the corset or monetary base control—would simply push banking activity offshore.[56] This, however, was not sufficient justification for 'abandoning our plan to dismantle exchange control'.[57]

The greatest disagreement was not whether or not to relax exchange controls, but which controls to relax first. Against claims that this liberalization was intended to boost the global prospects of the City, the Bank, DoT, and Lawson were pushing for caution in dismantling portfolio controls, which most frustrated

---

[51] Ibid.; emphasis in original.   [52] TNA PJ 1/93, Joseph to Howe, 1 June 1979.
[53] TNA PJ 1/93, Note of a Meeting, 17 May 1979.
[54] TNA T 388/203, Hancock to Lawson, 4 June 1979.
[55] TNA PJ 1/95, Department of Trade paper, 31 July 1979.
[56] Christchurch College, Oxford, Lawson MSS, Lawson 1 f363, Lawson to Howe, 4 October 1979, https://www.margaretthatcher.org/document/113284.
[57] Ibid.

the City's activities.[58] This was due to fear of a massive diversification by overseas investors out of sterling. On the other hand, the DoI was eager for 'substantial and early progress towards full dismantlement'.[59] Following the Conservative government's first round of liberalization in July, it was Lawson who pushed for complete abolition in October, convincing the Chancellor and an initially hesitant Prime Minister.[60] While this full liberalization would bring the UK in line with EEC directives, it would also please the US state, which had felt that the form in which UK exchange control relaxation had taken place thus far had discriminated against the US market in favour of Europe.[61]

Contrary to the claims of Helleiner (1994) and Germain (1997), the Thatcher government's advocacy of exchange control liberalization was not chiefly driven by a desire to consolidate the City's position as a global financial centre or a commitment to neoliberal principles. Instead, this chapter follows Christopher Bellringer and Michie (2014: 122) in arguing that 'no evidence can be uncovered that the decision was designed to improve the competitive position of the London Stock Exchange', nor other sectors of the City. Furthermore, while key figures in the government were certainly ideologically opposed to controls, the most immediate and pressing concern was the dire lack of export competitiveness. The Thatcher government intended temporarily to alleviate the stress on British exporters by placing downward pressure on the pound through exchange control liberalization—a strategy that they hoped would not jeopardize their monetary tightening. The final section of the chapter will explore the Conservatives' strategy for overcoming the barriers that had restricted their predecessors' deregulatory agenda.

The Winter of Discontent and Spooking the Market

If the Callaghan and Thatcher governments both shared the same motivation in pursuing exchange control liberalization—to provide palliative relief to the British economy so as to maintain political legitimacy during the profitability crisis—then what of the impediments to full deregulation that the former administration had faced? This section will argue that, while the domestic political constraint had significantly eased, the problem of volatile currency markets remained. Yet, unlike its predecessors, the Thatcher government crafted a rhetorical strategy that

---

[58] BOE G3/372 F17, Richardson to Howe, 11 May 1979, https://www.margaretthatcher.org/document/113157; TNA T 388/203, Lawson to Howe, 2 May 1979.

[59] TNA PJ 1/93, Joseph to Howe, 1 June 1979.

[60] Christchurch College, Oxford, Lawson MSS, Lawson 1 f363, Lawson to Howe, 4 October 1979, https://www.margaretthatcher.org/document/113284; TNA PREM 19/437, Howe to Thatcher, 9 July 1979.

[61] TNA T388/203, Lawson to Howe, 2 May 1979.

it believed would allow it to circumvent the latter obstacle. By publicly emphasizing the administration's ideological commitment to laissez-faire principles, the
Thatcher government intended to create the policy space to pursue currency
depreciation without spooking the markets.

Domestically, Thatcher was less constrained by the unions than Callaghan. To
some extent, this was due to the public relations defeat suffered by the unions
following the Winter of Discontent. As Gamble (1994a: 94–5) observed, the 'myth
of the Winter of Discontent, with its images of closed hospitals, rubbish piling up
in the streets, and dead bodies rotting unburied in graveyards', reinforced the
popular notion of the bankruptcy of benign state collaboration with the unions.
A directly oppositional policy towards the union movement was now not only
possible but electorally savvy: the 'old Tory disadvantage of a cold and distant
relationship with the union movement...turned into an asset' (Dorfman, 1983:
20). This calamitous event, combined with 'rising unemployment and de-
industrialisation', meant that 'Mrs Thatcher inherited a strong strategic position
in relation to the trade unions' (Marsh, 1992: 64). Indeed, the government 'used
their obvious political leverage over trade unionism' to enact a radical overhaul of
macroeconomic strategy 'without so much as consulting nor considering trade
union views' (Dorfman, 1983: 20). Whereas the Callaghan government had
moved tentatively on the issue of exchange control relaxation because of tense
government–union relations, the Thatcher administration in fact believed that the
abolition of exchange controls would 'help the Government's position vis-a-vis
the trade unions, by showing that the Government were determined that investors
should be allowed to put their money where they can earn the best return'.[62]

The external economic constraint, however, remained. The attempt to effect a
currency depreciation via exchange control relaxations in the context of a floating
exchange rate system was, as Lawson admitted in October 1979, 'bound to be a
leap in the dark'.[63] There remained a sense of unease throughout the different
branches of the government about the proper tools for managing a floating rate.
The Official Committee on External Economic Affairs—memories of past sterling
crises fresh in their minds—insisted that exchange control relaxation measures
should be gradual 'in order to avoid the risk of a foreign exchange crisis'.[64] The
Overseas Trade Board concurred, arguing that government intervention to lower
the rate 'could easily get out of hand because of speculative action, and it might be
very difficult to halt'.[65] Despite the accumulation of foreign reserves in recent
years, the authorities still feared that the floating-rate system ruled out a managed
devaluation of the pound because any overt government intervention to alter the

---

[62] TNA T 388/208, Note of a meeting, 18 October 1979.
[63] TNA T 388/207, Note for the record, 4 October 1979.
[64] TNA PJ 1/92, Coates to Lanchin, 1 March 1979.
[65] TNA PJ 1/92, Wilks to Pliatzky, 5 April 1979.

exchange rate could prompt rapid capital flight out of sterling (Rogers, 2012: 203). As a Treasury official commented in May, 'he would be a bold man who would say with complete confidence that we have put balance of payments troubles behind us for a decade or more because of North Sea oil' (quoted in Needham, 2014: 140).

The Thatcher administration concocted a rhetorical strategy to neutralize these dangers. By justifying the abolition of exchange controls under the banner of 'good housekeeping'—which meant a combination of responsible, forward-looking policy and a commitment to laissez-faire principles—they could manu-facture a sterling depreciation in a covert and seemingly unintentional manner. This would, it was hoped, reduce the chance of depreciation spooking the markets or painting the government as hypocrites. In June, Hancock wrote to Lawson, explaining that there was considerable debate within the Treasury on the possible impact of exchange control liberalization on the exchange rate. Regardless, he argued, 'it is risky for Government spokesmen to *say* that it [exchange control relaxation] was intended to secure a depreciation in the exchange rate. Once that feeling got abroad, the short term consequences for the exchange rate could be very destabilizing'.[66] For this reason, the government should avoid 'the argument that exchange control relaxation is intended as a means of increasing competi-tiveness'.[67] Lawson agreed that:

> reasoning based on the premise that the exchange control relaxations would help prevent this country catching the 'Dutch disease' should be avoided; *while the Financial Secretary sees some merit in the argument, it is not one that he would want to use publicly* and prefers instead to contend that the revenue from north sea oil should be used to build up overseas investments whose future earnings can provide a stream of foreign-generated income which will ultimately be able to replace the revenue from North Sea oil. *In this way the exchange control relaxa-tions can be presented as good housekeeping.*[68]

In August, Lawson explained to Howe that, while he favoured a strong (yet not inexorably rising) pound for anti-inflation purposes, he proposed 'a bonfire of most (if not all) of the remaining exchange controls this autumn'.[69] This liberal-ization should be pursued as an end in itself, yet it had the added advantage that it '*might*' slow sterling's rise without overtly signalling that 'we are unhappy at the strength of the £', which 'would quickly lead to a very serious loss of confidence in our resolve to stick to [anti-inflationary] policy'.[70]

---

[66] TNA T388/203, Hancock to Lawson, 4 June 1979; emphasis in original.   [67] Ibid.
[68] TNA T 388/203, Diggle to Hancock, 11 June 1979; emphasis added. Dutch disease, in this context, refers to the rise in price of a national currency caused by the exploitation of a natural resource.
[69] TNA T 388/59, Lawson to Howe, 28 August 1979.   [70] Ibid.; emphasis in original.

John Nott, Secretary of State for Trade, demonstrated this strategy in an interview with BBC Radio 4 after the first round of relaxations in July. In response to a question about whether this relaxation was an attempt to depreciate sterling, Nott responded:

> it's very difficult to say whether overseas opinion will take this further measure of liberalism, liberalisation with exchange control, in such a way that it thinks that the pound is all the more worth-while buying, because it is an act of self confidence, or whether they will say 'well, this means there's going to be a little bit more money going out of the country into overseas investment and therefore, we must sell the pound'. Now which way it'll go is very difficult to predict... What the strong pound has enabled us to do is pursue what I regard as the correct policies in themselves.[71]

Similarly, speaking to the House of Commons, Howe insisted that the aim was not to weaken the pound, but rather to build up overseas income streams for the future and to provide greater 'freedom of choice' to 'companies and individuals'.[72] The strong pound merely helped to facilitate this move. This strategy was also visible following the final abolition of controls in October. At a press conference, Lawson was questioned on the relationship between exchange control abolition and the price of sterling, but he 'refused to speculate about the possible outflows or impact on sterling from the changes' (Riddell, 1979c).

The government's pursuit of this rhetorical strategy must be understood in the context of the rise of new classical economics, with its emphasis on the importance of 'policy credibility' (Grabel, 2000). Propelled by several pivotal articles in the late 1970s, this approach argued that rational agents 'assess the credibility of an announced policy' before acting (ibid.: 3). Particularly influential for the Thatcher government was Patrick Minford's 'rational expectations' model, which too stressed the centrality of perceived credibility to the art of policymaking (Cooper, 2012: 39–40). Indeed, this rhetorical strategy was convincing, due to the perceived sincerity of the Thatcher administration's commitment to free market principles. The Conservatives had ruled out a pragmatic depreciation of sterling for export competitiveness purposes in their 1976 manifesto *The Right Approach*: 'We reject the simplistic argument that a depreciating currency is required to maintain competitiveness. Internal inflation is the real enemy of successful competition. A falling exchange rate makes internal inflation worse.' In addition, key figures in the administration had previously denounced exchange controls as a matter of principle. At a November 1978 Commons debate, Howe had decried the controls as 'a bureaucratic hallmark of a society that has no

---

[71] TNA PJ 1/94, BBC Radio 4 interview, 19 July 1979.
[72] Hansard, House of Commons, vol. 968, cc235–64, 12 June 1979.

confidence in itself', while in his autobiography he characterized them as 'totalitarian' and kept in place by 'forces of ignorance, timidity and inertia' (Howe, 1994: 140–1). Lawson too had publicly expressed his disdain for exchange controls, condemning them first in his 'maiden speech' as Opposition Treasury Spokesman in November 1977 and then in a *Financial Weekly* article at the height of the 1979 election campaign (Lawson, 1992: 38). Immediately following both the July and October 1979 deregulations, the *Financial Times* published front page stories that repeated the government's rhetoric. Peter Riddell reported on 19 July that 'the latest moves are not designed as a response to the recent sharp rise in the rate' (Riddell, 1979b). In October he went further, arguing that the 'Government has decided to go all the rest of the way now because Minsters believe it is right on its own merits to give additional freedom to investment' (Riddell, 1979c).

So successful was this rhetoric that the Thatcher government's 'neoliberal orientation' and dedication to the 'free market' is still one of the dominant explanations for the abolition of exchange controls in the political economy literature (Helleiner, 1994: 150; Germain, 1997). To paraphrase Gamble (1989: 351), the large gap between rhetoric and actions is not specific to Thatcherism, yet what is novel is the unusual degree to which the Thatcher governments were able to convince even their critics that this gap was much smaller than it really was. This is not to deny that figures like Howe and Lawson were ideologically committed to exchange control abolition—both indicated in private that they wished to see the controls abandoned as a matter of principle.[73] Yet this does not explain the ease with which this liberalization gained support at all levels of the civil service, nor why the ideological motivation was the only justification used publicly, despite the overwhelming desire to see these relaxations exert a downward pressure on sterling.

*   *   *

The abolition of exchange controls, much like CCC before it, was not a resounding success. Instead of gently depreciating sterling—or at least halting its appreciation—and thus providing palliative relief to Britain's struggling industrial exporters, there was in fact 'no discernible downward pressure on sterling at the time that the controls were removed' (Britton, 1994: 47). Sterling continued to appreciate for another year, due to the government's tightening of monetary policy, reaching a peak of $2.46 in October 1980 and provoking the Director General of the CBI to threaten the Thatcher government with a 'bare knuckle fight' if it did not take measures to address the exchange rate (Needham, 2014: 184). In addition, this financial liberalization would play havoc with the money supply

---

[73] In October, Howe wrote to Thatcher: 'Obviously the effect of abolishing exchange controls would be to permit outflows which, especially if they proved substantial, would cause the rate to be lower than otherwise. That is a necessary consequence of the achievement of our aim to abolish exchange control' (TNA T 388/207, Howe to Thatcher, 11 October 1979).

figures, rendering them 'increasingly unreliable' at a time when the Thatcher government was introducing a flagship governance project (MTFS) premised upon their fundamental reliability (OECD, 1989: 54).

Nevertheless, despite this comedy of errors, it is important to understand the scrapping of exchange controls for what it was: not a policy driven by blind neoliberal distrust of regulation nor a gift to the City, but a strategy to govern the contradictory imperatives of world value relations and human need during a period of profound global downturn. In the context of the profitability crisis, the strong pound after 1977 presented policymakers with a dilemma. The rise of sterling acted as an automatic disciplining mechanism that acted to purge inflation from the domestic economy, yet at the risk of plunging Britain into a politically unacceptable recession. As such, Callaghan and Thatcher endeavoured to ease exchange controls as a part of a palliative strategy to depreciate sterling, boost the competitiveness of exporters, and ease the recession. However, they faced the challenge of a vehemently opposed union movement and volatile global currency markets. While these obstacles impeded the Callaghan administration, the Thatcher government believed that by justifying the dismantling of exchange controls with rhetoric about 'good housekeeping', they could pragmatically boost export competitiveness while reducing the risk of a collapse in sterling's position. The accidental result of this strategy was to powerfully propel the dynamics of financialization.

6

The Big Bang

On the twentieth anniversary of the Big Bang, the *Financial Times* recited the 'conventional wisdom' that these reforms had 'saved the City from a slow slide into irrelevance': the Big Bang, it was claimed, had transformed Britain's financial sector into 'probably the nearest thing to a true meritocracy' (Larsen, 2006). The twenty-fifth anniversary commemorations in 2011 assumed a very different tone. As hundreds of protesters marked the occasion by demonstrating in Canary Wharf and at the 'Occupy' encampment outside the LSE, *The Economist* (2011) wrote: 'In the 25 years since Big Bang, the mood in the City has changed from optimism to anxiety'. In just five years, the memorialization of this event had transformed from an exercise in self-congratulation to a cautionary tale.

What has remained undisputed, however, is that the Big Bang represented a crucial policy change in propelling processes of financialization both in Britain and globally. By 27 October 1986, the LSE had undergone a dramatic liberalization. Monopolistic fixed commissions on the trading of securities were abandoned and barriers to the entry of foreign firms into the LSE were removed (Plender, 1986: 39). These changes in turn resulted in the scrapping of the single capacity system, which had barred jobbers (who traded wholesale on their own account) from performing the same role as brokers (who traded on behalf of their clients) (Vogel, 1996: 97). The results of this transformation were colossal. The cost of doing business in the LSE fell rapidly, with transaction costs of large trades dropping by 30 per cent between 1986 and 1987; while the average daily turnover of UK equities increased from £500 million in 1986 to £2 billion in 1995 (Laurence, 2001: 83). Overseas banks flooded into the LSE, with a sharp spike in the foreign acquisition of firms following the Big Bang (Fuller, 2016: 68). By 2007, the financial sector accounted for 8.3 per cent of Britain's GDP and, more importantly, trade in financial services yielded a surplus of £36.9 billion compared to the deficit of £89 billion in traded goods (Eglene, 2011: 33–4). By disrupting the cartel-like workings of the LSE and allowing for the globalization of the City, this liberalization accelerated the expansion of Britain's financial sector.

Despite its radical implications, 'Big Bang' is perhaps a misnomer, considering the gradual and winding institutional pathway by which this liberalization came into existence. The legal process that resulted in the Big Bang began with Heath's passing of the 1973 Fair Trading Act that established the Office of Fair Trading (OFT) (Moran, 1991: 69). The Wilson administration then extended the jurisdiction of this legislation in 1976 to cover 'virtually all services', without exempting

Governing Financialization: The Tangled Politics of Financial Liberalization in Britain. Jack Copley, Oxford University Press.
© Jack Copley 2022. DOI: 10.1093/oso/9780192897015.003.0006

the LSE.[1] As a result, the Director General of the OFT, Gordon Borrie, came under legal obligation to refer the LSE's rulebook to the Restrictive Practices Court (RPC), which he did in February 1979. The Chairman of the LSE, Goodison, consequently launched a campaign to lobby the government for an exemption. Goodison's pleas were rejected by the Callaghan administration, but the LSE expected a more sympathetic audience once the Conservatives won the 1979 election. However, in autumn 1979, the Thatcher administration refused to exempt the LSE. Goodison, frustrated but undeterred, continued to lobby the government. Finally, in summer 1983, under the stewardship of a new Chancellor and Secretary of State for Trade and Industry, the Thatcher government relented to the LSE's requests and halted the RPC case. In return for exemption, the LSE agreed to several fundamental changes to its rules, which were to be implemented by October 1986 (Moran, 1991). As such, in contrast to the abruptness of the Big Bang's enactment and its radical implications, the formulation of this landmark piece of liberalization was surprisingly slow, hesitant, and punctuated by periods of inactivity.

The Big Bang is widely understood as an archetypal case of state propulsion of financialization. As Talani (2012: 63) claims, the 'Big Bang represented the final stage of a process which had already begun in the mid 1970s: the definitive submission of productive capital to financial capital'. This liberalization was pursued, according to the mainstream literature, because of the Thatcher government's neoliberal orientation and as a response to the 'competitive deregulation dynamic' unleashed by the 1975 deregulation of the New York Stock Exchange (NYSE) (Helleiner, 1994: 151). This pressure led the Bank to push for the exemption of the LSE from the RPC case, out of fear that the City would lose market share to New York (Laurence, 2001: 75, 80). In contrast to these accounts, this chapter will lend support to Bellringer's and Michie's claim that the 'government's focus' in implementing the Big Bang 'was *not* on sparking a process to propel the Stock Exchange, and as a consequence the City of London, to a position of global influence' (2014: 126; emphasis added). Rather, this liberalization formed one element of the Thatcher government's broader strategy to chart a course between the opposed imperatives of global market viability and national political legitimacy—the impersonal domination of world value relations and people's stubborn assertion of their needs—during the deepest trough of the profitability crisis.

After its referral to the RPC in early 1979, the LSE began lobbying the government for an exemption from RPC jurisdiction. The Thatcher administration was torn over how to respond. While granting this exemption would ensure that the government could continue to sell its debt—gilt-edged securities—on the

---

[1]   TNA FV 73/148, Thatcher to Wilson, 10 November 1980.

LSE uninterrupted, which was an important instrument of monetary control, this very public favour for the City would make a mockery of the government's competition rhetoric. The political considerations won out in 1979 and Thatcher refused the LSE's request. However, the balance of forces shifted with the creation of the MTFS in 1980. MTFS was a self-imposed policy straitjacket that would lock the government into a four-year path of severe contractionary measures, in an attempt to purge the British economy of inflation and render Britain competitive on the world market. As a strategy of depoliticized discipline, MTFS required that certain money supply targets were met each year—so as to prove that the policy was working, and thus justify the painful deflation.

Yet this plan went disastrously wrong: the ensuing recession was deeper than expected and the government was unable to restrain the money supply. In the context of deepening recession and erosion of its legitimacy, the Thatcher administration lost its resolve and loosened monetary policy. Without the interest rate weapon, the government was forced to discover a different method for reducing the money supply, or else risk the total failure of MTFS. They found this instrument in a process called 'overfunding', whereby more government debt was sold on the LSE than required by current levels of state expenditure. This acted to soak up excess liquidity in the banking system and lower the money supply. In turn, overfunding required a smoothly functioning stock exchange, which could not be reconciled with the continuation of the RPC case against the LSE. As such, from 1982, the Thatcher government endeavoured to negotiate an exemption for the LSE, which was finally announced in July 1983. The decision that led to the Big Bang, then, was in large part a result of the government's need to rescue its ailing, ill-thought-out, depoliticized disciplining strategy.

'Hooked on Competition'

As discussed in Chapter 4, from the 1960s, pressure began to build across the partisan divide in British politics for the introduction of greater competition into Britain's cartelized financial system. This desire for heightened competitiveness, itself partly a response to the perception of British decline, played a role in motivating the CCC and exchange control liberalizations—though, this book has argued, more pragmatic concerns predominated. While the rise of the Eurodollar market and the sterling-denominated secondary banking sector, as well as CCC's dismantling of the clearing bank cartel, had made British banking more competitive, the securities industry—with its locus in the LSE—was able to resist the encroachment of competitive logics. This changed in 1979, when the OFT began its investigation of the LSE's restrictive practices. This gradual rise in influence of pro-competition ideology, combined with the immediate competitive threat to the British securities industry posed by the 1975 liberalization of the NYSE, acted as the initial spark for the drawn-out legal process that would finally result in the Big Bang. However, it was not a foregone conclusion that the Thatcher government would allow the LSE to be transformed by the incursion of restrictive practices legislation. As this chapter will demonstrate, what ultimately led the government to propel the Big Bang liberalization was not its genuine commitment to economic competition, but its practical struggle to respond to the governing contradictions churned up by the profitability crisis.

When the Conservatives arrived in office in May 1979, they faced a dire economic situation—as detailed in Chapter 5. The British experience of the global profitability crisis had entered its second phase, whereby the strong pound, propped up by North Sea oil and the IMF's seal of approval, was aiding in the government's attack on inflation (which nevertheless remained high), while simultaneously eroding companies' already low rates of profit. In these conditions, the RPC's legal action against the LSE presented the Thatcher administration with a dilemma. One the one hand, the government needed a smoothly functioning stock exchange both to sell its own debt and so that companies could sell their securities (Dutta, 2017). This was crucial for two reasons: in the context of accelerating inflation, the sale of government debt helped to control the money supply by soaking up excess liquidity; and in the context of dwindling corporate liquidity, companies needed to raise funds for investment. This suggested that the government should shield the LSE from the potential disruption that could be caused by a protracted court case. Yet, on the other hand, the Thatcher administration had been elected on a platform of increasing the competitiveness of the British economy as a whole—this was ostensibly to be its solution to the interminable problem of stagflation—and the high-profile exemption of a cosy cartel such as the LSE from legal scrutiny would represent an embarrassing U-turn on this stated objective. As Steven Vogel (1996: 103) observed, the new government did 'not want to be seen as too close a friend of the City'. Indeed, it was the apparent conviction of the Thatcher government's rhetoric on free competition that had given it the political cover to attempt to manipulate the pound through the abolition of exchange controls. The interplay of these contradictory pressures explains the Thatcher government's decision not to exempt the LSE from official scrutiny in 1979.

Upon its election, the Thatcher government was immediately warned by Treasury and Bank officials as to the dangers of the RPC case. On 10 May, Treasury official R. H. Seebohm wrote to Treasury Under Secretary Michael Bridgeman, explaining that an

> effective secondary market in gilts is highly desirable to support the funding of the PSBR…There is a genuine risk of financial anarchy in the event of an adverse Court decision before a new system is developed, during which period

there could be a hiatus in gilt sales. The secondary market is also important for company securities.[2]

Indeed, Bridgeman recognized that 'there is a risk, which may be small, of severe damage to the present Government's key element in its macro-economic strategy, control of the money supply'.[3] This reflected his observation earlier in the year that '[n]o Government which was committed to control of the broader monetary aggregates as a major element in its macro-economic policy and so a substantial programme of gilt sales could run the risk of such an hiatus'.[4] This problem was recognized by the Bank months before the Conservatives had arrived in office. In June, Bank Governor Richardson wrote to Chancellor Howe. Richardson argued that the 'outcome of such a review could be far reaching and unless very carefully handled could seriously disturb markets generally and the gilt-edged market in particular'.[5]

Against this advice, however, Howe was also repeatedly warned of the political embarrassment that would accompany an exemption of the LSE (Vogel, 1996: 102–3; Bellringer and Michie, 2014: 125). A Treasury note on 17 May warned that an 'amendment to the Services Order would require an Affirmative Resolution in both Houses and there could be political embarrassment for the Government (which could be accused either of abandoning the policy enshrined in the Fair Trading Act 1973 or of being selective in the support for stronger competition powers generally)'.[6] Two weeks later, Nott repeated this fear to Howe. He agreed that the RPC was the wrong forum to examine the LSE's practices, but emphasized that the legal process was 'already in train' and interrupting it now while claiming to want to 'strengthen competition policy generally…might be fiercely criticised'.[7] The Bank, despite voicing its support for exemption, was also beginning to realize the extent of the government's bind. Peter Cooke, Head of Banking Supervision, was informed by a Bank official after a meeting with Conservative ministers in mid June that the 'topic is going to be decided on political grounds by Ministers hooked on competition'.[8]

An attempt to reconcile the funding and political imperatives was made, however, in the form of a 'stay of execution' clause to the Competition Bill that was to be unveiled in 1980.[9] This legal amendment would grant the LSE time to adjust to the changes if its rulebook was deemed restrictive by the RPC, thus avoiding an initial period of chaos that could endanger gilt sales. A Treasury note

---

[2] TNA T 386/684, Seebohm to Bridgeman, 10 May 1979.
[3] TNA FV 73/147, Bridgeman to Durie, 21 June 1979.
[4] BOE 6A385/12, Bridgeman to PS/Chief Secretary, 30 January 1979.
[5] TNA T 386/684, Richardson to Howe, 4 June 1979.
[6] TNA FV 73/146, Treasury note, 17 May 1979.
[7] TNA FV 73/146, Nott to Howe, 30 May 1979.
[8] BOE 6A385/13, CEC to Cooke, 14 June 1979.
[9] TNA T 386/684, Note by Gilmore, 23 July 1979.

explained that this clause 'seems to remove the main difficulties of allowing the reference to proceed, without incurring the difficulties of immediate exemption'.[10] While this proposal was endorsed by Financial Secretary Lawson[11], the Bank was not convinced, with Richardson insisting to Howe that the stay of execution was a 'valuable improvement' but still deeply insufficient.[12]

A split began to emerge between Howe and Richardson on one side, and Lawson and Nott on the other. Howe wrote to Nott in late May, voicing his strong opposition to Nott's hesitancy about exemption. After numerous discussions, Howe's position softened somewhat. On 8 August, he explained to Nott that he was unable to 'simply accept the danger to our funding programme which a hiatus in gilt sales would represent...an effective market in gilts and in equities is essential to the economy'.[13] As such, he urged Nott to accept the stay of execution immediately and to keep open the option of exemption when the opportunity presented itself. Yet Nott felt that the political considerations should take precedence: 'The press (the Guardian and the Economist) had stated explicitly that they would regard the Government's actions with respect to the Stock Exchange as the key test of its commitment to [competition] policy'.[14] The Bank came to believe that Nott had isolated himself from his colleagues and advisers. There was talk in the Bank that Treasury Permanent Secretary Wass had 'spoken to the Chancellor who had urged Nott to reconsider this approach but Nott had said "no"'.[15] Furthermore, a DoT official had hinted to the Bank that 'DOT officials' advice to their Minister had been opposed to the line Nott was now taking'.[16] However, despite his possible isolation, Nott could rely on support from Lawson and, more importantly, Thatcher. The latter explained that while she was content for Nott and Howe to resolve the issue among themselves, she was 'inclined to agree with Mr. Nott that it would be hard to justify not having the Stock Exchange investigated by the Restrictive Practices Court...at this juncture'.[17] Nott revealed his decision not to exempt the LSE to Goodison on 16 October, to the latter's dismay.[18]

In the context of the second phase of British stagflation, in which the high pound was pushing the British economy deeper into recession, the RPC's case against the LSE left the government in a quandary. Exempting the LSE would allow continued sales of government bonds and company securities, which helped

[10] Ibid.   [11] TNA T 386/684, Lawson to Howe, 25 July 1979.
[12] TNA FV 73/147, Richardson to Howe, 15 August 1979.
[13] TNA T 386/684, Howe to Nott, 31 July 1979.
[14] TNA T 386/684, Note for the record, 31 August 1979.
[15] BOE 6A385/14, Note for the record, 4 September 1979.   [16] Ibid.
[17] TNA FV 73/146, Lankester to Durie, 4 June 1979.
[18] TNA FV 73/148, Note of a meeting, 16 October 1979. The LSE had a functional but somewhat uneasy working relationship with the DoT. As one official put it: 'The Stock Exchange Council is jealous of its independent status. The Chairman in particular tends to give the impression of that somewhat arrogant contempt for the world of Westminster and Whitehall which is not untypical of City institutions' (TNA FV73/214, Elizabeth Llewellyn-Smith to PS/Secretary of State, 10 July 1981).

in the battle against inflation and in keeping companies afloat despite dire profitability. Yet this exemption would directly contradict the Thatcher government's pro-competition rhetoric, and thus threaten its political legitimacy. In 1979, the government decided to postpone this dilemma. The immediate legitimacy concerns were considered to take priority, while the dangers associated with debt sales were somewhat allayed by the stay of execution clause. However, in the following years, the balance of forces was to change in significant ways, with the sale of government debt becoming an increasingly central element in the government's attempt to discipline British social relations in line with world market standards and thus revitalize the stagnant economy. This in turn rejuvenated the debate surrounding the RPC case.

The 'Political Economy' of MTFS

The archival record shows a curious lull in discussion of the RPC case within the Treasury, DoT, and Bank after Nott's decision in late 1979.[19] Yet in 1982 this debate reignited with a greater fervour than before. While this period of inactivity is generally explained in the existing literature as deriving from the ideological disposition of the Secretaries of State for Trade who held office at the time—Nott and John Biffen supposedly shared a lack of sympathy for the LSE's plight, while Arthur Cockfield and Cecil Parkinson were more predisposed to take the City's side (Moran, 1991; Vogel, 1996)—this chapter advances a different explanation. The re-emergence of interest in the RPC case was primarily driven by the necessity to support the government's MTFS policy: a depoliticized strategy to restructure British society according to the competitive dictates of global value relations and therefore respond to the profitability crisis. The government's need to prop up MTFS required them to ensure that there was no disruption in the gilt market resulting from a negative RPC decision.

MTFS was the policy framework upon which the Thatcher government's notorious monetarist experiment was based. It consisted of a four-year plan that set a series of annually declining targets for the money supply and PSBR, with the stated overall goal of reducing inflation. Not only were the money supply targets extremely ambitious, but the key monetary aggregate chosen as a target—£M3—had a very loose relationship with inflation. Indeed, there were concerns within the Bank, Treasury, and Civil Service Committee that the 'relationships between

[19] The exception to this generalization is the intervention made by Wilson following the publication of the Wilson Committee's *Review of the Functioning of Financial Institutions* in 1980. Wilson urged Thatcher, with Goodison's backing, to reconsider the RPC case in light of the report's findings. Thatcher, however, was unconvinced that the report offered any information that would cause the government to reverse its 1979 decision (TNA FV 73/148, Wilson to Thatcher, 17 October 1980; TNA FV 73/148, Thatcher to Wilson, 10 November 1980).

(any particular definition of) monetary growth and nominal incomes were too fragile a basis for such a long-term commitment' (Goodhart, 1995: 103). As Needham points out, while there was little econometric evidence suggesting that control of £M3 would allow the government to rein in inflation, there was a 'tolerably robust' relationship between another aggregate—M1—and nominal incomes. Yet Lawson, the policy's progenitor, chose the former as a target because prioritizing M1 would have given more interest rate setting power to the Bank, further cementing its autonomy from Treasury and ministerial control (Needham, 2014: 147). In addition, the raft of financial liberalizations that had preceded MTFS—most significantly the abolition of exchange controls—seriously under-mined the ability of policymakers to have any definite impact upon the money supply. Such practical concerns, however, were 'brushed aside' by the government in their determination to implement this new policy framework (Goodhart, 1995: 103).

The government's unwillingness to be deterred by the technical deficiencies of MTFS has often been interpreted as evidence of its ideological commitment to monetarism. The ideas of monetarist economists such as Friedman (with whom Thatcher personally corresponded) had exerted a growing influence over key figures within the Conservative Party during their time in opposition, particularly Joseph and Thatcher herself. Such ideas had, since the 1970s, been propagated by think tanks such as the Institute of Economic Affairs, the Centre for Policy Studies, and the Adam Smith Institute (Cooper, 2012: 36–41). The goal of these organizations was to 'socialise the British elite and ultimately the wider population to this kind of economic thinking and practice' (Best, 2020: 7). Articulating the perceived influence of such monetarist ideas on the Thatcher government, Healey, in an anti-Semitic barb, accused Howe in May 1980 of following the 'half-understood, half-baked theories of that Jewish leprechaun Milton Friedman'.[20]

Yet while the spread of monetarist ideas was doubtlessly important in motiv-ating MTFS, it is important not to overstate the case. What this focus on ideology misses is the fundamentally *political* character of the monetarist experiment. MTFS should be understood not simply as a reflection of the Thatcher adminis-tration's stubbornness and ideological fervour, but as an attempt to commit the government to a strict disciplining project that would confront the profitability crisis head-on, without undermining the government's legitimacy. John Fforde, Bank Executive Director (Home Finance), articulated this in a fascinating speech to the New York Federal Reserve in 1982. He distinguished between the 'practical macroeconomics' and 'political economy' of monetary targeting. While the former was concerned with the stability of relationships between monetary aggregates and inflation, the latter referred to the construction of coherent political strategies

---

[20] Thatcher Papers, Churchill College, Cambridge, THCR 2/6/2/141, Wolfson Note to MT, 23 May 1980, https://www.margaretthatcher.org/document/119476/.

that would allow the 'macroeconomic executive' to govern effectively (Fforde, 1982: 200). The challenge faced by the British state for more than a decade had been to govern 'a democratic society' in 'an economic environment characterized by sluggish or zero growth, a very large public sector, persistent and volatile inflation', and 'pronounced external constraints' (ibid.: 200–1). It was this dilemma that the *political economy* of MTFS sought to navigate. Fforde argued that the success of MTFS would lie not in 'particular developments in this or that [monetary] aggregate', but rather in the 'refusal of the authorities to stimulate demand in "Keynesian" fashion, or to "reflate", as conditions develop that would in the past have justified and provoked such a response' (ibid.: 207).[21]

By basing its macroeconomic strategy upon a select few monetary targets, the government was committing itself to transform policy if changes in financial conditions meant that the targets were in danger of being missed. As Thain (1985: 269) argues, this represented a 'deliberate abdication of power to the financial and exchange rate markets'. MTFS, as such, allowed the state to redis-cover 'automatic rules or pilots to manage the economy' (Bulpitt, 1986: 32). This policy straitjacket would nullify the 'need for an incomes policy and with it, direct and continuous political negotiations with trade unions': '[w]orkers who con-tinued to demand wage rises above the rate of inflation would be automatically forced to change their expectations or price themselves out of a job' (Flinders and

---

[21] Fforde's comments echoed Volcker's statement to the House of Representatives two years earlier, in which he insisted that his version of monetarism was not an exact science based upon precise relationships between monetary aggregates and inflation. Instead, monetarism was about signalling to the various sections of civil society that the state would not give in to their demands to artificially reflate the economy:

the world at large—the real world of huge prolonged deficits, of wage bargaining building in rising costs for years ahead, of enormous pressure to protect established competitive positions and living standards even when productivity cannot support them—will not focus on the technicalities of the various M's, the precise targets, or short-run fluctuations about those targets. What we must do is convey a general sense—and make good on that message—that excessive money and credit creation will not underwrite the inflationary process.

(TNA PREM 19.180, Volcker statement to the House of
Representatives, 19 November 1980)

Similar sentiments were expressed by one of Volcker's predecessors at the Federal Reserve, Arthur Burns, who could hardly be accused of being an ardent monetarist. Burns (1979: 14–15) claimed that '[r]ising economic expectations of people, wider citizen participation in the political arena, government commitments to full employment, liberal income maintenance programs, expanding government regulations, and increasingly pressing demands on government for the solution of economic and social problems' had 'transformed economic life and brought on secular inflation'. Faced with this problem, 'every central banker has learned from the world's experience that . . . excessive creation of money will over the long run cause or validate inflation . . . but this knowledge stops short of mathematical precision' (ibid.: 17). Yet despite the fact that 'the Federal Reserve System had the power', and the knowledge, 'to abort the inflation at its incipient stage fifteen years ago or at any later point', it had been obstructed by political concerns (ibid.: 15). What was needed, Burns (ibid.: 25) argued, was 'a binding endorsement of restrictive monetary policies until the rate of inflation has become substantially lower'. In other words, what was required was a strategy to discipline an enfranchised and entitled domestic population, eager for their social needs to be met, through a form of rules-based depoliticization.

Buller, 2006: 305). In addition to depoliticizing financial discipline, the policy's creators also believed—to the incredulity of certain officials within the Treasury—that MTFS could defeat inflation without terrible economic pain (Needham, 2014: 147). In accordance with the principles of the rational expectations hypothesis, discussed in Chapter 5, it was believed (or, perhaps more accurately, hoped) that the public announcement of £M3 and PSBR targets would provoke investors and wage earners to adjust their expectations and demands in line with the new financial environment—resulting in a downward spiral of inflation without the need for massive unemployment (Best, 2019: 632).[22]

While the policy had its detractors, its political character was widely recognized.[23] Discussing MTFS in early 1980, Sir Kenneth Berrill, head of the Cabinet Office's Central Policy Review Staff, communicated to Thatcher what was at stake in implementing this policy:

> This battle (which has only just begun) is between the irresistible force (trades union power) and the immovable object (the money supply). Given British conditions, it could be a very bloody battle indeed with interest rates, exchange rate, reduced investment, bankruptcies, at unknown levels. By declaring its determination to plough on with its monetary targets regardless the Government is giving itself very little elasticity... *This is one of the many decisions which is, in the end, more a matter of political than economic judgement.*[24]

Yet this lack of elasticity, which concerned Berrill, was exactly what attracted Lawson. He argued that this reduction in the government's 'room for manoeuvre as circumstances changed... was the point of the whole exercise. MTFS was intended to be a self-imposed constraint on economic policy-making'. It was a mistake to think, as many cynical Conservatives did, that previous Labour

---

[22] Several important figures, however, have denied that the rational expectations hypothesis played a large role in the formulation of MTFS. Lawson (1992: 69), in his memoirs, argued that this theory was 'scarcely known by either Ministers or officials in the crucial formative period'. Wass, in advising Thatcher on the best way to navigate the deeply recessionary effects of MTFS in November 1980, claimed: 'I have never myself believed that the statement of the commitment to a deceleration in monetary growth would, through expectations, lead rapidly and as it were on its own to a fall in wage settlements... [T]he pressures on wage bargainers and price fixers has to be through powerful financial and economic forces—in short an inability of the customer (employer) to afford the goods or services in question at the price that would otherwise be offered' (TNA PREM 19/174, Wass paper for Howe, 5 November 1980). This supports the notion that MTFS was primarily designed to defeat inflation through painful discipline.

[23] Governor Richardson urged Thatcher and Howe against the adoption of MTFS at a meeting in March 1980. While he recognized that the policy was designed to lock the government into a stable 'path through the difficulties ahead', he reminded them that it 'was hard enough to set a monetary target for one year ahead: it was much harder for a four year period' (TNA PREM 19/177, Lankester to Wiggins, 10 March 1980).

[24] TNA PREM 19/177, Berrill to Lankester, 25 February 1980; emphasis added.

governments 'foolishly over-expanded the money supply simply out of ignorance or sheer perversity'. Rather, Lawson emphasized, it was 'political pressures' that blew these governments off course (Lawson, 1992: 67). By committing itself to four years of economic stringency, MTFS would insulate the government from these political pressures. This represented, as Howe (1994: 163) observed, 'a natural follow-through from the sensible lesson that the IMF had imposed upon our predecessors'. The 1980/81 Financial Statement and Budget Report thus stated that 'there would be no question of departing from the money supply policy, which is essential to the success of any anti-inflationary strategy' (HM Treasury, 1981). As Thatcher (1993: 97) insisted, echoing the logic of the rational expect- ations hypothesis, rather than resting on a solid relationship between economic variables, MTFS depended upon a downward reappraisal of economic expect- ations that would only occur if the government was seen to be committed to strict and continued financial discipline: 'MTFS would only influence expectations in so far as people believed in our determination to stick to it: its credibility depended on that of the Government—and ultimately, therefore, on the quality of my own commitment . . . [that] I would not bow to demands to reflate'.

The Thatcher government's monetarist experiment should be understood as a strategy of depoliticized discipline, whereby the government would lock itself in to a contractionary programme that would limit policymakers' ability to fold in the face of popular outcry. This would allow the government to discipline domestic social relations in line with the impersonal pressures of a system of global value relations in deep crisis, without being impeded by the intrusion of concrete human needs. This strategy was predicated upon the achievement of certain technical monetary objectives, which would in turn justify the economic restruc- turing, and required a degree of faith that a shift in economic actors' expectations would allow inflation to be brought down without too much pain. However, as will be examined next, the practical shortcomings of this programme would ultimately push it to the brink of collapse.

When the Rubber Hit the Road

In order for MTFS to successfully depoliticize the government's disciplining strategy in response to the profitability crisis, Conservative politicians needed to be able to demonstrate that the policy was working towards its stated goal of tackling monetary growth, and ensure that the ensuing economic contraction was not too painful. The symbolism of hitting the £M3 and PSBR targets would justify the government's disciplining measures and help them resist political pressures to reflate the economy. As Fforde (1982: 204) explained, 'the "political economy" of the strategy seemed to require a demonstration of quite close [monetary] control, and an absence of intolerable side-effects'. However, this plan foundered immediately upon implementation, devastating the government's disciplining strategy.

In 1980, Britain entered the worst recession since 1921. Razor-thin company profits shrank even further, as they were squeezed by both a pound priced at over $2.40 and interest rates that stood at 16 per cent (Needham, 2014: 154). Manufacturing investment fell by 26 per cent, GDP dropped by 4.6 per cent, and unemployment climbed above two million for the first time since the 1930s (Needham, 2014: 154; Britton, 1994: 49). Richardson explained the problem in stark terms to Thatcher, Howe, and Lawson in October: 'Profitability was at an appallingly low level: although pre-tax rates of return had fallen in all countries, in the UK it was only about half of what it was elsewhere ... there was a danger [in some sectors] that the UK would lose industrial capacity altogether'.[25] This was exactly the kind of 'bloody battle' that Berrill had warned of. Indeed, in an April 1980 letter, Hayek had personally cautioned Thatcher against a 'gradual' monetarist strategy like MTFS because he foresaw that it would result in such protracted 'misery no government could last out'.[26] For this fundamentally political reason, he insisted that monetarist penance 'can be carried out only by an instantaneous act', and indeed should be pursued only after organized labour had been defeated.[27] In the context of the unprecedentedly deep 1980 recession, it became essential that the Thatcher government could at least point to the success of MTFS in meeting the money supply objectives. Yet the monetary aggregates showed no sign of responding to MTFS. In contrast to the target range of 7–11 per cent, £M3 grew by 19.1 per cent between February 1980 and April 1981, while inflation averaged 18.1 per cent throughout 1980 (Cobham, 2002: 43, 12). By September 1980, Thatcher was expressing 'serious concern that the money supply would be seen to be out of control'.[28] Her fears were founded. As the *Observer's* economics editor William Keegan pointed out that month: 'We have managed to achieve a seemingly impossible feat: monetary growth far in excess of what our monetarist ministers said was necessary to bring inflation down, yet a squeeze which is half killing British industry' (Keegan, 1980).

MTFS was being torn apart at the seams. Its disciplining effects had been even greater than expected, as the monetary tightening had caused a further appreciation of sterling, which was imposing an extreme contraction upon British businesses. Furthermore, the ensuing recession could not be justified by pointing to the government's success in meeting the monetary objectives, as £M3 was well above the target range. Confronted with this dilemma, the Thatcher administration's resolve was weakened. MLR was reduced from 17 per cent to 16 per cent in

[25] TNA PREM 19/179, Lankester to Wiggins, 14 October 1980.
[26] Hoover Institution, Hayek MSS, Box 101, Folder 26, Hayek to Thatcher, 24 April 1980, https://www.margaretthatcher.org/document/112692/.
[27] Ibid.   [28] TNA PREM 19/178, Pattison to Wiggins, 3 September 1980.

July 1980 and then to 14 per cent in November, in spite of the £M3 and inflation numbers, so as to allow ailing businesses to access cheaper credit and to assuage the important Conservative constituency of mortgagors (Temperton, 1991: 115; Tomlinson, 2007: 9). The political sensitivity of increases in MLR meant that the government had to rely on other mechanisms to attempt to meet the MTFS targets. As such, the March 1981 Budget announced a series of sharp cuts in public expenditure as well as indirect and income tax increases, in an attempt to combat the government's contribution to the growth in the money supply and shift resources from the personal to the corporate and state sectors. This in turn allowed Howe to reduce MLR to 12 per cent and thus ease the pressure on companies and the mortgage market (Temperton, 1991: 115). As Needham (2014: 153–4) notes, MTFS came to resemble much more a *fiscal*, rather than monetary, strategy.

The recession bottomed out in early 1981, with output reaching its lowest point in spring (Britton, 1994). Between April and July, major riots broke out amongst the racialized poor in London, Liverpool, and Manchester, followed by less serious upheavals in Birmingham, Sheffield, Nottingham, Hull, Slough, Leeds, Bradford, Leicester, and Derby (Scarbrough, 2000: 150–1). Consequently, the economic outlook began to gradually improve: GDP rose for the first time since 1979, sterling reached a four-year low of $1.76 in August, £M3 rose by 13.7 per cent (which was still well above the 6–10 per cent MTFS target), and inflation averaged 11.9 per cent (Cobham, 2002: 43, 12). However, by the start of 1982, bank lending had begun to grow rapidly. Driven chiefly by a desperate company sector as well as house buyers, this sharp acceleration in bank lending threatened to throw the MTFS targets into chaos just when the government seemed to be getting to grips with the economic situation (Dow, 2013: 198). Combined with the stubborn continued rise in unemployment, which began to approach three million, this represented a worrying challenge to the Conservatives' chances in the 1983 election.

In order to preserve the presentational coherence of MTFS, it was crucial that bank lending be restricted without further increasing unemployment, jeopardizing the timid recovery in business investment, or alienating mortgagors. As Richardson and Howe both acknowledged, 'for the sake of the corporate sector, there would have to be some reduction in interest rates; but it was questionable whether this could be reconciled with sticking to the figures in the medium-term financial strategy'.[29] Furthermore, not only had MLR increases been deemed too politically sensitive, but the government had very few methods for tightening monetary policy left at its disposal, having abolished exchange controls on capital movements in 1979 and 'corset' controls on bank lending in 1980. The success of

[29] TNA PREM 19/179, Lankester to Wiggins, 14 October 1980.

MTFS as a strategy of depoliticized discipline required the discovery of a more politically neutral instrument that could give the government some measure of control over the money supply.

Overfunding and the Stock Exchange

The Thatcher administration discovered an imperfect resolution to this dilemma in a monetary instrument called overfunding. Overfunding was a 'peculiarly British practice' that involved the government selling more debt than it needed to fund its expenditure (Lawson, 1992: 449). The authorities would sell a large volume of government debt to the non-bank private sector—principally house-holds and companies—which these investors would pay for by drawing from their bank accounts, restricting the growth of bank deposits (Cobham, 2002: 25; Howson, 1994: 252). Overfunding thus had the effect of soaking up liquidity in the financial system. This aided in reducing the money supply without politically difficult increases in MLR. In broader terms, overfunding would allow the Thatcher administration to meet their monetary targets, which would in turn justify the pain of the government's depoliticized disciplining strategy to purge stagflation from the British economy.

Goodhart, Bank chief adviser during this period, observed that because 'the government [had] shrunk from the option of pushing up interest rates high enough', they were forced to rely on large sales of gilt-edged securities to pick up the slack (Goodhart, 1995: 106). The government's fiscal tightening was proving insufficient to counteract the rise in bank lending, as the Treasury's Rachel Lomax argued in November 1981: 'If bank lending continues to grow rapidly, the task of meeting the MTFS target will be difficult, even if the PSBR falls relative to GDP, as planned. We may only be able to restrain the growth in £M3 by persistently overfunding the PSBR'.[30] Overfunding became a crucial tool in the Thatcher administration's arsenal, with the government selling an excess of £2.5 billion in debt more than was needed to fund the PSBR in 1981–2 (Bank of England, 1982: 201). Indeed, Lawson (1992: 72) wrote that the MTFS objectives for 1982 and 1983 'were met only after the targets had been raised, and then by somewhat artificial means (the technique known as "overfunding")'. Similarly, former Bank advisor Christopher Dow noted the importance of this method of monetary control when he commented that the increase in bank lending in 1982 'would have had to be accompanied by even more rapid growth of bank deposits— and hence of £M3—than in fact occurred had we not sold debt on an enormous scale' (Dow, 2013: 198). The centrality of overfunding to the government's

---

[30] BOE 13A173/3, Pirie to Minister of State (Commons), 3 November 1981.

macroeconomic strategy was explained in May 1982 to Howe by Treasury Deputy Secretary Middleton in a revealing letter:

> The abolition of exchange controls has greatly restricted our ability to do anything about one counterpart—the growth of bank lending. If direct controls are imposed the banking system would continue to expand offshore beyond our control. We have a completely free banking system for the first time in living memory... We have not thought it either feasible or desirable to attempt to reduce bank lending over the medium term by letting short term interest rates rise... So, for a given fiscal policy, *we are left with only one instrument to control £M3 and the wider aggregates—funding in all its forms.*[31]

The need to use government debt sales to control the money supply increased even further in July, when the hire purchase controls on bank lending were abolished (Britton, 1994: 62).

This heavy intervention in the gilts market created a greater necessity for a functioning stock exchange. As a result, interest in pursuing the exemption of the LSE from the RPC revived within the Treasury and DoT in 1982, after little attention had been paid to the issue since autumn 1979. Wass wrote to Bank Deputy Governor McMahon in March, arguing that the problem was not simply that a negative ruling by the RPC could create a temporary disruption in the sale of government debt. Rather, there was an additional problem that meant an unconditional exemption which maintained the status quo would also be unworkable, namely that the LSE's outdated and monopolistic practices had rendered the existing stock market too small to adapt to the government's overfunding requirements: 'The jobbers, as you have often told us, are not highly capitalised, and could not be expected to run sizeable books, particularly of long-dated stock... [This lack of] capital base imposes a serious constraint on our freedom to experiment with new techniques of selling [debt]'.[32] Governor Richardson urged Howe in late June that 'the Court proceedings ought to be stopped and replaced by a rapid independent enquiry'.[33] Furthermore, he assured Howe that he had 'obtained Mr Goodison's informal and confidential assurance that he would be prepared to work for the implementation of the findings of any such enquiry'.[34] By the end of June, Howe decided to take action to accelerate the process by asking 'for a speedy paper from Treasury officials to consider inter alia a forum other than... Restrictive Practices Court for examining the Stock Exchange's restrictions'.[35]

---

[31] TNA T 521/42, Middleton to Howe, 13 May 1982; emphasis added.
[32] TNA T 521/42, Wass to McMahon, 15 March 1982.
[33] TNA T 521/44, Seebohm to Pirie and Monck, 2 July 1982.   [34] Ibid.
[35] TNA FV 73/215, Note for the file, 1 July 1982.

Political considerations concerning a visible U-turn on competition policy, which had stopped the government from exempting the LSE in 1979, had still not faded completely from sight. By August 1982, Howe had arrived at the 'provisional conclusion' that 'primary or secondary legislation to interrupt the case would be very difficult politically'.[36] As such, 'the best of an unpromising range of options may be to encourage "without prejudice" discussions with a view to settlement out of Court'.[37] Secretary of State for Trade Cockfield, Biffen's successor, shared the same sentiment, explaining to Howe that he 'thought it impossible to withdraw or block the case: and that the only possible way out was for the Stock Exchange to put its house in order and for what amounted to a consent judgement to be given on that basis'.[38]

Similar developments took place during this period within the Bank, which was concerned with the 'trading of gilt-edged securities' and 'the overall health of the City' (Vogel, 1996: 103–4). David Walker was appointed Executive Director for Industrial Finance and consequently started to investigate ways to circumvent the RPC (ibid.). Walker began corresponding with Philip Brown, DoT Deputy Secretary, on the topic of a possible exemption. Considering the political sensitivity, Brown insisted that the DoT believed 'the right way to talk is "talks about talks"'—yet Walker commented that 'even "talks about talks" will be difficult to launch'.[39] Furthermore, Cockfield was wary of the Treasury taking the lead on the case because the 'Treasury could not be relied upon to adopt a wholly independent posture on Bank proposals', as 'Treasury perceptions would be dominated by the likely effect of any proposals upon the gilts market'.[40]

Growth in monetary aggregates slowed in the second half of 1982, possibly dampening the sense of immediacy about exempting the LSE, which is reflected in a period of quiet in the archival record. Yet in early 1983 the situation worsened. From March to May, £M3 grew by 15.7 per cent, flouting the MTFS targets (Bank of England, 1983: 173). The most important reason for this monetary growth was a sharp and unexpected increase in the PSBR and mortgage lending. In order to counter this, the government sold £3.1 billion in gilt-edged securities between March and May (ibid: 174). In early May, Howe, Cockfield, and Richardson met and decided that the 'next step should be for the Treasury and DOT officials, in consultation with the Bank, to produce, as a matter of urgency, a draft negotiating brief'.[41] As a Treasury paper stressed again in June, the government required 'an efficient market for gilts not only as a source of finance but as an instrument of

---

[36] TNA FV 73/215, Rutter to Rhodes, 3 August 1982.   [37] Ibid.

[38] TNA FV 73/215, Whitlock to Linstead, 15 August 1982.

[39] TNA FV 73/215, Brown to Walker, 23 August 1982; TNA FV 73/215, Walker to Brown, 26 August 1982.

[40] TNA FV 73/215, Madelin to Brown, 19 November 1982.

[41] TNA PREM 19/1005, Record of a discussion, 9 May 1983.

monetary control'.[42] In order to maintain (or rescue) the appearance of MTFS as an economically sound strategy, rather than a device to depoliticize disciplining measures, the government desperately needed the capacity to control monetary growth by selling debt to the non-bank private sector.

The Conservatives' election victory on 9 June spurred the process further, as Lawson became Chancellor and Parkinson was appointed as Secretary of State for Trade and Industry (Moran, 1991: 70–1). Parkinson was strongly opposed to the RPC case, a position that was motivated by his fear that the 'Stock Exchange would become a peripheral institution on the world financial scene': ironically, Parkinson argued, the LSE was being 'prevented from changing by a legal action designed to promote change' (Parkinson, 1992: 244). Eager to maintain the momentum that had been built up before the election, Parkinson looked to arrange a meeting with Lawson and Richardson to discuss the next steps. In preparation for this meeting, Treasury Under Secretary for Home Finance, Nicholas Monck, emphasized to Treasury officials—including Middleton, the new Permanent Secretary—that the 'Treasury has an interest in the subject both because of the macro-economic importance of an efficient and effective capital market and because of our interest in an effective and cheap mechanism for marketing gilt-edged stock as a means of controlling the growth of the broad monetary aggregates'.[43]

In addition to the energy injected by the new post-election appointments, the political considerations surrounding the exemption of the LSE had changed significantly. The fear of damaging political repercussions if the government was seen to contradict its competition rhetoric had subsided after the election victory. Furthermore, a new political concern was emerging. If the case went all the way to court it could expose a deep division between the Treasury and Bank. On 22 June, Monck told Lawson:

> Apart from the argument of substance, continuation of a Court case could produce severe embarrassment. The Bank feel that if they had to give evidence, they would have to support the status quo ... There would be a choice between the Treasury giving evidence in favour of the status quo and a more or less public disagreement with the Bank. It would be preferable to avoid this and the Department of Trade proposal offers a way of doing so.[44]

Monck emphasized to Lawson that he should endorse the DoT's proposal 'provided the negotiations yield sufficient change to be politically presentable'.[45]

---

[42] TNA T 486/12, Monck to Cassell, 2 June 1983.
[43] TNA T486/12, Monck to Principal Private Secretary, 14 June 1983.
[44] TNA T 486/12, Monck to Lawson, 22 June 1983.   [45] Ibid.

As such, at a meeting between Parkinson, Lawson, and Richardson on 24 June, a plan of action was set out, which would include speaking first with Borrie and then beginning negotiations with Goodison: 'The aim would be to move as fast as possible with the Stock Exchange Council'.[46] Less than one month later, a deal was struck: the Goodison–Parkinson agreement was announced on 19 July 1983 (Vogel, 1996: 106). Borrie was bitterly opposed to this deal, which invalidated the years of work his staff had put in on this matter, and he refused to withdraw the OFT's case against the LSE. This in turn forced the government to 'introduce immediate legislation extricating the Exchange from the clutches of the OFT and the Restrictive Practices Court' (Moran, 1991: 71). On 13 March 1983, Parliament approved this measure (Vogel, 1996: 106).

*   *   *

Financial liberalization and monetarism are commonly understood as integral elements of neoliberalism's initial 'roll-back' assault on the Keynesian status quo (Peck, 2010: 26). Yet several accounts have correctly pointed out that these two ingredients of the neoliberal policy prescription did not complement one another upon implementation: 'financial deregulation policies undermined the monetarist assumption that government had the requisite policy levers to control the money supply' (Clift, 2020: 292). As we have seen, this was certainly the case with regards to the abolition of exchange controls and MTFS, as the former eroded the stable monetary foundations upon which the latter was based. The fact that financial liberalization and monetarism were still pursued by Thatcher, despite their functional incoherence, contributes to the widely held assumption that they must have been driven by a blinkered commitment to the foundational tenets of neoliberal doctrine. It was, as Evans (2004: 21) wrote, 'the ultimate triumph of ideology over common sense'.

This chapter, however, has demonstrated that Thatcher's two flagship monetarist and financial liberalization projects of the 1980s—MTFS and the Big Bang—were not simply ideologically related, but practically and functionally intertwined. More specifically, the Big Bang was propelled to a significant extent by a pragmatic attempt to prop up MTFS—itself a policy framework that was proving contradictory, politically divisive, and fundamentally unworkable. The British state did not pursue this liberalization simply to boost the City's competitive position or out of neoliberal conviction, as the interest-based and ideational approach to the politics of financialization claims. In fact, at times the 'competitiveness' angle was used as a post hoc justification for the decision to set the Big Bang in motion, suggesting that it was more important as a means to generate political capital after the fact than as a motivating factor. This was expressed clearly by John Redwood, who became Thatcher's chief policy adviser after the Goodison–Parkinson

---

[46]   TNA PREM 19/1005, Record of discussion, 24 June 1983.

agreement and a man whose politics can be summed up by the fact that he was the only politician to ever hold the title of Shadow Secretary of State for Deregulation. In October 1983, Redwood argued: 'Now that the Stock Exchange has approved the deal struck with the Secretary of State for Trade and Industry ... [w]e should claim more credit for breaking a cosy cartel and introducing competition and innovation ... So far, we have failed to capitalise on the radical nature of the deal'.[47]

Yet if the Big Bang was not simply propelled by City lobbying and pro-market ideas, neither was this policy an attempt to placate the capitalist class by freeing up credit in times of crisis or to place Britain on a new path of finance-based accumulation, as the functionalist approach would insist. Rather, the Big Bang must be understood in relation to the contradiction between the impersonal domination of global value relations during a period of crisis and the demands by people for their immediate needs to be met. MTFS was an ill-thought-out political strategy to discipline domestic social relations in line with world market imperatives, in a depoliticized manner that would insulate political legitimacy— and the Big Bang should be conceptualized as, in significant part, an ad hoc attempt to support this ailing strategy.

In sum, the exemption of the LSE from the RPC became a political priority for the Thatcher government following the calamitous implementation of its depoliticized disciplining strategy. MTFS was designed to lock the government into a four-year policy straitjacket, whereby severe economic contraction could be pursued without the government being blown off course by legitimacy concerns. In order to justify this disciplining, it was crucial that MTFS be seen to successfully meet its stated objective of reducing the money supply. However, due to the Thatcher government's unfamiliarity with monetary aggregates and dismissal of the Bank's advice, it selected an aggregate—£M3—that was notoriously difficult to control. As such, MTFS pushed the British economy into an unprecedentedly deep recession without a commensurate fall in £M3. In response, the Thatcher administration loosened monetary policy, in order to provide palliative relief to companies and mortgagors. Yet this left the problem of how to reduce £M3 so as to maintain MTFS's presentational coherence. The government discovered this strategy in overfunding, whereby excess liquidity would be soaked up through the sale of government debt on the LSE and consequently the money supply would be reduced. By applying the bandage of overfunding to MTFS, this deeply flawed strategy of depoliticized disciplining could stagger on without being branded a total failure. For this reason, it became essential for the government to ensure that their enormous debt sales were not interrupted by the RPC's case, which led to the eventual exemption of the LSE. This in turn set in motion the Big Bang's radical transformation of the City.

---

[47] TNA PREM19/1005, Redwood to Turnbull, 18 October 1983.

7

The Financial Services Act

The FSA stands in contrast to the other policies studied in this book, in that it consisted of a profound consolidation of formal state regulation over the City. It was, nonetheless, fundamentally a financial *liberalization*, as this extension of state regulatory infrastructure allowed for the growth, globalization, and heightened competitiveness of the City in the proceeding years. 'Freer markets', as Vogel (1996) put it, require 'more rules'. Yet despite the crucial role of the FSA in acting as the *re*regulatory counterpart to the Big Bang's *de*regulation, it has rarely been mentioned in discussions of financialization.

Prior to 1986, British financial services were regulated by a fragmented combination of self-regulation, informal supervision by the Bank, and weak legal protections for investors. The securities industry was ostensibly subject to the 1958 Prevention of Fraud (Investments) Act, enforced by the DoT and then after 1983 the Department of Trade and Industry (DTI); however, many important market actors—including most clearing banks, merchant banks, and the LSE— were exempt from this regulation (Pimlott, 1985: 143–5). Instead, 'first tier' banks were supervised by the Bank, which relied on informal meetings with leading bankers, observation of market indicators, and self-regulation on the part of the practitioners; while 'second tier' banks were overseen by the Treasury (Vogel, 1996: 96). The LSE, on the other hand, was self-regulating: it policed its own members according to its rulebook, which became the subject of the RPC case discussed in the last chapter. The Bank and DoT/DTI formally oversaw this self-regulation.

In contrast, FSA introduced a coherent and extensive statutory framework for regulating the securities industry. In other words, it brought statute law—which requires the approval of both Houses of Parliament as well as Royal Assent—to bear on City affairs, instituting formality where informality had previously reigned supreme. FSA produced three institutional layers. Firstly, actors in the securities industry were grouped into five organizations called Self-Regulatory Agencies (SRAs). These SRAs required that all investment firms within their branch of the industry were authorized and acted according to that SRA's rules (Laurence, 2001: 87). Secondly, these rules, created and enforced by individual SRAs, had to comply with the general directives set by a broader body: the Securities and Investments Board (SIB). The SIB was a limited company comprising City practitioners, yet it exercised public authority in carrying out the following tasks: authorizing the SRAs, creating broad rules for these SRAs to follow,

Governing Financialization: The Tangled Politics of Financial Liberalization in Britain. Jack Copley, Oxford University Press.
© Jack Copley 2022. DOI: 10.1093/oso/9780192897015.003.0007

supervising their registration of businesses, and policing and prosecuting offences (Moran, 1991: 59). Finally, these public powers were delegated to the SIB by the Secretary of State for Trade and Industry, who alongside the Bank Governor appointed the Chairman and members of this body. The Secretary of State was in turn subject to Parliamentary scrutiny (Singh, 2007: 11).

This transformation heralded by FSA boosted processes of financialization in two ways. Firstly, by instituting a clear set of rules for global actors to adhere to, FSA allowed the City to exploit its new-found potential, following the Big Bang, of attracting transnational financial capital (Thatcher, 1993: 311–12). The globalization of the City thus required this extension of formal legal structures. Secondly, and perhaps more importantly, the *form* that this regulation took engendered an enduring 'light-touch' approach, which ensured that regulatory power remained with City practitioners rather than the state. As Engelen et al. (2011: 143) argue, FSA was 'discredited by successive regulatory failures, and above all by the massive failure of light-touch regulation to foresee and forestall the crash of the House of Baring in 1995'. Moreover, although this framework was significantly changed by New Labour's transformation of the SIB into the Financial Services Authority in 1997, the new system of regulations built upon the 1986 FSA's system of delegation of public powers to non-state intermediaries. This perpetuated serious institutional fragilities, as the 2008 financial crisis revealed (Daripa, Kapur, and Wright, 2013).

This chapter will explore the governing motivations that underpinned FSA. More specifically, it will explain 1) why this reform—a dramatic and unprecedented financial *re*regulation—was deemed necessary and 2) why this reregulation took an arm's-length, light-touch, quasi-governmental form. The key to these puzzles lies in the preceding fifteen years of financial liberalization. CCC had broken up the clearing bank cartel, scrapped the state's preferential system for distributing credit to strategic sectors, and been followed by the marketization of Bank Rate; the abolition of exchange controls had dismantled the state's controls over inflows and outflows of capital; and the Big Bang had done away with the LSE's outdated rulebook and opened up the UK's securities industry to global market actors. These cumulative changes spurred a growing divergence between the trajectories of the British industrial and financial sectors, leading to a pattern of growth increasingly dependent upon financial accumulation. As evidenced by the litany of banking scandals and financial crises that followed this raft of liberalizations, Britain's model of financialized accumulation has proven to be deeply volatile. FSA must therefore be understood as an attempt to create a system of financial regulation appropriate to Britain's new financialized status quo—a status quo accidentally arrived at through the state's pursuit of strategies to govern the dilemmas emerging from the global profitability crisis.

In 1981, following several fraud scandals in the City, the DoT commissioned Professor Laurence Gower to review Britain's financial regulations (HM Treasury,

2002: 228). Gower's first set of proposals, advocating self-regulation within a statutory framework, was deemed to be too interventionist by the government, Bank, and City practitioners alike. Yet this attitude changed with the signing of the 1983 Goodison–Parkinson agreement, which set the stage for the Big Bang's rapid globalization of the City, forcing these actors to recognize the necessity of a rigorous legal framework. Gower's next publication, which suggested that existing self-regulation be supplemented by the DTI's direct supervision and statutory backing, caused the government more concern. By placing the DTI at the centre of this framework and invoking statute law, the Prime Minister's office worried that government ministers would be held politically responsible for future financial crises—crises that they felt unable to prevent following the cumulative liberalizations studied in this book. Such a regulatory failure could shatter the government's legitimacy.

As such, Thatcher and her advisers set out to depoliticize Gower's proposals by convincing the DTI, which was in charge of formulating a new regulatory structure, to insulate the government from direct supervision of the City. Simultaneously, the Bank set up a group of City practitioners to devise recommendations to put to the DTI. The Bank used the findings of this group, which stressed the City's dislike of government intervention, to push its own institutional agenda of maintaining its autonomy from government and insulating its network of informal regulatory relationships. The Bank's proposals chimed with Number 10's depoliticization agenda, and both of these powerful groups pushed the DTI to devise a new regulatory framework based on these principles. The resulting White Paper successfully depoliticized Gower's original proposals by erecting a three-tier system of regulation that allowed the government to maintain a sizeable distance from City activities and which gave the Bank a veto over important decisions. FSA should be understood as a kind of regulatory tidying up, whereby a new form of financial governance was instituted that was appropriate to the financial order bequeathed by the previous fifteen years of liberalization.

Tying a Bow on an Era of Liberalization

As explained in Chapters 4 and 6, the political desire to infuse the British financial system with greater competitive impulses was not solely a feature of the Thatcher governments. Pressure had been building in this direction since the 1960s, before reaching its apotheosis in the 1980s. Another long-term development that became most fully expressed during the Thatcher years was the 'incremental juridification and codification' of the regulations governing the City (Moran, 1991: 64). In part, this increasing role of law in financial governance was driven by changes within the Bank. While the Bank had traditionally preferred to govern the British financial system through an informal network of personal relationships with the very institutions it was tasked with monitoring—a form of governance that it jealously guarded from democratic oversight—this regulatory style was gradually eroded in the postwar era. The Bank became increasingly professionalized and integrated into the state's macroeconomic policymaking apparatus. It 'ceased to be an appendage of the City', becoming more like a public agency (ibid.: 67).

Perhaps more important than the transformation of the Bank in propelling the juridification of financial regulation, though, was the series of politically damaging financial scandals during the 1970s and early 1980s. CCC, as this book has discussed, contributed to the 1973–5 Secondary Banking Crisis, which was in turn followed by the near collapse of the bank Slater Walker Limited and its rescue by the Bank in 1977 (Grady and Weale, 1986: 162–3). In the aftermath of these events, the authorities sought to strengthen their supervision of the financial system. The Bank introduced several internal changes, yet more impactful was the passing of the 1979 Banking Act (Rawlings, Georgosouli, and Russo, 2014: 11). This Act introduced statute law into banking regulation and created two tiers of authorization of deposit-takers—recognized banks and licensed deposit-takers— both of which were covered by the new Deposit Protection Scheme. Nevertheless, this was proceeded by the 1981 failure of the investment management firm Norton-Warburg, resulting in the loss of £4.5 million of its clients' money, which was met with considerable public outrage (Laurence, 2001: 86).

It was in this context that the policymaking process that would result in FSA was set in motion. Yet FSA did not emerge preformed. It was instead the product of a period of deliberation that spanned 1981–86, which can be split into three phases:

Phase I: In July 1981, following several fraud scandals in the City, the DoT was tasked with commissioning company law expert Professor Gower to review the existing securities regulations (HM Treasury, 2002: 228). Gower, who had recently retired from the post of Vice Chancellor of Southampton University, had published his seminal work *Principles of Company Law* in 1954 and had previously participated in Wilson's Royal Commission on the Press. Gower's first publication as part of the DoT's commission, a discussion document released in January 1982, condemned the existing system and proposed a fusion of self-regulation with a new system of statutory controls.

Phase II: In January 1984, Gower released his full report. A number of SRAs would supervise day-to-day affairs within their particular spheres of financial services, while statutory powers would be delegated to these SRAs by an umbrella supervisory body, which Gower argued should be the DTI   (Pimlott, 1985: 153).

Phase III: After discussing Gower's report for nearly one year, the DTI published a White Paper in January 1985. This accepted the broad thrust of Gower's proposals with one major exception: the umbrella body would not be the DTI or any government agency, but rather two *private* bodies, the SIB and the Marketing of Investments Board (MIB). Following debates with Conservative MPs, the White Paper's recommendations were amended so as to merge the SIB and MIB, and consequently grant the SIB powers to investigate and prosecute offences. These changes were crystallized in the 1986 FSA.

Crucially, through these three phases of deliberation, FSA was transformed from a regulation administered by the state, to one that operated with a tremendous degree of autonomy from state authority.

This chapter will demonstrate that the arm's-length character of FSA emerged from a desire by the state authorities for a depoliticized system for governing Britain's increasingly globalized and fragile financial system. Following the July 1983 Goodison–Parkinson agreement, whereby the government and the LSE agreed to the changes to the LSE's rulebook that would be implemented in the 1986 Big Bang reform, the Thatcher government faced a governing predicament. The impending liberalization of the LSE necessitated a complementary system of laws for global actors to follow when operating in the City. Without clear, statutory regulations, there was the risk both that foreign financial firms would be discouraged from operating in London and that dubious practices could result in a damaging scandal or full-scale financial crisis. On the other hand, by creating a system whereby the state directly regulated the City, governments would risk being seen as responsible for financial crises, thus endangering political legitimacy. The dilemma for the Thatcher government was how to govern a financialized pattern of accumulation—inherited from previous strategies to govern the profitability crisis—without risking the collapse of popular legitimacy during financial scandals. It is through this lens that the deliberations over FSA must be framed.

Phase I: Gower's Discussion Document and the Big Bang

Less than a year after being commissioned by the DoT to review British securities regulation, Gower published his initial discussion document in January 1982. This document was circulated amongst City practitioners and officials at the DoT, OFT, Treasury, and Bank. Although relatively vague on specifics, this document rejected the principle of *caveat emptor* (the buyer is responsible for their purchase) and insisted that some statutory system was needed to supplement existing self-regulation. This document received an almost universally icy reception across Whitehall and the City. The City was opposed to legal intervention, the government was concerned about the impact of Gower's proposals on the drawn-out and expensive RPC investigation of the LSE, and the Bank was wary of forfeiting its informal regulatory networks. However, the impending globalization of the City provoked by the Goodison–Parkinson agreement of July 1983 forced all parties to recognize the need for some form of statutory intervention.

The City, unsurprisingly, had the coldest response to Gower's document. At a meeting with Bank Governor Richardson on 5 January, the Chairman of the Accepting Houses Committee stated his anxiety regarding the potential 'erection of a new tier of bureaucracy in the field of investment management'.[1] It appeared that this sentiment was widely shared. DoT official Elizabeth Llewellyn-Smith informed Secretary of State Biffen in March that '[o]pinion in the City seems to be hardening against Professor Gower's scheme for a constellation of "self-regulatory" bodies within a loose statutory framework'.[2] Indeed, the following day Goodison, Chairman of the LSE, explained to Biffen that 'Professor Gower's proposals were unnecessarily elaborate. There was no occasion to interfere with the Stock Exchange procedures, which were working satisfactorily'.[3] The City Capital Market Committee provided a clearer explanation of their anxieties about the Gower document. While they acknowledged that his proposals 'might have merit in theory', they feared that the abolition of exchange controls ruled out a statutory approach, because 'too tight a control might frighten people away'.[4]

Despite commissioning Professor Gower to carry out this inquiry, DoT officials were also unconvinced by his initial findings. Of particular concern was the possibility that Gower's overhaul of City institutions could overrule the OFT inquiry into the LSE's rulebook. As OFT official Timothy Pratt observed, a clash between Gower's report and the OFT's activities 'could cause the Department some embarrassment'.[5] This was especially the case, OFT Director General Borrie observed, due to the 'time, money and thought [that] have been expended by the Stock Exchange and Government in preparing the case for the court'.[6] The DoT also supported the Bank's plans to update its traditional self-regulation, as a way to negate the need for statutory intervention. As Deputy Secretary Brown explained to Secretary of State Cockfield in November, 'the attempt to improve the present self-regulatory structure is wholly desirable, and if it does produce a system which we can later recommend to Ministers as a reliable alternative to more statutory supervision, that is all to the good'.[7]

The Bank's response to the discussion document was both fearful and pragmatic. Walker, Executive Director for Industrial Finance within the Bank, explained to the Bank's Court of Directors in April that Gower's 'statute-based framework . . . would involve unwelcome government intrusion, would require a

---

[1] BOE 7A15/4, Note of a meeting, 5 January 1982.
[2] TNA FV 73/215, Brief for a meeting, 17 March 1982.
[3] TNA FV 73/215, Note of a meeting, 19 March 1982.
[4] BOE 7A15/4, Note of a meeting, 23 March 1982.
[5] TNA FV 73/214, Note of a meeting, 5 January 1982.
[6] TNA FV 73/214, Borrie to Brown, 6 January 1982.
[7] TNA FV 73/215, Brown to Cockfield, 10 November 1982.

substantial administrative overhead and would not in the end be as flexible or effective as better self-regulation'.[8] The task for the Bank to pursue in the coming months was to 'strengthen the City's self-regulating agencies, thus weakening or largely removing any case for extensive legislation' and minimizing the 'risk of intrusion by statute'.[9] Walker himself led this initiative, setting out his proposed alternative to the DoT in late March, which entailed self-regulation remaining the dominant form of City policing, with occasional licensing of fringe investors by the DoT.[10] Yet while the Bank appeared confident that it could undermine Gower's recommendations through its own efforts at self-improvement, Cockfield was less sure, warning Richardson in November that 'it was quite possible Professor Gower's next recommendations would be for a higher proportion of statutory regulation'.[11]

However, while the government and the Bank displayed a clear opposition to Gower's proposed statutory regulations, this sentiment began to change following the 1983 Goodison–Parkinson agreement that started the countdown to the Big Bang. As examined in the previous chapter, this agreement involved a compromise whereby the LSE agreed to abolish both fixed commissions on securities trading and barriers to the entry of foreign firms in return for the government exempting the LSE from an anti-monopolization court case brought by the RPC in 1979. The City was thus preparing itself for a period of rapid liberalization and globalization, characterized by massive increases in financial flows through London and the domination of Britain's financial sector by transnational actors.

As argued by Norman Tebbit, Secretary of State for Trade and Industry, the Goodison–Parkinson agreement 'heaved a massive brick into the once tranquil waters of the City'.[12] This '"financial services revolution"', the DTI explained, 'is rapidly altering the institutional structure of the City of London', resulting in 'increasing international competition in the provision of financial services'.[13] The City's fragmented and club-like regulations were unsuitable for a globalized financial market, in which foreign actors, unschooled in informal British regulatory customs, would need clear rules to follow. As Moran (1991: 78) explains, 'the Goodison/Parkinson agreement meant that new sources of regulatory authority were urgently required'. Faced with the prospect of the globalization of a once cosy British market, the government came to recognize the necessity of a non-preferential infrastructure of statutes (Lawson, 1992: 400). As such, the DTI argued that the 'Government needs to take action now' by introducing a 'statutory framework' which 'inspire[s] investor confidence by ensuring that the UK financial services sector both is and is clearly seen as, a competitive and "clean" place in

---

[8] BOE 3A161/199, Williams to Dawkins, 29 April 1982. [9] Ibid.
[10] TNA FV 73/215, Walker to Brown, 30 April 1982.
[11] TNA FV 73/215, Note of a meeting, 15 November 1982.
[12] Hansard, House of Commons Debate, vol. 64, cc49–114, 16 July 1984.
[13] TNA PREM 19/1461, DTI note, 12 July 1984.

which to do business'.[14] Sentiment even began to change within the Bank. Treasury officials noted that four months after the Goodison–Parkinson agreement was signed, 'the Bank, who were at an earlier stage strongly critical, have of late struck a more forthcoming note, without yet going so far as to endorse the Gower package'.[15] This, the Treasury observed, 'may suggest that the [Gower] report's main proposals could command more widespread acceptance than seemed likely earlier'.[16]

While Gower's 1982 Discussion Document met a wall of resistance due to its proposals for statutory intervention in the City, the impending Big Bang forced the government and Bank to reconsider their opposition. The globalization of the City implied by this liberalization, building on the previous liberalizations passed during the profitability crisis, made it necessary to institute a clear and unbiased legal framework within which global actors could operate in London. The next section deals with the political debates over what form this reregulation should take, following the publication of Gower's 1984 Report.

Phase II: Depoliticizing Gower's Proposals

Gower's full report, published in January 1984, outlined a comprehensive system of self-regulation within a statutory framework. SRAs, some of which would be based upon already existing City organizations, would regulate day-to-day financial activities, while the whole system would be overseen by a central organization which would delegate its statutory powers to these SRAs (Pimlott, 1985: 153). Politically, Gower's proposals already ensured a significant degree of distance between the government and the City, due to the emphasis the report placed on self-regulation. Yet Gower was insistent that the central supervisory body should be the DTI—a state department.

Four groups were tasked with assessing the Gower Report and advising Tebbit as to the form that a future financial services bill should take: the Gower Report Group (GRG), the Number 10 Policy Unit, the Bank's City practitioner group, and Alexander Fletcher's (Under Secretary of State for Trade and Industry) insurance industry practitioner group. These groups were not all clearly defined; for example, Fletcher set up the insurance practitioner group but was also instrumental in the GRG. Nor were these groups equally influential; there is little evidence of the impact of Fletcher's insurance industry practitioner group on Tebbit's thinking, and thus it is not analysed in this chapter. Finally, there is an unequal availability of archival evidence about these groups; there is no documentary record of the internal discussions of either practitioner group. However, these

---

[14] Ibid.   [15] TNA T 471/171, Saunders to Pirie and Lawson, 17 November 1983.   [16] Ibid.

groups hint broadly at the networks of politicians and civil servants that trans-formed Gower's proposals into the depoliticized 1985 White Paper.

The GRG and the Number 10 Policy Unit

The first group to begin digesting the Gower Report was the GRG. Made up primarily of DTI officials, with one Bank and one Treasury official (Dawkins and W. R. Pirie, respectively), this group met from December 1983 to June 1984. In its first preliminary meeting, Fletcher clearly expressed the DTI's anxiety about the political implications of assuming extensive control over City activities. He acknowledged that a legal framework was necessary but noted that 'self-regulation was important as the government was not an enthusiastic regulator'.[17] Furthermore, Fletcher was 'opposed to the establishment of an independent Securities Exchange Commission [SEC]'—referring to the US federal government agency created as part of President Franklin D. Roosevelt's New Deal—because it 'would lead to an extra layer of regulation, as the government would not be able to stand back entirely'.[18] Expressing a similar sentiment, a Treasury note in January 1984 explained that '[i]f regulation is imposed comprehensively, Ministers will be unable to avoid an enhanced degree of responsibility for regulatory arrangements, even when these are largely self-regulatory'.[19] Yet not all GRG members shared this anxiety about the politicization of regulation. In fact, later in January, DTI official Reid expressed concern that the existing Gower proposals would take too much power out of ministers' hands: the 'yielding of the necessary wide powers to a [SEC-style] Commission would not be welcome either to MPs or to Ministers—who would wish to retain their control over such a crucial area of policy. Political reality in the UK was that direct accountability to Parliament, through a Government Department, was the most acceptable form of regulation'.[20]

The next group to begin analysing the Gower Report was the Number 10 Policy Unit. Redwood served as Director of this group, while David Willetts—who would later contribute to the marketization of English higher education under Prime Minister David Cameron—also played an active role. Similar to the GRG, the chief concern of the Policy Unit, and of Thatcher herself, was the threat of politiciza-tion. On 6 April, Redwood wrote to Thatcher, voicing his unease:

---

[17] TNA T 520/117, Note of a meeting, 15 December 1983.
[18] Ibid. Redwood would similarly caution Thatcher against adopting any regulatory system that resembled the US SEC: 'One of the reasons why London is picking up some American business is because the SEC tends to over-regulate. Alan Walters' [Thatcher's former economic adviser] thoughts on the SEC are unprintable' (TNA PREM19/1461, Redwood to Thatcher, 11 May 1984).
[19] TNA T 471/171, Pirie to Dell, 17 January 1984.
[20] TNA T 471/171, Note of a meeting, 20 January 1984.

The intention behind Gower of setting up a series of self-regulatory bodies beneath an umbrella organisation with responsibility ultimately flowing back to the Department of Trade and Industry is a dangerous one. It would mean that the Government would start to assume responsibility for all the foibles and problems of the market place. People would expect the Government to offer them redress. People would expect the Government to make sure there were no crooked operators. It is not within the Government's power to ensure either of these things.[21]

Rather than directly intervening in City affairs, the Government should instead restrict its role to ensuring against fraud and embezzlement and guaranteeing that market operations were as transparent as possible. Thatcher annotated her agreement with Redwood's points.[22] Four days later, Number 10 informed the DTI of Thatcher's concern: 'She wonders just how closely the Government should become involved in taking responsibility for the proposed self-regulatory bodies as there is a risk that ultimately the Government could be blamed for any malpractice in the City'.[23] During the remainder of April, Willetts drafted a paper that both critiqued Gower and put forward an 'alternative minimalist approach' to financial regulation. Redwood sent this paper to Fletcher on 4 May, in an effort to influence the DTI's assessment of Gower. Willetts's central criticism of the Gower Report was that:

it conflicts with one of the fundamental tenets of this Government—that *Government should not appear to take on responsibility for matters which are not actually under its control.* Under Professor Gower's proposals, the DTI registers, directly or through SRA members, all those permitted to carry out investment business. This must inevitably become a seal of approval... If and when a registered investment business is found to have been engaging in criminal malpractices, it will be claimed that the DTI and the Ministers responsible have not been doing their job properly.[24]

In contrast to Gower's proposals, Willetts's approach involved forgoing any register of investment businesses, while supporting the principle of *caveat emptor* with tough legal enforcements, preferably through the creation of a new 'investigation and prosecution agency' with powers to prosecute 'breaches of criminal law'.[25] This approach, Willetts emphasized, 'goes with the grain of the Government's philosophy' by entailing 'no suggestion of government endorsement' of any City firms.[26]

---

[21] TNA PREM 19/1461, Redwood to Thatcher, 6 April 1984.   [22] Ibid.
[23] TNA PREM 19/1461, Turnbull to McCarthy, 10 April 1984.
[24] TNA PREM19/1461, Redwood to Fletcher, 4 May 1984; emphasis in original.   [25] Ibid.
[26] Ibid.

The GRG reacted to efforts to depoliticize Gower's proposals with some scepticism. The group explained that the 'Government would inevitably have some responsibility; if offences were created to influence City behaviour Government could not wash its hands of having created them'.[27] Yet, interestingly, the group pointed out that '[i]f one was trying to limit political embarrassment the SRA approach might be rather useful'.[28] This suggests that they recognized that the self-regulatory element of Gower's approach already involved a significant depoliticization of financial regulation.

Tebbit responded at length to Number 10's concerns in July, via a DTI note on financial regulation. The paper set out five policy objectives that a future regulation must meet: the City must be 'able to provide services to UK industry and commerce, private investors and the Government' cheaply and competitively; market forces must be free to stimulate competition and innovation; the 'regulatory framework must provide effective protection for investor[s]', without becoming protectionist; regulation must 'inspire investor confidence' through transparency; and regulation must be predictable and flexible.[29] Crucially, this regulation was also required to meet three *political* objectives: 'the Government should not appear to take responsibility for the activities of City practitioners'; a regulatory body should be made up of 'the minimum number of civil servants'; and this regulatory framework should entail 'the minimum number of quangos'.[30] Overall, Tebbit emphasized that '[p]hilosophically I favour standing as close to reliance on market forces as we can defend politically'.[31] The regulation would as such be made up of voluntary SRAs operating 'at arms-length [sic] from Government'.[32] With regards to an intermediate umbrella body supervising these SRAs, Tebbit was ambivalent at this stage: 'I leave that question open at the moment until I hear what the Governor's Group may have to say'.[33] Yet at a Treasury meeting the following day between Tebbit, Lawson, Bank Governor Robin Leigh-Pemberton, and other officials, the attendees agreed that 'it was becoming increasingly likely' that the 'most acceptable form could well be a number of SRAs plus an umbrella body'.[34] Number 10 received Tebbit's note with measured enthusiasm. Willetts commented: 'It is much closer to the Prime Minister's thinking than the earlier work done by the DTI'.[35] Furthermore, he wrote, 'at least Mr Tebbit emphasises that the SRAs will operate at arm's-length from Government'.[36] He encouraged Thatcher to agree with Tebbit's proposals, which she did.

The Prime Minister's office, and to a lesser extent several DTI officials within the GRG, expressed a clear and urgent desire to depoliticize the Gower Report so

[27] TNA T 520/118, Note of a meeting, 25 June 1984.   [28] Ibid.
[29] TNA PREM 19/1461, Tebbit to Thatcher, 12 July 1984.   [30] Ibid.   [31] Ibid.
[32] Ibid.   [33] Ibid.   [34] BOE 15A91/6, Note of a meeting, 13 July 1984.
[35] TNA PREM 19/1461, Willetts to Turnbull, 13 July 1984.   [36] Ibid.

as to avoid blame for future financial scandals. This occurred months before the Bank put the recommendations of its practitioner group to the DTI—the event that most accounts of FSA point to as key in establishing its arm's-length character (Vogel, 1996: 110; Laurence, 2001: 88). In the context of a radically deregulated financial system, following a decade and a half of cumulative liberalizations, the Thatcher administration intended to institute a depoliticized mode of financial governance that would insulate the government's legitimacy from crises. However, while the government sought to depoliticize Gower's proposals, it was not clear how this could be achieved. As the next section will demonstrate, it was the Bank that proposed that this objective could be attained through the creation of institutional shock absorbers between the government and the City.

The Bank's Practitioner Group

While certain figures within the Bank had reacted very negatively to Gower's 1982 discussion document—due to fears of government encroachment in their informal regulatory networks—Bank officials had a more conciliatory response to Gower's full report. This compromising tone resulted from two factors: the impending Big Bang and the Bank's fear that an oppositional approach to Gower's findings would isolate them from the decision-making process. Indeed, in January 1984, Walker explained that if the Bank did not appear to be attempting to reform their networks of informal regulation, 'there was a risk that the introduction of more intrusive structures would be precipitated'.[37]

In May 1984, the Bank took the first concrete steps towards directly intervening in the debates surrounding the Gower Report. On 10 May, Bank Governor Leigh-Pemberton wrote to Thatcher, expressing his desire 'to invite, on my own initiative and without committing Government, a small number of senior City practitioners...to form an advisory group' on future financial regulation.[38] This request was not received warmly in the Treasury. Treasury official M. A. Hall expressed his distrust of the Bank's initiative to Chancellor Lawson: 'There has been no collective discussion by Ministers, yet the appointment of a group from the City implicitly rules out the statutory approach...And the recommendations of such a high powered group would be difficult to reject'.[39] Thatcher's Principal Private Secretary Andrew Turnbull alerted her to the Treasury's displeasure and speculated as to the Bank's motives: 'I detect some ill feeling in the Treasury about this letter. They feel that there has been a deal between the Bank and DTI without

[37] BOE G4/211, Minutes of a meeting, 27 January 1984, https://www.bankofengland.co.uk/sitemap/minutes.
[38] TNA PREM 19/1461, Leigh-Pemberton to Thatcher, 10 May 1984.
[39] TNA T 520/118, Hall to Lawson, 10 May 1984.

bringing them in ... I suspect that the purpose [of the group] is that the Bank will provide the secretariat, enabling them to write the script'.[40] This discontent must be understood within the context of the Bank's long-standing desire, since its nationalization in 1946, to gain greater autonomy from government (see Burn, 1999). Indeed, this circumvention of the Treasury's input may explain Lawson's subsequent disavowal of FSA, which he described as 'cumbersome and bureaucratic' (Lawson, 1992: 401). Nevertheless, Thatcher was encouraged by both Redwood and Tebbit to endorse the Governor's plans, without associating the government with the group.[41] As such, Thatcher gave Leigh-Pemberton her blessing on 18 May, while insisting that the group's 'recommendations would in no way restrict the Government's options in looking at a wider range of possible regulatory arrangements'.[42]

For the following three months, the Bank's practitioner group carried out private and undocumented deliberations, chaired by banker Sir Martin Jacomb (Vogel, 1996: 110). Before the group's conclusions were unveiled, Walker began hinting that the Bank was moving ever closer to Gower's proposals. He told the Court of Directors on 23 August that 'it was hard to conceive any sensible way forward that did not involve both continuing self-regulation and statutory underpinning'.[43] This sentiment was echoed weeks later, when on 6 September Leigh-Pemberton announced the practitioner group's findings to the Court. He referred to the 'unreality of the so-called choice between self regulation [sic] and statutory regulation. In practice, neither represents a serious option on its own'.[44] Therefore, the Governor proposed a strategy for depoliticizing the Gower proposal's fusion of self-regulation and statutory control, through the insertion of a private body between the government and the City: 'The preference of the advisory group, and one which I fully share, would be for securities regulation to be headed by a *private sector body*, recognised as the competent authority by government and, on being so recognised, left to get on with the job'.[45] Yet even this depoliticization of Gower's plans did not allay City anxieties over government encroachment, due to the lack of Bank participation in this supervisory body:

> in the absence of the insulation that would be provided by the continuous prominent involvement of the Bank, there would be risk that Ministers and officials would persistently interfere in a way that would undermine the effectiveness of such a private sector body and the readiness of major practitioners to

[40] TNA PREM 19/1461, Turnbull to Thatcher, 11 May 1984.

[41] TNA PREM 19/1461, Tebbit to Thatcher, 11 May 1984; TNA PREM 19/1461, Redwood to Thatcher, 11 May 1984.

[42] TNA PREM 19/1461, Thatcher to Leigh-Pemberton, 18 May 1984.

[43] BOE G4/211, Minutes of a meeting, 23 August 1984, https://www.bankofengland.co.uk/sitemap/minutes.

[44] BOE 3A161/199, Minutes of a meeting, 6 September 1984.   [45] Ibid; emphasis added.

be committed to it. The [group's] argument is that a structure for which the bank had a clear responsibility would largely eliminate this risk and would thus be very desirable.[46]

However, while Leigh-Pemberton sympathized with this concern, he explained that Bank officials had 'strong arguments against assumption by the Bank of a formal statutory responsibility for supervision in this area. In any event, I doubt whether government and Parliament would be ready to give the Bank such power even if we ourselves sought it'.[47] As Vogel (1996: 110) argues, the Bank was wary of assuming formal responsibilities due to the difficulties of governing this complicated array of financial institutions. In order to resolve this problem, he suggested that the Bank could be given greater veto power over the staffing of the private supervisory body:

> a structure could be put in place under which, with the power of appointment of the chairman and council of the regulatory body reposing in the Governor, and clear delegation by the government through recognition of the body as competent authority, the Bank would be in a position to exert influence in our conventional and informal way to the extent that this were necessary. I am planning to put advice on broadly these lines to Ministers in the near future.[48]

Leigh-Pemberton thus used his practitioner group's recommendations to advise the DTI to ensure that two principles were at the heart of a future system of regulations. Firstly, a private body should insulate the Bank and City from government prying; and secondly, the Bank should have a veto over the makeup of this body so as to maintain the Bank's traditional autonomy.

Drawing on the Bank's recommendations, Tebbit began creating a fully-formed framework for what would become the 1985 White Paper (Tebbit, 1989: 296). He explained the make-up of the future regulation to Thatcher on 9 October. Tebbit came down firmly in favour of Gower's principle of self-regulation through SRAs within a statutory framework, yet he insisted that the government delegate its supervisory capacities to two non-state bodies: the SIB and MIB.[49] These bodies would be given statutory backing 'on the condition that they satisfied basic principles of conduct to be laid down by Government'.[50] These bodies' decisions on licensing and disciplining of investors would need to be verified by an 'independent tribunal whose members I would appoint'.[51] This arm's-length approach should also ensure against the DTI 'being too closely involved in answering

---

[46] Ibid.   [47] Ibid.   [48] Ibid.
[49] TNA PREM 19/1461, Tebbit to Thatcher, 9 October 1984.   [50] Ibid.   [51] Ibid.

to Parliament'.[52] Tebbit ended the letter by disclosing that he had discussed the matter with Lawson, who agreed with the plan.

Within Number 10, Tebbit's proposals were met with ringing endorsement. Willetts exclaimed to Thatcher on 10 October, in explicit depoliticization terms, that 'Mr Tebbit's particular solution is ingenious ... [H]is supervisory bodies can check up on the performance of SRAs, *whilst acting as a lightning conductor for City scandals so they are not blamed on the Government*'.[53] After requesting clarification on certain issues concerning Tebbit's proposed framework later in October, Thatcher informed the DTI in November that she was 'broadly content with the line your Secretary of State is taking'.[54] Yet she continued to push for greater depoliticization: 'In her view, the role of the Government—and, indeed, the House of Commons—should be to satisfy themselves about the general conduct of City regulation', and as such 'the Government should steer clear of involvement in individual cases, and should not be answerable for these in the House of Commons'.[55]

The decision to depoliticize Gower's proposals through the creation of the SIB (and the short-lived MIB) resulted from the coincidental harmonization of interests between Number 10 and the Bank. The Prime Minister's office was keen to ensure that government ministers were politically insulated from future crises, which were more likely to occur following the cumulative liberalizations studied in this book. The Bank was keen to preserve its informal networks of financial regulation against the encroachment of government ministers, officials, and Parliament. These interests coalesced around the same depoliticization agenda, whereby a 'lightning conductor' body would be erected between the government and the City, and the Bank would play a crucial role in deciding which people occupied this body. Tebbit, whose department shared some of the government's concerns about the dangers of politicized financial regulation, heeded the demands of these powerful advisers during the creation of the 1985 White Paper. The following section will examine how this depoliticized reform became law.

Phase III: Defending Depoliticization

While the depoliticized approach contained in the 1985 White Paper satisfied the interests of Number 10, the Bank, and the DTI, it was heavily criticized in the House of Lords, House of Commons, and even on the Conservatives' own back benches. The Lord Chancellor, Lord Hailsham, wrote to Tebbit on 9 January 1985, expressing that he feared Tebbit 'may have underestimated the criticism which

---

[52] Ibid.   [53] TNA PREM 19/1461, Willetts to Thatcher, 10 October 1984; emphasis added.
[54] TNA PREM 19/1461, Flesher to Thompson, 14 November 1984.   [55] Ibid.

will be mounted against your proposal that the legislation should enable you to delegate your regulatory powers to the proposed Securities and Investments Board and Marketing of Investments Board'.[56] This framework would mean these boards 'would be law-making bodies without any sort of Parliamentary accountability'—a form of 'sub-delegation to a quango' that was 'unprecedented' except 'under the Emergency Powers (Defence) Act 1939'.[57] Lord Gowrie, Chancellor of the Duchy of Lancaster, shared the same concern. Writing to Tebbit days later, Gowrie explained that 'we may be vulnerable to criticism' due to the lack of accountability to government entailed in the White Paper: 'I wonder whether we can expect Parliament to sign so open a cheque'.[58]

Upon presenting the core elements of the White Paper to the House of Commons on 24 April, Tebbit received backlash from both sides of the partisan divide. Conservative MP Anthony Beaumont-Dark decried the 'constitutional outrage' entailed by granting the Bank the power to overrule the Secretary of State's decisions with regards to the SIB.[59] Anthony Nelson, another Conservative MP, expressed his agreement with Beaumont-Dark about the growing power of the Bank: 'There is great concern that the proposals for the SIB ... effectively give a power of veto to the Governor of the Bank of England ... Many of us are concerned about the steady encroachment of the Bank of England in this area'.[60] This sentiment was echoed by Labour politician John Smith, Shadow Secretary of State for Trade and Industry, who nevertheless put a party-political spin on his critique. Smith suggested that 'the purpose of the Bank of England veto', which was a 'monstrous proposition', was 'to guard against what a Labour Secretary of State might do' in the future.[61] The fear on the part of Labour was that by hiving off the government's power to both the SIB and the Bank, the Thatcher administration was effectively foreclosing the future, by preventing a Labour government's incursion into City affairs. Of course, this anxiety was proven to be misplaced, given that when Labour finally arrived in power under the leadership of Tony Blair, his government made clear that it had no interest in intervening in the City or reversing the Thatcherite liberalizations, as will be discussed in Chapter 8.

The greatest formal challenge to Tebbit's framework, however, was mounted by Conservative backbenchers during the Committee stage of the Financial Services Bill, following Tebbit's replacement as Secretary of State for Trade and Industry by Leon Brittan (September 1985–January 1986) and Paul Channon (January 1986–June 1987). Conservative MPs Nelson and Tim Smith made several amendments to the DTI's proposals, including the scrapping of the

---

[56] TNA PREM 19/1461, Hailsham to Tebbit, 9 January 1985.   [57] Ibid.
[58] TNA PREM 19/1461, Gowrie to Tebbit, 15 January 1985.
[59] Hansard, House of Commons, vol. 77, cc885–964, 24 April 1985.   [60] Ibid.   [61] Ibid.

MIB. Yet the most serious of these amendments gutted the regulatory framework of its depoliticizing characteristics and effectively 'made the SIB a conventional government agency—with its budget, staffing and powers under full departmental control'.[62] In April 1986, Channon suggested to Lawson that these backbenchers could be appeased by granting a number of concessions related to the SIB. These concessions included solidifying the SIB's regulatory capacities against accusations of being light-touch, by granting the SIB statutory powers to investigate and prosecute illegal investment activities.[63] Ironically, in an attempt to assuage Conservatives who were worried about the government's loss of control over City regulation, Channon was advocating a further delegation of public powers to a private body. Thatcher recognized this point, writing: 'This is a fundamental change...Are there any other *private bodies* with *prosecuting* powers?'[64] Yet Channon's initiative was successful, as the concessions were accepted by Nelson and Smith, paving the way for the bill to make smoother progress through the remaining stages of the legislative process.[65] FSA finally gained Royal Assent on 7 November.

*   *   *

In contrast to its high-profile counterpart, the Big Bang, FSA received little attention in the aftermath of the 2008 financial crisis. This belies the powerful influence of this liberalization in kick-starting the expansion and globalization of the City and in creating an enduring light-touch regulatory framework that would facilitate the worst excesses that took place in London up to and beyond 2008. Nevertheless, this chapter has demonstrated that FSA's arm's-length form cannot be explained solely by reference to the pro-finance ideology of the Thatcher government or to politicians' capture by City elites. To the extent that FSA was designed to promote the City, this was because, as Redwood and Willetts explained to Thatcher, the City was 'a successful, profitable area of the economy' and the 'Government should reap political benefits from associating itself with this success story'.[66] FSA, this chapter argued, is better understood as an attempt to create a system of financial governance appropriate to Britain's newly globalized financial order—imparted by the array of earlier liberalizations studied in this book—yet in a manner that would shield the government from the political fallout arising from future City crises. As those actors involved with formulating the policy understood, the stakes were high: 'If Big Bang goes off successfully, it will

[62] TNA PREM 19/1718, Griffiths and Willetts to Thatcher, 11 April 1986.
[63] TNA PREM 19/1718, Channon to Lawson, 17 April 1986.
[64] TNA PREM 19/1718, Norgrove to Thatcher, 18 April 1986; emphasis in original.
[65] TNA PREM 19/1718, DTI note, 7 May 1986.
[66] TNA PREM 19/1461, Redwood and Willetts to Thatcher, 29 June 1984.

be seen as a showpiece for Government policy on deregulation and increased competition; if it leads to scandals and liquidations, it will be labelled the unacceptable face of unpopular capitalism'.[67]

Although the government and Bank were initially resistant to Gower's 1982 proposal for statutory regulation of the UK's financial sector, the impending Big Bang underlined the necessity of a clear and firm system of rules for the City. However, the Thatcher administration feared that Gower's 1984 proposals would hold government ministers responsible for future financial crises, despite having less power to prevent them. Number 10 and the DTI endeavoured to overcome this dilemma by depoliticizing Gower's proposals. The Bank, desiring to protect its regulatory relationships from government intervention, proposed that this depoliticization could be achieved through the insertion of a private agency between the Government and the City. This coalition of interests explains the transformation of the 1984 Gower Report's proposals for direct government oversight into the arm's-length, delegated oversight of the 1985 White Paper. While the resulting depoliticized framework met diverse opposition, the government was able to resist pressures to repoliticize the scheme after certain political manoeuvring, and this in turn outsourced even more regulatory power away from the British state.

---

[67] TNA PREM 19/1718, Griffiths and Willetts to Thatcher, 3 June 1986.

8
Conclusion

Reflecting on the early 1980s, Thatcher's first Chancellor characterized policy-making as 'not the product of any initially coherent strategic inspiration but rather the result of what looks in retrospect like a trudge through a seemingly endless series of multiple choice exam questions' (Howe, 1994: 191–2). This dreary description jars with the dominant narrative of the politics of financialization, which tends to present financial liberalization as part of a grand, ambitious blueprint to dismantle the institutions of postwar industrial capitalism and forge a new pattern of financialized accumulation. Thatcher—the 'Queen Mother of global austerity and financialization'—occupies a special place in this narrative (Hudson and Sommers, 2013). Her crimes were twofold, it is said, as she opened the state's doors to financial lobbyists and ushered in a new ideological paradigm predicated upon radically deregulated markets.

Yet the archival evidence presented in this book demonstrated that Howe's metaphor has considerable resonance. The governments of Thatcher, Callaghan, and Heath—responsible for landmark policies of financial liberalization—were not enacting a coherent script, but rather haphazardly responding to the various dilemmas of their time. British policymakers from the late 1960s to early 1980s were forced to govern a political economy that had entered a deep crisis. Global profitability fell as Britain's ability to compete eroded, national economic indicators became erratic and distorted, domestic groups pressed their demands upon the state in an increasingly militant manner, and the traditional Keynesian tools of macroeconomic management proved progressively less effective. In this context, policymakers attempted to craft strategies that would reproduce the state's economic and political bases by both recreating the necessary conditions for Britain's global economic viability and ensuring the state's appearance as a neutral referee between the partisan demands of civil society. The policies of financial liberalization studied in this book constituted elements of these broader strategies of desperate crisis governance.

The form that these strategies took was ideologically inflected, influenced by factional political struggles, and defended publicly with rhetoric that connected them to greater blueprints for British prosperity. At the same time, the archives reveal that the motivations to pursue such policies were relatively consistent across Labour and Conservative governments and fundamentally driven by pragmatic governing concerns. The historical record cautions us against explanations of the state's role in financialization that assign undue causal power to the

Governing Financialization: The Tangled Politics of Financial Liberalization in Britain. Jack Copley, Oxford University Press.
© Jack Copley 2022. DOI: 10.1093/oso/9780192897015.003.0008

ideologically driven machinations of politicians or the nefarious power of financial lobbyists. Rather, the characters in this book appeared to struggle with impersonal forces that had escaped the control of even the most powerful groups in society. Nevertheless, the evidence similarly warns against functionalist interpretations of British financial liberalization. The state did not simply act as a track switch, automatically facilitating Britain's shift from a path of ailing productive accumulation to a new trajectory of speculative financial accumulation. Policymakers instead wielded these liberalization measures in an attempt to muddle through an intractable governing paradox—one that has generated enduring consternation within liberal political economy—namely the need to enforce the painful adjustments dictated by the world market and ensure a stable domestic politics.

Governing Contradictions

It is rare that a contemporary political economy concept crosses over into mainstream usage. 'Globalization' is the most obvious example, having been employed ad nauseam by politicians and commentators since the 1990s. To a lesser extent, 'neoliberalism' has also gained significant popular cachet. It is premature to add 'financialization' to this list of crossover concepts, yet it too has displayed the potential to seep from an originally rather narrow set of scholarly debates into wider usage. Furthermore, like globalization and neoliberalism, financialization denotes a broad, seemingly tectonic shift in economic life that implies a worrying set of limits on the democratic process. Within the social sciences, however, no ambiguity exists about the traction of this term. A broad and diverse array of studies, often grouped under the umbrella of political economy, have explored the contours of the phenomenon of financialization.

Within this large body of literature, this book engaged with accounts that focus on the state's role in mediating the twin processes of productive stagnation—understood as the faltering performance of 'real' economic indicators in various advanced capitalist economies since the 1970s—and financial expansion. Two broad schools of thought can be discerned. The first relies on an interest-based and ideational understanding of state behaviour to argue that financial elites have captured the levers of state power, directly or through the diffusion of pro-finance ideology, and consequently utilized the state to liberalize finance and facilitate financial capital's expropriation of productive capital. The second approach adopts a functionalist state theory to claim that states reacted automatically to the crisis of productive capital by liberalizing the financial sector in order to boost credit expansion and offer capitalists the option of profiting through speculative investments. Neither explanation leaves significant room for an examination of political and social struggle nor the strategizing of policymakers. An important exception to these pluralist/functionalist approaches to the politics of financialization is the work of Streeck (2014) and Krippner (2011), both of whom have sought to conceptualize states' roles in liberalizing finance as a matter of the strategic reconciliation of economic imperatives and legitimacy concerns. This book extended Streeck's and Krippner's strategic approach to the archetypal case of Britain's financial liberalization agenda in the 1970s and 1980s. At the same time, this book has sought to ground these scholars' piercing empirical insights in a broader theory of capitalist domination and liberal governance.

The concept of domination reoccurs in discussions of the politics of financialization. While interest-based and ideational approaches insist that states have become dominated by financial elites and beholden to pro-finance policy norms, functionalist approaches understand states as dominated by the collective behaviour of the capitalist class more generally. In contrast, this book drew from the value-form Marxist tradition to argue that domination in capitalist society is not only exercised directly by identifiable social groups, but also emanates impersonally from capitalism's basic social relations. Value, for Marx, is a relationship of radical equality between diverse types of human labour that emerges when the products of labour are exchanged for money. By comparing tangible goods as merely different quantities of human labour in general, monetized commodity exchange creates averages of labour productivity that impose themselves upon individual market participants as a seemingly external necessity to produce more in less time. In a historical context in which money is the dominant form of socialization, that is, in which the market presents the only possibility for social reproduction, this 'law of value' sets society in motion in a perpetual competitive struggle. As Isaak Rubin (2010: 81) argued: 'Value is the transmission belt which transfers the movement of working processes from one part of society to another, making that society a functioning whole'—a functioning whole in which the unending drive to produce faster than one's competitors becomes the condition for survival. This dominating pressure derives not from any particular agent, institution, or class, but from the totality of monetary exchange relations.

Capitalism is double-sided. The driving impulse of this uniquely dynamic form of society is the production of value—an intangible, abstract substance that reflects average labour productivity within the entire economy. Yet value can only exist through the production of useful goods. Thus, two radically different forms of wealth—value and usefulness—coexist simultaneously within the commodity. The tension between them, for Marx, is the source of capitalist crises. In chasing the expansion of value, individual capitals seek to outdo their competitors through the introduction of labour-saving technologies. The resulting increases in labour productivity lead to a growing abundance of useful goods but a stagnating quantity of value, a dynamic expressed as the simultaneous overproduction of commodities and falling average rate of profit. The system of value, especially during these periods of crisis, confronts society as simply unfit for purpose. To advance their real aspirations, preserve their mental wellbeing, and often simply survive, people continually refuse value's dictates and instead assert their heterogeneous needs. They deny the blind expansion of value and demand a world geared towards tangible ends. Capitalist society is thus fundamentally antagonistic.

Capitalism's monetized relations are daily reproduced by the actions of states. States and state-delegated political authorities construct and govern national hierarchies of money and international exchange rate regimes. In doing so, they unconsciously forge the law of value on a world scale, which in turn rebounds upon them, exposing them to unrelenting competitive dictates. The governments and policymakers occupying the state apparatus are thus forced to continually augment the competitivity of their national territory on the world market or face a range of impersonal sanctions, including balance of payments crises, speculation against the national currency, capital flight, and prohibitive global borrowing costs. Yet this necessity to discipline national social relations in line with global productivity averages runs up against the need for the state to ensure a governable social order at home by meeting the demands of civil society. This contradiction is heightened in moments of global crisis. The liberal tradition grasps this dilemma as a scalar tension between national politics and global economics: 'A major reason why the international monetary system is afflicted with problems is that the nations that participate in it are politically independent but economically dependent' (Solomon, 1982: 6). Yet this is but a surface expression of the deeper antinomy contained within the commodity form itself—between the concrete usefulness of goods and the abstract social value embodied in them.

Confronted with this paradox, policymakers deploy governing strategies that fall on a spectrum between two poles: depoliticized discipline and palliation. The former strategy attempts to restructure domestic social relations in line with global averages while neutralizing the consequent political backlash, while the latter seeks to delay the bite of world market imperatives in the name of maintaining domestic social peace. Depoliticized discipline is a strategy advocated with considerable clarity by the neoliberal tradition. For neoliberals, the historic achievement of the world market can only be sustained through measures that 'encase' its often painful adjustment mechanism from the forces of politicization—a task that requires an authoritative, depoliticized state (Slobodian, 2018). As Bonefeld (2016: 16) suggests, that which Marx criticises about politics under the dominion of capital, neoliberalism espouses 'as the political principle of capitalist society'. The Keynesian strand of liberalism, on the other hand, understands that unrelenting discipline is unsustainable, and that the state is at times required to ease the population's pain through palliative measures in order to preserve the market itself. Forced to steer between the contradictory imperatives of global value relations and national political legitimacy, especially in moments of world economic crisis, states implement depoliticized discipline and palliation strategies in a haphazard manner—sometimes in sequence and sometimes simultaneously. It is through this conceptual lens that this book explored the policies enacted by the British state that fuelled processes of financialization both nationally and on the global scale.

The Politics of Liberalizing Finance in Britain

It is important to differentiate between the long decline of British imperial power and world market share, on the one hand, and the steep economic crisis that beset Britain from the late 1960s, on the other. This latter phenomenon, notoriously characterized by both grinding stagnation and high inflation, was the national manifestation of the profitability crisis that plagued the world capitalist economy during this period. This book offers a novel periodization of the stagflation crisis in Britain. From 1967 to 1977, the British economy was rocked by recurrent sterling crises, generated in part by the impact of falling profitability and rising inflation on the balance of payments; while from 1977 to 1983, sterling remained strong due to the effects of the IMF's intervention and the flow of North Sea oil, but the domestic economy was pushed into a deep recession. Governments during this era attempted to negotiate Britain's path through this global crisis by employing strategies that sought to reconcile the need to both purge inflation from the UK economy through disciplining measures and maintain political legitimacy. British governments—from Wilson to Thatcher—either oscillated between strategies of depoliticized discipline and palliation or employed them in tandem. The four key financial liberalization policies that were implemented during this period—CCC, the abolition of exchange controls, the Big Bang, and FSA—must be understood as measures that constituted part of these broader governance strategies.

The first major financial liberalization of the postwar era was CCC in 1971. This was a hugely transformative policy, which saw the British state relinquish most of its direct controls over credit creation and instead rely on partly marketized interest rates to govern lending. This directly contributed to the first serious financial crash of the postwar era—the 1973–5 Secondary Banking Crisis. In the context of the early stages of the global profitability crisis, Britain's worsening trade performance had resulted in a series of currency crises, to which Wilson's government responded in 1967 by devaluing sterling. In aid of devaluation, the government enacted a series of contractionary measures, designed to reduce demand for imports and thus promote a balance of payments recovery. An important element of this disciplining strategy was the tightening of monetary policy, chiefly pursued through state-imposed ceilings on the amount banks could lend. However, two obstacles stood in the way of this governing objective. Firstly, people proved resistant to this reduction in their living standards, and thus endeavoured to combat income losses by extending their bank borrowing.

Secondly, due to falling profitability, companies faced a liquidity crisis that threatened to undermine their investment and thus derail Britain's export recovery. As such, the state authorities sought to use the lending ceilings to both restrict credit to persons and extend credit to companies, that is, to operate a simultaneously disciplining and palliative credit policy. This hybrid strategy was extremely difficult to operate with the blunt monetary instruments at hand, especially considering the ongoing transformations in the British financial sector, whereby the traditional institutions that the lending ceilings affected were losing market share to new, unregulated secondary banks. In addition to the functional inadequacies of the existing lending controls, they were also becoming increasingly politicized and painful for the authorities to operate. Consequently, the Treasury and Bank sought to discover a better system of monetary governance. It was the Bank that designed the uniquely arm's-length CCC proposals, partly to consolidate its own institutional autonomy. Yet these proposals were accepted by the Treasury and government in significant part because they appeared to offer a depoliticized mechanism through which the state could redistribute credit resources from persons to companies in aid of augmenting Britain's world market competitiveness.

The abolition of exchange controls between 1977 and 1979 transformed the British and global economies by ushering in a new era of mobile capital flows and offshore financial markets. Following the IMF's 1976 bailout of the UK and the advent of North Sea oil in 1977, sterling began to appreciate precipitously. While the rise in sterling's price helped to discipline the domestic economy and reduce inflation, it also pushed British exporters to the brink of collapse and therefore threatened to cause widespread political disaffection. Governments during this period thus faced a choice between embracing the strong pound and tackling inflation, on the one hand, and combating the pound's rise in order to maintain political legitimacy, on the other. The governments of both Callaghan and Thatcher sought to navigate carefully between these two options. By getting rid of exchange controls, these governments hoped that investment would flow out of Britain, causing a moderate fall in the price of sterling. This would aid in making Britain's exports more competitive without generating a spike in inflation that would likely result from an overt sterling devaluation. While the Callaghan administration partially dismantled exchange controls, it was held back from totally abolishing them by a resistant trade union movement. Thatcher, however, was able to fully scrap these controls due to the historic defeat of the trade unions following the 1979 Winter of Discontent. In addition, Thatcher sought to reassure global financial markets that this policy was *not* an attempt to lower sterling's value, but was rather driven by a genuine faith in laissez-faire principles. The abolition of exchange controls should thus be understood as a palliative strategy to protect government legitimacy by providing temporary relief to Britain's ailing export sector.

Thatcher's famous 1986 Big Bang liberalization of the LSE was the single most important policy in transforming the City into a truly global financial centre and, in turn, providing international financial actors with a radically liberalized space in which to conduct their operations. This policy was the result of a winding institutional process that began in 1979 when the RPC began a case against the LSE for non-competitive practices. While the LSE pleaded that Thatcher exempt them from this court case, the Prime Minister refused, because it would contradict the government's pro-competition rhetoric. However, things changed following the government's implementation of its notorious monetarist experiment: MTFS. MTFS was a strategy to discipline the British economy in a depoliticized manner, by locking the government into years of financial stringency based on a series of policy rules. In order for this strategy to be successful, the government had to meet certain monetary targets, which would justify the painful measures. Yet this plan went awry immediately, as the economy was plunged into a deep recession and the government failed to hit these targets. To prevent the complete presentational collapse of MTFS, the government began to make massive sales of government debt on the Stock Exchange in order to soak up excess liquidity in the banking system and meet the monetary targets that way. This in turn made it crucially important that the normal functioning of the Stock Exchange was not disrupted by a drawn-out court case. Consequently, the Thatcher government finally decided to exempt the Stock Exchange from this investigation in 1983, which began the countdown to the 1986 Big Bang liberalization. The decision that led to the Big Bang was thus, to a significant extent, a desperate attempt to protect the government's broader strategy of depoliticized discipline—MTFS—which had sought to restructure the British economy in line with global competitive pressures.

FSA, introduced in 1986, was a key complement to the Big Bang that totally restructured Britain's system of financial oversight by instituting a light-touch and arm's-length form of regulation—one that would come to be widely denounced as partly responsible for Britain's outsized role in the 2008 financial crisis. In 1981, the government commissioned a legal academic, Professor Gower, to investigate Britain's financial regulations and make recommendations on future amendments. Gower proposed a system of self-regulation that would be directly supervised by a government body. This form of state oversight was met with disapproval by the government and Bank. However, the impending Big Bang changed policymakers' opinions. This radical liberalization would invite global actors to operate in the City, which in turn necessitated the creation of an impartial and legally enforced system of rules. Nevertheless, the Thatcher government was concerned that Gower's proposals would make it politically responsible for future financial crises, while the Bank worried that its informal relations with the City would be interrupted by government meddling. As such, the government and Bank worked to depoliticize Gower's plans by inserting a private body between the government and the City, and thus insulate policymakers from legitimacy problems that would result from financial crises. FSA can thus be understood as an attempt to create a depoliticized framework of financial governance that would simultaneously provide a clear legal framework for Britain's newly liberalized financial system and protect the state authorities from the political backlash accompanying this financialized pattern of growth.

Afterlives of Liberalization

The liberalizations explored in this book supercharged processes of financialization. As described in Chapters 4 to 7, these policies allowed Britain's financial sector to expand rapidly in size and to become increasingly global in nature. By 2006, UK banking assets had swelled to more than 500 per cent of GDP, while the City had higher rates of foreign ownership than Tokyo or New York (Bell and Hindmoor, 2015: 104; Pandit, Cook, and Ghauri, 2006: 90). Furthermore, as Adam Tooze (2018b: 82) argued, 'UK liberalization not only freed up UK markets but acted as a crowbar to dislodge regulation worldwide'. Partly responding to the earlier deregulations by the US, the British state's scrapping of controls on cross-border flows and its globalization of the City spurred a worldwide dynamic of competitive liberalization. As growing capital mobility saw financial investment criss-cross national territories, nations with strong financial centres were incentivized to pursue liberalization in order to attract these deterritorialized flows (Cerny, 1994). On the other hand, nations without such advantages felt the sanctioning power of financial flows—they were pressed to either continually tighten capital controls and face declining regulatory competitiveness or abandon controls altogether (Goodman and Pauly, 1993). States found themselves 'effectively competing for the right to regulate capital' (Andrews, 1994: 199). Finally, in addition to fuelling financialization both nationally and globally, these liberalizations left a lasting imprint upon Britain's system of financial governance. The successive liberalizations studied in this book contributed to the construction of a powerful path dependency, steering British regulations in the direction of light-touch, arm's-length mechanisms, with disastrous consequences. This will be briefly explored below.

Following the Secondary Banking Crisis in 1973–5, itself spurred by the CCC liberalization, the 1979 Banking Act was passed. While all authorized institutions were now subject to Bank oversight, the Act represented a fusion of statute law with the continuation of the Bank's informal regulatory approach (Turner, 2014: 192–3). As the DoT put it in 1983: 'The Bank of England has exercised a traditional informal but highly effective supervision of banking activity for well over a century. The traditional system was reinforced by statute in the Banking

Act 1979'.[1] The inadequacies of this updated regulatory system were exposed when Johnson Matthey Bankers, the banking arm of a large precious metals dealer, almost collapsed in 1984, forcing the Bank to rescue it. This embarrassing episode led to another inquiry, culminating in the 1987 Banking Act (Peeters, 1988: 377–8). The 1987 Act scrapped two-tiered authorization and raised the threshold for institutions to be considered a bank. Among other provisions, it also furnished the Bank with new powers to acquire information on any area of banks' dealings and to determine banks' corporate governance structures (Turner, 2014: 194–5). While this introduced more formality into the Bank's operations— requiring the Bank to submit an annual report to the Treasury and creating the Board of Banking Supervision, partly staffed with non-Bank members—the explicit aim of the Act was 'to create a statutory framework within which the previous, informal supervision of the traditional banks could be continued' (quoted in Rawlings, Georgosouli, and Russo, 2014: 14). The 1986 FSA and the 1987 Banking Act together provided the overarching framework for the governance of the financial sector in Britain in the late 1980s and 1990s—both characterized by light-touch, depoliticized structures. 'For in the end', Redwood claimed in 1985, 'the only people who know whether a business is being well run or badly run, whether it is corrupt or fair, whether it is exploiting or performing a good service, are the people running the business itself.'[2]

Predictably, this regulatory system was shaken by two serious scandals. The first involved a foreign bank. Bank of Credit and Commerce International (BCCI) was a financial firm incorporated in Luxembourg but with its effective head office in London (Rawlings, Georgosouli, and Russo, 2014: 15). Referred to by some as Bank of Cocaine and Criminals International, BCCI had offices in seventy-three countries, including Colombia, where it laundered money for the Cali and Medellin drug cartels, as well as providing banking services to Panamanian dictator Manuel Noriega. Despite senior BCCI executives standing trial for these crimes in the US from 1988, the Bank failed to take decisive action on its UK operations until 1991, when the Bank finally shut down its British branches and froze its deposits after damning reports of systematic illegal activity (Heffernan, 2005: 376–8).

The second scandal arose from the most traditional of City institutions. Barings Bank was the oldest merchant bank in Britain, founded in 1762 and remaining an important force in the City until its abrupt collapse in 1995. It was brought down by the activities of a single trader, Nick Leeson, operating from its Singapore branch, who racked up colossal losses from the trading of derivatives on the Singapore and Tokyo Exchanges (Nelson, 2008: 114–15). Leeson's malfeasance was facilitated by a total failure of Barings' management practices, which the Bank

---

[1] TNA T520/117, DoT Paper, December 1983.
[2] TNA PREM 19/1461, Redwood article, 18 September 1985.

failed to recognize due to its confidence in 'verbal assurances from senior management' at Barings that its business was in good shape (Tickell, 1999: 13). The Bank did not bail Barings out—although it did facilitate its purchase by the Dutch ING Bank—ultimately deciding that this mid-sized bank did not present a systemic financial risk. Yet in a statement that appears darkly prescient in the aftermath of 2008, Andrew Large, then chairman of the SIB, pondered in 1995: '[W]hat if Barings had had a balance sheet 10 times or 50 times its size?...What would have happened then?' (quoted in Tickell, 2000: 93).

Of course, from the vantage point of the post-2008 world, we know that the warnings of the early to mid 1990s were not properly heeded. The state reacted to Barings by launching two formal inquiries. One by the Board of Banking Supervision voiced only mild criticism of the Bank, but the other, by the House of Commons Treasury Select Committee, pointed to structural failings in Bank oversight and called for the Bank's supervisory duties to be concentrated in a separate body (Tickell, 1999: 15). Upon the election victory of Blair's New Labour in 1997, Chancellor Gordon Brown used this momentum to grant the Bank operational independence and at the same time centralize the different regulatory duties held by the Bank and other supervisory bodies under a single third-party 'mega-regulator': the Financial Services Authority (Han, 2016: 97). This new body, alongside the Treasury and Bank, formed Britain's 'tripartite' system of financial regulation: the Bank was responsible for ensuring the system's overall stability, the Treasury was tasked with governing the general structure of regulation and its underpinning legislation, and the Financial Services Authority was to supervise and regulate particular financial institutions (Bank of England, 2006).

Despite Brown's claims to have sought to replace the 'informal old boys' network' with rigorous 'professional monitoring', this new agency was effectively a renamed SIB (Brown, 2017: 120). The Financial Services Authority—a company limited by guarantee but wielding public powers—operated according to the same philosophy of self-regulation within a statutory framework discussed in Chapter 7. This new framework, then, cemented the depoliticized, arm's-length regulatory structure that was introduced by the 1986 FSA—'not just a light touch but a limited touch', in Brown's words (quoted in Turner, 2014: 218). It was this limited touch that allowed London to become the centre of Euro-denominated financial activity after the creation of the European Monetary Union in 1999, attracted double the number of foreign banks to the City as to Wall Street by 2007, and meant that some of the riskiest and most destructive financial practices were conducted by the London branches of global banks (Thompson, 2017: 217; Tooze, 2018b: 83). Peter Gowan (2009: 15) put it starkly: 'London thus became for New York something akin to what Guantánamo Bay would become for Washington: the place where you could do abroad what you could not do back home'.

The global financial crisis would reveal the fundamental failure of Britain's tripartite regulatory system, with the Financial Services Authority labelled as the 'watchdog that didn't bark' (Treanor, 2013). None of the three bodies, the Treasury admitted, 'had the responsibility, authority or powers to oversee the financial system as a whole' (HM Treasury, 2011: 12). Its structural inadequacies were most stunningly demonstrated by the collapse and subsequent nationalization of Northern Rock in 2007–8—the first run on a British bank since 1866. As a 2008 House of Commons report concluded, the Financial Services Authority had 'systematically failed in its duty as a regulator' in relation to this troubled bank (House of Commons Treasury Committee, 2008: 34). Unsurprisingly, the Conservative and Liberal Democrat coalition government that won power in 2010 quickly moved to dismantle New Labour's regulatory project. The Financial Services Authority was abolished and its duties divided between two new bodies—the Prudential Regulation Authority and the Financial Conduct Authority—both technically companies but the former wholly owned by the Bank (Burnham, 2017: 182–3). The Financial Policy Committee was also established within the Bank to combat systemic risks within the UK financial system. Finally, the Independent Commission on Banking's 2011 recommendation to 'ring-fence' banks' retail and investment arms was accepted and implemented by 2019 (Bell and Hindmoor, 2015: 300). These post-crisis reforms represented a shift to macroprudential supervision—a focus on *systemic* financial risks—as well as a victory for the Bank in clawing back responsibilities for financial regulation and broader economic management. Nevertheless, the basic trajectory of Britain's arm's-length regulatory structure remained unchanged, with policymakers forced to reconcile economic stability with the maintenance of the City's global competitiveness (ibid.: 11).

In addition to entrenching a pattern of depoliticized financial governance, which meant that London would play a crucial role in incubating the 2008 crisis, the liberalizations explored in this book also contributed to the distinctly housing-centric nature of Britain's trajectory of financialization. Since the 1980s, housing in Britain has expanded beyond the role of a public good and instead become an important engine of economic growth. The median house price in England and Wales rose by 259 per cent between 1997 and 2016, in a context in which earnings increased by just 68 per cent and welfare provisions have been retrenched (ONS, 2017). Housing has thus become a vital source of wealth for homeowners, spurring their consumption and thus propping up demand within the economy. Matthew Watson (2010) has referred to this dynamic as 'house-price Keynesianism', whereby rising house prices and the subsequent wealth effects have come to replace the state's Keynesian demand stimulus measures typical of the postwar boom years. The flipside of this dynamic, however, has been a growing wealth gap between homeowners and renters, which has further exacerbated racial, generational, and regional cleavages. This distorted status quo was most starkly demonstrated by the 2017 Grenfell Tower disaster, whereby fatally neglected and overcrowded social housing was located in a London borough with an average property price in excess of £2 million (Smith, 2018).

House-price Keynesianism depends on a massive availability of credit for mortgage lending, and thus is only possible due to Britain's highly liberalized financial system. The 1971 CCC measures, by abolishing quantitative limits on lending, fuelled a mortgage lending boom that saw house prices rise by 77 per cent between 1971 and 1973 (Konzelmann, Fovargue-Davies, and Wilkinson, 2013: 89). This was to be a preview of the mortgage finance explosion of the 1980s and beyond (see Fuller, 2016). The abolition of exchange controls, the Big Bang, and FSA together facilitated the globalization of the City, as foreign financial companies moved to London to exploit its permissive environment. US investment banks set up mortgage lending subsidiaries in Britain, introducing financial practices like securitization that supercharged mortgage lending capacity (Wainwright, 2012: 103). Yet the liberalizations studied in this book are only part of the story of financialized housing in Britain. A critical role was played by the 1980 Housing Act, known as 'Right to Buy', which introduced the right for public housing tenants to purchase their homes, as well as restructuring housing subsidies. This large scale privatization of housing was complemented by the 1986 and 1997 Building Societies Acts. The former allowed building societies to 'demutualize' (change from mutual societies into public companies), undertake mergers, and expand into other financial services, while the latter permitted these institutions to engage in an even broader array of financial activities (Cowan, 2011: 41–2). One building society to take advantage of this relaxed regulatory environment was Northern Rock, which demutualized in 1997 (House of Commons Treasury Committee, 2008: 11). These housing-specific financial liberalizations, however, lie beyond the scope of this book.

* * *

The conditions of economic stagnation wrestled with by the policymakers explored in this book were somewhat eased from the late 1980s to the 2000s. A series of developments, some quite extraordinary—from the elimination of backward enterprises and devaluation of capital through deep economic contraction, to the immiseration of the global working class through recession and structural adjustment, to the relocation of manufacturing to the Global South, to the rise of the information technology industry, to the historic entry of China into global capitalist relations, to the tremendous credit creation unleashed by cumulative financial liberalizations—had been sufficient to spark a limited recovery in profitability. When this upswing ran out of steam, capped spectacularly by the 2008 crisis, grinding stagnation again became the status quo. In such conditions, the business sector has grown increasingly bifurcated between a handful of monopolistic superstars and 'legions of companies condemned to a ghostly existence on the edges' (Smith, 2020: 53). Today a few giant corporations (chiefly in information technology, energy, pharmacy, and finance) headquartered in the richest countries capture the lion's share of global profits by cornering markets and earning monopoly rents. The rest (especially firms in labour- and capital-intensive sectors like textiles and automobiles) struggle to achieve profitability in hyper-competitive global markets, with many only surviving by taking on rising debt (Dobbs et al., 2015; Christophers, 2020). In a desperate attempt to breathe some dynamism into this polarized and pallid global economy and thus maintain social stability, central banks have continued to keep the taps of monetary policy open in the post-2008 era. The result has been the further swelling of financial markets and ongoing inflation of asset price bubbles, which, as even mainstream economists have observed, may simply be the price that must be paid to achieve anything resembling a socially acceptable level of economic growth (Teulings and Baldwin, 2014).

This warped, financialized society is one that appears more than ever subordinated to 'the rule of the number' (Caffentzis, 2005: 100). The poor and the middle class take on a growing volume of debt, the former to survive another day and the latter to acquire residential property that may act as a bulwark against weak wage growth. The rich, for their part, plough their capital into financial ventures in search of elusive yield. Everyone is playing a numbers game: the indebted are stalked by personal credit scores or national bond ratings, while investors monitor asset performances from the screens of their electronic devices.

The origin story of this financialized order is a political one. States facilitated the expansion of finance through policies of liberalization. Britain was among the first to lead this charge, imposing radical measures that both unleashed the domestic financial sector and put pressure on other states to follow suit. Yet in pursuing these policies, the state was not favouring the interests of finance capital over industry, nor was there an attempt to institute a new finance-based growth model. This book's archival study revealed no smoking guns, in this sense. Instead, the British state turned to financial liberalization as an immediate, practical fix to the opposed political and economic pressures churned up by the profitability crisis. The politics that birthed financialization were a conjunctural expression of the broader politics of liberal governance during moments of severe crisis.

Capitalist society is not rigged by the financial sector—perhaps this would be a more reassuring conclusion. Rather, under capitalism, people are compelled to dance to the tune of their own monetized relationships with one another. These intangible relations dominate their concrete activities: 'illusion dominates reality', as Theodor Adorno (1976: 80) observed. States are not autonomous from this dynamic of unconsciously self-imposed domination. States accidentally reproduce their own subordination to this system on the world scale through the forging and management of international money relations. Yet people's aspirations do not map onto the dictates of value, nor can they be synchronized with the booms and busts of capitalist development. Thus, particularly during global crises, the state is torn between the material and ideological reproduction of capitalism; between the meeting of abstract dictates and concrete demands. The secret of British financial liberalization policies in the era of financialization lies in this banal reality. No totalizing subservience to financial lobbyists, hardly enough room for manoeuvre to implement a coherent neoliberal blueprint—just a 'trudge through a seemingly endless series of multiple choice exam questions' (Howe, 1994: 191–2). The liberalizations studied in this book were employed to either temporarily escape the present dilemma or impose social restructuring in a depoliticized manner. The tremendous expansion of global financial markets that these policies unleashed was largely unintentional.

Many critiques of the politics of financialization miss this point. They are committed to a game of political whack-a-mole, in which the enemy appears here as Thatcher and there as Friedman. The quest to locate the moment of state capture by financial elites is perpetually frustrated and catharsis postponed. This is because such critiques commit a category error. In their justified anxiety about the synthetic nature of financial wealth and their desire for the creation of an economy that serves tangible purposes, they personalize a form of domination that is ultimately impersonal; they concretize that which is fundamentally abstract. This is a political dead end. An adequate critique of the politics of financialization must begin by examining what it is about our society that made such liberalizations appear rational in the first place. This requires a critique of the basic social relations of capitalist society.

Annex

List of Names

Allen, Douglas	HM Treasury, Permanent Secretary, 1968–74
Armstrong, Robert	Prime Minister's Principal Private Secretary, 1970–75
Barber, Anthony	HM Treasury, Chancellor of the Exchequer, 1970–74
Barnett, Joel	HM Treasury, Chief Secretary to the Treasury, 1974–79
Barratt, F. Russell	HM Treasury, Deputy Secretary
Beaumont-Dark, Anthony	Conservative Member of Parliament, 1979–92
Berrill, Sir Kenneth	Cabinet Office, Head of Central Policy Review Staff, 1974–80
Biffen, John	HM Treasury, Chief Secretary, 1979–81; Department of Trade, Secretary of State, 1981–82
Blair, Tony	Prime Minister, 1997–2007
Borrie, Gordon	Office of Fair Trading, Director General, 1976–92
Bridgeman, Michael	HM Treasury, Under Secretary, 1975–81
Brittan, Leon	Department of Trade and Industry, Secretary of State, 1985–86
Brown, Gordon	HM Treasury, Chancellor of the Exchequer, 1997–2007
Britton, Andrew	HM Treasury, Senior Economic Adviser; HM Treasury, Under Secretary, 1981–82
Brown, Philip	Department of Trade, Deputy Secretary
Butler, M. D.	Foreign and Commonwealth Office
Callaghan, James	Prime Minister, 1976–79
Cameron, David	Prime Minister, 2010–16
Cassell, Frank	HM Treasury, Home Finance Adviser
Channon, Paul	Department of Trade and Industry, Secretary of State, 1986–87
Cockfield, Arthur	Department of Trade, Secretary of State, 1982–83
Cooke, Peter	Bank of England, Head of Banking Supervision, 1976–85
Dawkins, Douglas	Bank of England, First Deputy Chief of Exchange Control, 1972–79; Chief of Exchange Control, 1979–80
Dell, Edmund	Department of Trade, Secretary of State, 1976–78
Dixon, P. V.	HM Treasury, Industrial Economic Division
Dow, Christopher	Bank of England, Adviser to the Governors, 1981–84
Fforde, John	Bank of England, Executive Director for Home Finance, 1970–82; Adviser to the Governors, 1982–84

Figgures, Frank	HM Treasury, Second Permanent Secretary, 1968–71
Fletcher, Alexander	Department of Trade and Industry, Under Secretary, 1983–1985
Gill, George Malcolm	HM Treasury
Goodhart, Charles	Bank of England, Monetary Adviser, 1969–85; Chief Adviser, 1980–85
Goodison, Nicholas	London Stock Exchange, Chairman, 1976–86
Griffiths, Brian	Adviser to Margaret Thatcher
Hall, M. A.	HM Treasury
Hancock, David	HM Treasury, Under Secretary, 1975–80
Hattersley, Roy	Department of Prices and Consumer Protection, Secretary of State, 1976–79
Healey, Denis	HM Treasury, Chancellor of the Exchequer, 1974–79
Heath, Edward	Prime Minister, 1970–74
Hogg, Quintin	Second Viscount Hailsham; Lord Chancellor, 1979–87
Holland, David	Bank of England, Deputy Chief of the Economic Intelligence Department, 1975–80
Howe, Geoffrey	HM Treasury, Chancellor of the Exchequer, 1979–83
Jenkin, Patrick	HM Treasury, Financial Secretary, 1970–72
Jenkins, Roy	HM Treasury, Chancellor of the Exchequer, 1967–70
Joseph, Keith	Department of Industry, Secretary of State, 1979–81
Lanchin, Gerry	Department of Trade, Under Secretary
Large, Andrew	Securities and Investments Board, Chairman, 1992–97
Lawson, Nigel	HM Treasury, Financial Secretary, 1979–81; Chancellor of the Exchequer, 1983–89
Leigh-Pemberton, Robin	Bank of England, Governor, 1983–93
Liesner, Hans	Department of Trade, Chief Economic Adviser
Llewellyn-Smith, Elizabeth	Department of Trade
Lomax, Rachel	HM Treasury, Senior Economic Adviser
Lovell, Arnold	HM Treasury, Monetary Policy Division, 1965–70
Mason, Graham	CBI, Deputy Overseas Director
McMahon, Kit	Bank of England, Executive Director of External Finance, 1973–80; Deputy Governor, 1980–85
Middleton, Peter	HM Treasury, Under Secretary, 1976–80; Deputy Secretary, 1980–83; Permanent Secretary, 1983–91
Monck, Nicholas	HM Treasury, Under Secretary, 1977–84
Neale, Alan	HM Treasury, Deputy Secretary, 1968–71
Nelson, Anthony	Conservative Member of Parliament, 1974–97
Nott, John	Department of Trade, Secretary of State, 1979–81
O'Brien, Leslie	Bank of England, Governor, 1966–73

Painter, R. J.	HM Treasury, Under Secretary
Parkinson, Cecil	Department of Trade and Industry, Secretary of State, 1983
Pirie, W. R.	HM Treasury
Pliatzky, Leo	Department of Trade, Permanent Secretary, 1977–79
Posner, Michael	HM Treasury
Pratt, Timothy	Office of Fair Trading
Reading, Brian	Special Advisor to the Prime Minister, 1970–72
Redwood, John	Chief of Policy to the Prime Minister, 1982–87
Rees, Peter	HM Treasury, Minister of State, 1979–81
Reid [first name unknown]	Department of Trade and Industry, Companies Legislation Division
Richardson, Gordon	Bank of England, Governor, 1973–83
Ruthven, Grey	Second Earl of Gowrie; Chancellor of the Duchy of Lancaster, 1984–85
Sangster, John	Bank of England, Deputy Chief Cashier, 1975–79
Seebohm, R. H.	HM Treasury, Home Finance Division
Smith, John	Shadow Secretary of State for Trade and Industry, 1984–87
Smith, Tim	Conservative Member of Parliament, 1977–97
Stowe, Kenneth	Prime Minister's Principal Private Secretary, 1975–79
Tebbit, Norman	Department of Trade and Industry, Secretary of State, 1983–85
Thatcher, Margaret	Prime Minister, 1979–90
Turnbull, Andrew	Prime Minister's Private Secretary, 1983–85
Varley, Eric	Department of Industry, Secretary of State, 1975–79
Walker, David	Bank of England, Executive Director for Industrial Finance, 1981–88
Wass, Douglas	HM Treasury, Under Secretary; Deputy Secretary, 1968–73; Second Permanent Secretary, 1973–74; Permanent Secretary, 1974–83
Willetts, David	Prime Minister's Policy Unit, 1984–86
Wilson, Harold	Prime Minister, 1964–70, 1974–76

Archival Sources

The National Archives, Kew

T 326: HM Treasury: Finance, Home and General Division, 1953–74
T 326/791   Credit control of banks, 1968
T 326/961   Credit control of banks, 1968 January–1969 December
T 326/962   Credit control of banks, 1969 January–December
T 326/963   Credit control of banks, 1969 January–December

T 521: HM Treasury: Domestic Economy Sector, Home Finance Group, Financial Institutions Division, 1981–82

T 521/42   Changes in the securities market and monetary policy, 1981 January–1982 December

T 521/44   The Stock Exchange and the Restrictive Practices Court, 1982 January–December

PJ 1: Department of Trade: General Division, 1975–82

PJ 1/92   Exchange control: proposals for adjustment, 1977 January–1979 December

PJ 1/93   Exchange control: proposals for adjustment, 1979 January–December

PJ 1/94   Exchange control: proposals for adjustment, 1979 January–December

PJ 1/95   Exchange control: proposals for adjustment, 1979 January–December

FV 73: Department of Trade and Industry and successors, Fair Trading Division, 1963–89

FV 73/146   Stock Exchange: exemption from Restrictive Trade Practices Act 1976, 1979 January–December

FV 73/147   Stock Exchange: exemption from Restrictive Trade Practices Act 1976, 1979 January–December

FV 73/148   Stock Exchange: exemption from Restrictive Trade Practices Act 1976, 1979 January–December

FV 73/214   Restrictive trade practices: the Stock Exchange, 1980 January–1982 December

FV 73/215   Restrictive trade practices: the Stock Exchange, 1982 January–1983 December

FV 89: Department of Trade and Industry and successors, Central Secretariat, 1973–84

FV 89/2   Economic strategy: including policy on exchange rate controls, 1977 January–December

PREM 16: Prime Minister's Office, Correspondence and Papers, 1973–79

PREM 16/2108   Industrial policy, 1978 March–1979 April

PREM 19: Records of the Prime Minister's Office, Correspondence and Papers, 1976–93

PREM 19/29   Economic policy: 1979 Budget; part 1, 1979 May–June

PREM 19/174   Economic policy: Economic strategy; pay and prices; monthly economic report etc., 1980 September–December

PREM 19/177   Economic policy: Domestic monetary policy; monetary control; medium term financial strategy; part 3, 1980 January–May

PREM 19/178   Economic policy: Domestic monetary policy; monetary control; banking figures; part 4, 1980 May–September

PREM 19/179   Economic policy: Domestic monetary policy; monetary prospects; part 5, 1980 September–October

PREM 19/180   Economic policy: Domestic monetary policy; monetary control; improvements in funding methods; flexibility of short term interest rates; part 6, 1980 October–November

PREM 19/437   Economic policy: Exchange rate; exchange control policy; inflow controls; part 1, 1979 May–1981 October

PREM 19/1005 Economic policy: Restrictive Trade Practices Act 1976: exemption of Stock Exchange, 1979 May–1983 November

PREM 19/1461 Economic policy: Financial services: position of Stock Exchange etc., 1983 November–1985 September

PREM 19/1718 Economic policy: Financial Services Bill: Stock Exchange deregulation etc., 1986 February–September

Bank of England, Threadneedle Street

3A161: Committee of Treasury Files, 1922–98
3A161/199   The Council for the Securities Industry, 1976 December–1985 May

6A385: Stock Exchange: General, 1966–90
6A385/12   Stock Exchange: General, 1979 January–April
6A385/13   Stock Exchange: General, 1979 May–June
6A385/14   Stock Exchange: General, 1979 July–December

7A15: City Committee on Capital Markets and Company Law, 1979–94
7A15/4   1982 January–December

13A173: Housing Finance, 1979–86
13A173/3   Bank Lending for House Purchase Provision of Statistics, 1979 October–1981 December

15A91: Operation and Structure of the Stock Exchange: Post Restrictive Trade Practices (RTP)–inc. Big Bang, 1981–88
15A91/6   1984 July–1985 September

Hansard, UK Parliament

House of Commons Debate, vol. 64, cc49–114, 17 July 1984

House of Commons, vol. 77, cc885–964, 24 April 1985

House of Commons, vol. 968, cc235–64, 12 June 1979

Modern Records Centre, University of Warwick

Confederation of British Industry, Papers of the CBI Director General
MSS.200/C/3/DG2/22   Correspondence with the Treasury and Chancellor of the Exchequer, Anthony Barber, 1971 September–November
MSS.200/C/3/DG2/23   Correspondence with the Treasury and Chief Secretary, Patrick Jenkin, 1972 February–August

Confederation of British Industry, Directorates
MSS.200/C/3/ECO/2/7   Financial Policy Committee: Committee papers, incl. minutes, circulars and correspondence, 1973 August–November
MSS.200/C/3/ECO/2/29   Domestic monetary policy, 1969–71
MSS.200/C/3/ECO/11/24 Overseas Investment Committee, 1977–78
MSS.200/C/3/ECO/11/25 Overseas Investment Committee, 1977–78
MSS.200/C/3/ECO/11/26 Overseas Investment Committee, 1977 July–November

Trade Union Congress, Economic Committee Minutes
MSS.292D/462/3   Investments, 1976–78
MSS.292D/40.2LPMR/2   Minutes, reports and correspondence relating to the meetings of the TUC–Labour Party Liaison Committee, 1977–78

Bibliography

Abramovitz, M. (1994) 'Catch-up and convergence in the postwar growth boom and after', in W. Baumol, R. Nelson, and E. Wolff (eds), *Convergence of Productivity Cross-National Studies and Historical Evidence* (New York: Oxford University Press), pp. 86–125.

Adorno, T. (1976) 'Sociology and empirical research', in T. Adorno, H. Albert, R. Dahrendorf, J. Habermas, H. Pilot, and K. Popper (eds), *The Positivist Dispute in German Sociology* (London: Heinemann, 1976), pp. 68–86.

Aitken, R. (2007) *Performing Capital: Toward a Cultural Economy of Popular and Global Finance* (Basingstoke: Palgrave Macmillan).

Amin, S. (2003) *Obsolescent Capitalism: Contemporary Politics and Global Disorder* (London: Zed Books).

Anderson, P. (1964) 'Origins of the present crisis', *New Left Review*, 23: 26–53.

Andrews, D. (1994) 'Capital mobility and state autonomy: Toward a structural theory of international monetary relations', *International Studies Quarterly*, 38(2): 193–218.

Arrighi, G. (1994) *The Long Twentieth Century: Money, Power, and the Origins of Our Times* (London: Verso).

Arrighi, G. and B. Silver (1999) *Chaos and Order in the Modern World System* (Minneapolis: University of Minnesota Press).

Aveyard, S., P. Corthorn, and S. O'Connell (2018) *The Politics of Consumer Credit in the UK, 1938–1992* (Oxford: Oxford University Press).

Backhouse, R. and M. Boianovsky (2013) *Transforming Modern Macroeconomics: Exploring Disequilibrium Microfoundations, 1956–2003* (Cambridge: Cambridge University Press).

Bank of England (1982) 'Operation of monetary policy', *Bank of England Quarterly Bulletin*, June.

Bank of England (1983) 'Operation of monetary policy', *Bank of England Quarterly Bulletin*, June.

Bank of England (2006) 'Memorandum of Understanding for Financial Stability', https://www.bankofengland.co.uk/-/media/boe/files/news/2006/march/memorandum-of-understanding-for-financial-stability.

Bank of England (2018) 'A millennium of macroeconomic data for the UK', https://www.bankofengland.co.uk/statistics/research-datasets/.

Bank of England (2019) 'Balance of payments time series', 20 December, https://www.ons.gov.uk/economy/nationalaccounts/balanceofpayments/datasets/balanceofpayments/.

Bank of England (2020) 'Statistical interactive database—daily spot exchange rates against sterling', http://www.bankofengland.co.uk/BOEAPPS/IADB/Rates.asp?into=GBP.

Bayliss, K. (2014) 'The financialization of water', *Review of Radical Political Economics*, 46(3): 292–307.

Becker, J., J. Jäger, B. Leubolt, and R. Weissenbacher (2010) 'Peripheral financialization and vulnerability to crisis: a regulationist perspective', *Competition and Change*, 14(3–4): 225–47.

Beggs, M. (2017) 'The state as a creature of money', *New Political Economy*, 22(5): 463–77.

Bell, S. and A. Hindmoor (2015) *Masters of the Universe, Slaves of the Market* (Cambridge, MA: Harvard University Press).

Bellamy Foster, J. (2007) 'The financialization of capitalism', *Monthly Review*, 58(11): 1–11.

Bellringer, C. and R. Michie (2014) 'Big Bang in the City of London: an intentional revolution or an accident?', *Financial History Review*, 21(1): 111–37.

Benanav, A. (2015) 'A Global History of Unemployment: Surplus Populations in the World Economy, 1949–2010'. PhD dissertation, University of California, Berkeley.

Benko, R. (2011) 'October surprise: can gold be the Panama Canal treaty of 2012?', *Forbes*, 31 October, https://www.forbes.com/sites/ralphbenko/2011/10/31/october-surprise-can-gold-be-the-panama-canal-treaty-of-2012/#177d07522062/.

Best, J. (2004) 'Hollowing out Keynesian norms: How the search for a technical fix undermined the Bretton Woods regime', *Review of International Studies*, 30(3): 383–404.

Best, J. (2005) *The Limits of Transparency: Ambiguity and the History of International Finance* (Ithica, NY: Cornell University Press).

Best, J. (2019) 'The inflation game: Targets, practices and the social production of monetary credibility', *New Political Economy*, 24(5): 623–40.

Best, J. (2020) 'The quiet failures of early neoliberalism: From rational expectations to Keynesianism in reverse', *Review of International Studies*, 46(5): 383–404.

Biebricher, T. (2018) *The Political Theory of Neoliberalism* (Stanford: Stanford University Press).

Blackby, F. T. (1979) 'Narrative, 1960–74', in F. T. Blackby (ed.), *British Economic Policy, 1970–74: Demand Management* (Cambridge: Cambridge University Press), pp. 11–76.

Block, F. (1987) *Revising State Theory: Essays in Politics and Postindustrialism* (Philadelphia: Temple University Press).

Bonefeld, W. (1995) 'Monetarism and Crisis', in W. Bonefeld and J. Holloway (eds), *Global Capital, National State and the Politics of Money* (Basingstoke: Macmillan), pp. 35–68.

Bonefeld, W. (2010) 'Abstract labour: Against its nature and on its time', *Capital & Class*, 34(2): 257–276.

Bonefeld, W. (2014) *Critical Theory and the Critique of Political Economy* (London: Bloomsbury).

Bonefeld, W. (2016) *The Strong State and the Free Economy* (London: Rowman & Littlefield).

Bonefeld, W. and J. Holloway (eds) (1995) *Global Capital, National State and the Politics of Money* (Basingstoke: Palgrave Macmillan).

Booth, A. (1995) *British Economic Development Since 1945* (Manchester: Manchester University Press).

Bordo, M. (1993) 'The Bretton Woods international monetary system: A historical overview', in M. Bordo and B. Eichengreen (eds), *A Retrospective on the Bretton Woods System: Lessons for International Monetary Reform* (Chicago: University of Chicago Press), pp. 3–108.

Bordo, M. (2020) 'The imbalances of the Bretton Woods system 1965 to 1973: U.S. inflation, the elephant in the room', *Open Economies Review*, 31: 195–211.

Boyer, R. (2000) 'Is a finance-led growth regime a viable alternative to Fordism? A preliminary analysis', *Economy and Society*, 29(1): 111–45.

Brenner, R. (2006) *The Economics of Global Turbulence* (London: Verso).

Brenner, R. (2009) 'What is good for Goldman Sachs is good for America: The origins of the current crisis', https://escholarship.org/uc/item/0sg0782h/.

Brittan, S. (1971) *Steering the Economy: The Role of the Treasury* (London: Penguin).

Brittan, S. (1995) *Capitalism with a Human Face* (Cambridge, MA: Harvard University Press).

Britton, A. (1994) *Macroeconomic Policy in Britain: 1974–1987* (Cambridge: Cambridge University Press).

Brown, G. (2017) *My Life, Our Times* (London: Vintage).

Browning, P. (1986) *The Treasury and Economy Policy: 1964–1985* (Harlow: Longman).

Buller, J. (1999) 'A critical appraisal of the statecraft interpretation', *Public Administration*, 77(4): 691–712.

Bulpitt, J. (1986) 'The discipline of the new democracy: Mrs Thatcher's domestic statecraft', *Political Studies*, 34(1): 19–39.

Burn, G. (1999) 'The state, the City and the Euromarkets', *Review of International Political Economy*, 6(2): 225–61.

Burnham, P. (1990) *The Political Economy of Postwar Reconstruction* (Basingstoke: Palgrave Macmillan).

Burnham, P. (2001) 'New Labour and the politics of depoliticisation', *British Journal of Politics and International Relations*, 3(2): 127–49.

Burnham, P. (2006) 'Marx, the state and British politics', *British Politics*, 1(1): 67–83.

Burnham, P. (2007) 'The politicisation of monetary policy-making in postwar Britain', *British Politics*, 2: 395–419.

Burnham, P. (2011) 'Depoliticising monetary policy: The Minimum Lending Rate experiment in the 1970s', *New Political Economy*, 16(4): 463–80.

Burnham, P. (2017) 'The alternative externalisation strategy, operational independence and the Bank of England', *Parliamentary Affairs*, 70(1): 173–89.

Burns. A. (1979) *The Anguish of Central Banking*, The 1979 Per Jacobsson Lecture (Belgrade: Per Jacobsson Foundation).

Caffentzis, G. (2005) 'Immeasurable value? An essay on Marx's legacy', *The Commoner*, 5: 87–114.

Cairncross, A. (1995) *The British Economy Since 1945* (Oxford: Blackwell).

Cairncross, A. (1996) 'The Heath government and the British economy', in S. Ball and A. Seldon (eds), *The Heath Government, 1970–1974: A Reappraisal* (London: Routledge), pp. 107–38.

Cairncross, A. and P. Sinclair (1982) *Introduction to Economics* (London: Butterworth).

Callaghan, J. (2000) 'Rise and fall of the alternative economic strategy: From internationalisation of capital to "globalisation"', *Contemporary British History*, 14(3): 105–30.

Capie, F. (2010) *The Bank of England: 1950s to 1979* (Cambridge: Cambridge University Press).

Carchedi, G. (1991) *Frontiers of Political Economy* (London: Verso).

Carchedi, G. (2009) 'The fallacies of "new dialectics" and value-form theory', *Historical Materialism*, 17(1): 145–169.

CBI (1973) Press Release: 'Profits and Investment' (London: CBI).

CBI (1977) 'Industry and the City: The first-stage CBI evidence to the Committee to Review the Functioning of Financial Institutions' (London: CBI).

Cerny, P. (1993) 'The deregulation and re-regulation of financial markets in a more open world', in P. Cerny (ed.), *Finance and World Politics: Markets, Regimes and States in the Post-Hegemonic Era* (Cheltenham: Edward Elgar), pp. 51–85.

Cerny, P. (1994) 'The dynamics of financial globalization: Technology, market structure, and policy response', *Policy Sciences*, 27(4): 319–42.

Chakrabortty, A. (2011) 'Britain is ruled by the banks, for the banks', *The Guardian*, 12 December, https://www.theguardian.com/business/2011/dec/12/britain-ruled-by-banks/.

Christophers, B. (2015) 'The limits to financialization', *Dialogues in Human Geography*, 5(2): 183–200.

Christophers, B. (2020) *Rentier Capitalism: Who Owns the Economy, and Who Pays for It?* (London: Verso).

Chuǎng (2019) 'Red dust: The transition to capitalism in China', *Chuǎng*, Volume II: *Frontiers*, pp. 21–281.

Clapp, J. (2014) 'Financialization, distance and global food politics', *Journal of Peasant Studies*, 41(5): 797–814.

Clarke, S. (1988) *Keynesianism, Monetarism and the Crisis of the State* (Aldershot: Edward Elgar).

Clarke, S. (1991) 'State, class struggle and the reproduction of capital', in S. Clarke (ed.), *The State Debate* (Basingstoke: Palgrave Macmillan), pp. 183–203.

Clarke, S. (1994) *Marx's Theory of Crisis* (Basingstoke: Macmillan).

Clift, B. (2020) 'The hollowing out of monetarism: The rise of rules-based monetary policy-making in the UK and USA and problems with the paradigm change framework', *Comparative European Politics*, 18: 281–308.

Clift, B. and J. Tomlinson (2008) 'Negotiating credibility: Britain and the International Monetary Fund', *Contemporary European History*, 17(4): 545–66.

Clift, B. and J. Tomlinson (2012) 'When rules started to rule: The IMF, neo-liberal economic ideas and economic policy change in Britain', *Review of International Political Economy*, 19(3): 477–500.

Coakley, J. and L. Harris (1992) 'Financial Globalisation and Deregulation', in J. Michie (ed.), *The Economic Legacy: 1979–1992* (London: Academic Press), pp. 37–56.

Coates, D. (1980) *Labour in Power? A Study of the Labour Government 1974–1979* (London: Longman).

Coates, D. and J. Hilliard (1986) *The Economic Decline of Modern Britain: The Debate Between Left and Right* (Brighton: Wheatsheaf Books).

Cobham, D. (2002) *The Making of Monetary Policy in the UK, 1975–2000* (Chichester: John Wiley & Sons).

Cohen, B. (1977) *Organizing the World's Money* (Basingstoke: Macmillan).

Cohen, B. (1982) 'Balance-of-payments financing: Evolution of a regime', *International Organization*, 36(2): 457–78.

Collins, J. (1979) 'British abolish controls on foreign currency', *New York Times*, 24 October.

Cooper, J. (2012) *Margaret Thatcher and Ronald Reagan: A Very Political Special Relationship* (Basingstoke: Palgrave Macmillan).

Cowan, D. (2011) *Housing Law and Policy* (Cambridge: Cambridge University Press).

Crafts, N. (1988) 'British economic growth before and after 1979: A review of the evidence', CEPR Discussion Paper no. 292.

Crafts, N. (1995) 'The Golden Age of Economic Growth in Western Europe, 1950–1973', *Economic History Review*, 48(3): 429–47.

Crafts, N. (2012) 'British relative economic decline revisited: The role of competition', *Explorations in Economic History*, 49(1): 17–29.

Crafts, N. and G. Toniolo (2012) '"Les trentes glorieuses": From the Marshall Plan to the oil crisis', in D. Stone (ed.), *The Oxford Handbook of Postwar European History* (Oxford: Oxford University Press), pp. 356–78.

Crotty, J. (2000) 'Structural contradictions of the global neoliberal regime', *Journal of Radical Political Economics*, 32(3): 361–68.

Crotty, J. (2003) 'The neoliberal paradox: The impact of destructive product market competition and impatient financial markets on nonfinancial corporations in the neo-liberal era', *Review of Radical Political Economics*, 35(3): 271–79.

Crotty, J. (2009) 'Structural causes of the global financial crisis: A critical assessment of the "new financial architecture"', *Cambridge Journal of Economics*, 33(4): 563–80.

Crouch, C. (2009) 'Privatised Keynesianism: an unacknowledged policy regime', *British Journal of Politics and International Relations*, 11(3): 382–99.

Daripa, A., S. Kapur, and A. Wright (2013) 'Labour's record on financial regulation', *Oxford Review of Economic Policy*, 29(1): 71–94.

Davies, A. (2017) *The City of London and Social Democracy: The Political Economy of Finance in Britain, 1959–1979* (Oxford: Oxford University Press).

Davies, G. (2017) 'Whatever happened to secular stagnation?', *Financial Times*, 26 February, https://www.ft.com/content/33a5aa60-2fef-3724-92ad-34fe284e4cee/.

Davis, A. and C. Walsh (2016) 'The role of the state in the financialisation of the UK economy', *Political Studies*, 64(3): 666–82.

Davis, A. and C. Walsh (2017) 'Distinguishing financialization from neoliberalism', *Theory, Culture and Society*, 34(5–6): 27–51.

Dobbs, R., T. Coller, S. Ramaswamy, J. Woetzel, J. Manyika, R. Krishnan, and N. Andreula (2015) *Playing to Win: The New Global Competition for Corporate Profits* (New York: McKinsey Global Institute).

Dollar, D. and E. Wolff (1994) 'Capital intensity and TFP convergence by industry in manufacturing, 1963–1985', in W. Baumol, R. Nelson, and E. Wolff (eds), *Convergence of Productivity Cross-National Studies and Historical Evidence* (New York: Oxford University Press), pp. 197–224.

Dorey, P. (1995) *The Conservative Party and the Trade Unions* (London: Routledge).

Dorfman, G. (1983) *British Trade Unionism against the Trades Union Congress* (Stanford, CA: Hoover Institution Press).

Dow, C. (2013) *Inside the Bank of England: Memoirs of Christopher Dow, Chief Economist, 1973–84* (Basingstoke: Palgrave Macmillan).

Duménil, G. and D. Lévy (2002) 'The nature and contradictions of neoliberalism', *Socialist Register*, 38: 43–71.

Duménil, G. and D. Lévy (2004) *Capital Resurgent: Roots of the Neoliberal Revolution* (Cambridge, MA: Harvard University Press).

Dunn, B. (2018) 'On the prospects of a return to Keynes: Taking Keynes's political philosophy seriously', *Global Society*, 32(3): 302–323.

Dutta, S. (2017) 'Sovereign debt management and the globalization of finance: Recasting the City of London's "Big Bang"', *Competition and Change*, 22(1): 3–22.

Economist, The (2011) 'Banged about', 29 October, https://www.economist.com/britain/2011/10/29/banged-about/.

Edgerton, D. (2018) *The Rise and Fall of the British Nation: A Twentieth Century History* (London: Allen Lane).

Eglene, O. (2011) *Banking on Sterling: Britain's Independence from the Eurozone* (Plymouth: Lexington Books).

Eichengreen, B. (1997) 'The Bretton Woods system: Paradise lost?', in B. Eichengreen and M. Flandreau (eds), *The Gold Standard in Theory and History* (London: Routledge), pp. 224–34.

Eichengreen, B. (2008) *Globalizing Capital: A History of the International Monetary System* (Princeton: Princeton University Press).

Eichengreen, B., and P. Temin (2000) 'The Gold Standard and the Great Depression', *Contemporary European History*, 9(2): 183–207.

Eichengreen, B., D. Perkins, and K. Shin (2012) *From Miracle to Maturity: The Growth of the Korean Economy* (Cambridge, MA: Harvard University Press).

Engelen, E., I. Ertürk, J. Froud, S. Johal, A. Leaver, M. Moran, A. Nilsson, and W. Karel (2011) *After the Great Complacence: Financial Crisis and the Politics of Reform* (Oxford: Oxford University Press).

Engelen, E., R. Fernandez, and R. Hendrikse (2014) 'How finance penetrates its other: A cautionary tale on the financialization of a Dutch university', *Antipode*, 46: 1072–1091.

Epstein, G. (2005) 'Introduction: financialization and the world economy', in G. Epstein (ed.), *Financialization and the World Economy* (Cheltenham: Edward Elgar), pp. 3–16.

Evans, E. (2004) *Thatcher and Thatcherism* (London: Routledge).

Feenstra, R., R. Inklaar, and M. Timmer (2015) 'The Next Generation of the Penn World Table', *American Economic Review*, 105(10): 3150–3182, www.ggdc.net/pwt.

Feld, L., E. Köhler, and D. Nientiedt (2015) 'Ordoliberalism, pragmatism and the eurozone crisis: How the German tradition shaped economic policy in Europe', Freiburger Diskussionspapiere zur Ordnungsökonomik No. 15/04, Albert-Ludwigs-Universität Freiburg.

Fforde, J. (1982) 'Setting monetary objectives', *Bank of England Quarterly Bulletin*, June.

Flinders, M. and J. Buller (2006) 'Depoliticisation: principles, tactics and tools', *British Politics*, 1(3): 293–318.

Foroohar, R. (2016) 'American capitalism's great crisis', *Time*, 12 May, http://time.com/4327419/american-capitalisms-great-crisis/.

Foroohar, R. (2016) *Makers and Takers: The Rise of Finance and the Fall of American Business* (New York: Crown Business).

Foucault, M. (1995) *Discipline and Punish: The Birth of the Prison* (New York: Vintage Books).

Foucault, M. (2001) *Power* (London: Allen Lane).

Fuller, G. (2016) *The Great Debt Transformation: Households, Financialization, and Policy Responses* (Basingstoke: Palgrave Macmillan).

Gamble, A. (1989) 'The politics of Thatcherism', *Parliamentary Affairs*, 3(1): 350–61.

Gamble, A. (1994a) *Britain in Decline: Economic Policy, Political Strategy and the British State* (Basingstoke: Macmillan).

Gamble, A. (1994b) *The Free Economy and the Strong State: The Politics of Thatcherism* (Basingstoke: Macmillan).

Gamble, A. and P. Walton (1976) *Capitalism in Crisis: Inflation and the State* (Basingstoke: Macmillan).

Germain, R. (1997) *The International Organization of Credit: States and Global Finance in the World Economy* (Cambridge: Cambridge University Press).

Gola, C. and A. Roselli (2009) *The UK Banking System and Its Regulatory and Supervisory Framework* (Basingstoke: Palgrave Macmillan).

Goodhart, C. (1995) *The Central Bank and the Financial System* (Basingstoke: Macmillan).

Goodman, J. and L. Pauly (1993) 'The obsolescence of capital controls? Economic management in an age of global markets', *World Politics*, 46(1): 50–82.

Gore, C. (1854) *The Money Lender* (London: George Routledge and Co.).

Gowan, P. (2009) 'Crisis in the heartlands', *New Left Review*, 55: 5–29.

Grabel, I. (2000) 'The political economy of "policy credibility": The new-classical macroeconomics and the remaking of emerging economies', *Cambridge Journal of Economics*, 24(1): 1–19.

Grady, J. and M. Weale (1986) *British Banking, 1960–85* (Basingstoke: Palgrave Macmillan).

Green, J. (2016) 'Anglo-American development, the Euromarkets, and the deeper origins of neoliberal deregulation', *Review of International Studies*, 42(3): 425–49.

Green, J. (2020) *The Political Economy of the Special Relationship: Anglo-American Development from the Gold Standard to the Financial Crisis* (Princeton, NJ: Princeton University Press).

Gunnoe, A. and P. K. Gellert (2011) 'Financialization, shareholder value, and the transformation of timberland ownership in the US', *Critical Sociology*, 37(3): 265–84.

Haache, G. and C. Taylor (2013) 'Editors' Introduction', in G. Haache and C. Taylor (eds), *Inside the Bank of England: Memoirs of Christopher Dow, Chief Economist, 1973–84* (Basingstoke: Palgrave Macmillan), pp. 1–33.

Hall, P. (1993) 'Policy paradigms, social learning, and the state: The case of economic policymaking in Britain', *Comparative Politics*, 25(3): 275–96.

Hall, S. (1988) *The Hard Road to Renewal: Thatcherism and the Crisis of the Left* (London: Verso).

Han, M. (2016) *Central Bank Regulation and the Financial Crisis: A Comparative Analysis* (Basingstoke: Palgrave Macmillan).

Hansen, A. (1939) 'Economic progress and declining population growth', *American Economic Review*, 29(1): 1–15.

Hardie, I. (2011) 'How much can governments borrow? Financialization and emerging markets governments borrowing capacity', *Review of International Political Economy*, 18(2): 141–67.

Harmon, M. (1997) 'The 1976 UK–IMF crisis: The markets, the Americans, and the IMF', *Contemporary British History*, 11(3): 1–17.

Hay, C., J. M. Riiheläinen, N. Smith, and M. Watson (2008) 'Ireland: the outlier inside', in K. Dyson (ed.), *The Euro at Ten: Europeanization, Power and Convergence* (Oxford: Oxford University Press), pp. 182–203.

Hayek, F. A. (1945) 'The use of knowledge in society', *American Economic Review*, 35(4): 519–530.

Hayek, F. A. (1982a) *Law, Legislation, and Liberty*, Volume II: *The Mirage of Social Justice* (London: Routledge).

Hayek, F. A. (1982b) *Law, Legislation, and Liberty*, Volume III: *The Political Order of a Free People* (London: Routledge).

Heffernan, S. (2005) *Modern Banking* (Chichester: John Wiley & Sons).

Helleiner, E. (1994) *States and the Reemergence of Global Finance: From Bretton Woods to the 1990s* (Ithica, NY: Cornell University Press).

Helleiner, E. (1995) 'Explaining the globalization of financial markets: Bringing states back in', *Review of International Political Economy*, 2(2): 315–41.

Hirsch, F. (1965) *The Pound Sterling: A Polemic* (London: Victor Gollancz).

Hirsch, J. (1978) 'The state apparatus and social reproduction: Elements of a theory of the bourgeois state', in J. Holloway and S. Picciotto (eds), *The State and Capital: A Marxist Debate* (London: Edward Arnold), pp. 57–107.

HM Treasury (1981) *Financial Statement and Budget Report* (London: HM Treasury).

HM Treasury (2002) *Reforming Britain's Economic and Financial Policy: Towards Greater Economic Stability* (Basingstoke: Palgrave).

HM Treasury (2011) 'The Government Response to the Independent Commission on Banking', Cm 8252 (London: The Stationery Office), https://www.gov.uk/government/publications/government-response-to-the-independent-commission-on-banking-reforming-uk-banking-structure.

Holloway, J. (2002) 'Class and classification: Against, in and beyond labour', in A. Dinerstein and M. Neary (eds), *The Labour Debate: An Investigation into the Theory and Reality of Capitalist Work* (Aldershot: Ashgate), pp. 27–40.

Holloway, J. (2015) 'Read Capital: The first sentence', *Historical Materialism*, 23(3): 3–26.

Holmes, M. (1997) *The Failure of the Heath Government* (Basingstoke: Macmillan).

Hopkin, J. and K. A. Shaw (2016) 'Organized combat or structural advantage? The politics of inequality and the winner-takes-all economy in the United Kingdom', *Politics and Society*, 44(3): 345–71.

House of Commons Treasury Committee (2008) *'The Run on the Rock'. Fifth Report of Session 2007–08* (London: The Stationery Office).

Howe, G. (1994) *Conflict of Loyalty* (London: Macmillan).

Howson, S. (1994) 'Money and monetary policy in Britain, 1945–1990', in R. Floud and D. McCloskey (eds), *The Economic History of Britain Since 1700*, 2nd edn, Volume 3: *1939–1992* (Cambridge: Cambridge University Press), pp. 221–54.

Hudson, M. and J. Sommers (2013) 'The Queen Mother of global austerity and financialization', *Counterpunch*, April 8, https://www.counterpunch.org/2013/04/08/the-queen-mother-of-global-austerity-financialization/.

IMF (1992) *Report on the Measurement of International Capital Flows* (Washington, DC: International Monetary Fund).

Ingham, G. (1984) *Capitalism Divided: The City and Industry in British Social Development* (Basingstoke: Macmillan).

Jacobs, S. (1985) 'Race, empire and the welfare state: Council housing and racism', *Critical Social Policy*, 5(13): 6–28.

James, S. and L. Quaglia (2020) *The UK and Multi-Level Financial Regulation: From Post-Crisis Reform to Brexit* (Oxford: Oxford University Press).

James, T. S. (2018) 'Political leadership as statecraft? Aligning theory with praxis in conversation with British party leaders', *British Journal of Politics and International Relations*, 20(3): 555–572.

Jenkins, S. (2006) Thatcher and Sons: A Revolution in Three Acts (London: Penguin).

Jessop, B. (1988) *Thatcherism: A Tale of Two Nations* (Cambridge: Polity Press).

Jessop, B. (1990) *State Theory: Putting the Capitalist State in its Place* (University Park, PA: Pennsylvania State University Press).

Jessop, B. (1997) 'Twenty years of the (Parisian) regulation approach: The paradox of success and failure at home and abroad', *New Political Economy*, 2(3): 503–26.

Johnson C. (1991) *The Economy Under Mrs Thatcher: 1979–1990* (London: Penguin).

Kavanagh, D. (1990) *Thatcherism and British Politics: The End of Consensus?* (Oxford: Oxford University Press).

Keegan, W. (1980) 'Operation Fudge-Up', *The Observer*, 7 September.

Kettell, S. (2004) *The Political Economy of Exchange Rate Policy-Making: From the Gold Standard to the Euro* (Basingstoke: Palgrave Macmillan).

Keynes, J. M. (2013) *The General Theory of Employment, Interest and Money* (Cambridge: Cambridge University Press).

Keynes, J. M. (2019) *The Economic Consequences of the Peace* (Cham: Palgrave Macmillan).

Kliman, A. (2012) *The Failure of Capitalist Production: Underlying Causes of the Great Recession* (London: Pluto).

Konzelmann, S., M. Fovargue-Davies, and F. Wilkinson (2013) 'The United Kingdom: Thatcherism – 'a heavy hand and a light touch', in S. Konzelmann and M. Fovargue-Davies (eds), *Banking Systems in the Crisis: The Faces of Liberal Capitalism* (London: Routledge), pp. 80–106.

Krippner, G. (2007) 'The making of US monetary policy: Central bank transparency and the neoliberal dilemma', *Theory and Society*, 36(6): 477–513.

Krippner, G. (2011) *Capitalizing on Crisis: The Political Origins of the Rise of Finance* (Cambridge, MA: Harvard University Press).

Krugman, P. (1979) 'A model of balance-of-payments crises', *Journal of Money, Credit and Banking*, 11(3): 311–25.

Lake, R. (2015) 'The financialization of urban policy in the age of Obama', *Journal of Urban Affairs*, 37(1): 75–8.

Langley, P. (2004) 'In the eye of the "perfect storm": The final salary pensions crisis and financialisation of Anglo American capitalism', *New Political Economy*, 9(4): 539–58.

Langley, P. (2008) 'Financialization and the consumer credit boom', *Competition & Change*, 12(2): 133–47.

Larsen, P. (2006) 'Big Bang still brings much to London finance', *Financial Times*, 25 October, https://www.ft.com/content/c400bd64-644b-11db-ab21-0000779e2340/.

Laurence, H. (2001) *Money Rules: The New Politics of Finance in Britain and Japan* (Ithaca, NY: Cornell University Press).

Lawson, N. (1992) *The View from No. 11: Memoirs of a Tory Radical* (London: Transworld).

Lazonick, W. (2013) 'The fragility of the U.S. economy: The financialized corporation and the disappearing middle class', in D. Breznitz and J. Zysman (eds), *The Third Globalization: Can Wealthy Nations Stay Rich in the Twenty-First Century?* (New York: Oxford University Press), pp. 232–76.

Lazonick, W. and M. O'Sullivan (2002) 'Maximizing shareholder value: A new ideology for corporate governance', in W. Lazonick and M. O'Sullivan (eds), *Corporate Governance and Sustainable Prosperity* (Basingstoke: Palgrave), pp. 11–36.

Link, S. (2020) *Forging Global Fordism: Nazi Germany, Soviet Russia, and the Contest over the Industrial Order* (Princeton: Princeton University Press).

Longstreth, F. (1979) 'The City, industry and the state', in C. Crouch (ed.), *State and Economy in Contemporary Capitalism* (London: Croom Helm), pp. 157–90.

Lotz, C. (2014) *The Capitalist Schema: Time, Money, and the Culture of Abstraction* (Lanham, MD: Lexington Books).

Ludlam, S. (1992) 'The Gnomes of Washington: Four myths of the 1976 IMF crisis', *Political Studies*, 40(4): 713–27.

Maddison, A. (1995) *Monitoring the World Economy, 1820–1992* (Paris: OECD).

Maddison, A. (1997) 'Macroeconomic accounts for European countries', in B. Van Ark and N. Crafts (eds), *Quantitative Aspects of Post-War European Economic Growth* (Cambridge: Cambridge University Press), pp. 27–83.

Mann, G. (2018) *In the Long Run We're All Dead: Keynesianism, Political Economy, and Revolution* (London: Verso).

Marsh, D. (1992) *The New Politics of British Trade Unionism: Union Power and the Thatcher Legacy* (Basingstoke: Macmillan).

Martin, R., M. Rafferty, and D. Bryan (2008) 'Financialization, risk and labour', *Competition and Change*, 12(2): 120–32.

Marx, K. (1976) *Capital: A Critique of Political Economy*, Volume I (London: Penguin).

Marx, K. (1981) *Capital: A Critique of Political Economy*, Volume III (London: Penguin).

Marx, K. (1993) *Grundrisse* (London: Penguin).

Mattick, P. (2011) *Business as Usual: The Economic Crisis and the Failure of Capitalism* (London: Reaktion Books).

Mazzucato, M. (2018) *The Value of Everything: Making and Taking in the Global Economy* (London: Allen Lane).

McKelvie, I. (1971) 'More loans bid for more jobs', *Daily Express*, 1 July.

McNally, D. (2004) 'The dual form of labour in capitalist society and the struggle over meaning: Comments on Postone', *Historical Materialism*, 12(3): 189–208.

McNally, D. (2011) *The Global Slump: The Economics and Politics of Crisis and Resistance* (Oakland, CA: PM Press).

McNally, D. (2014) 'The blood of the commonwealth: War, the state, and the making of world money', *Historical Materialism*, 22(2): 3–32.

McNamara, K. (1999) *The Currency of Ideas: Monetary Politics in the European Union* (Ithaca, NY: Cornell University Press).

Mehrling, P. (2013a) 'The inherent hierarchy of money', in L. Taylor, A. Rezai, and T. Michl (eds), *Social Fairness and Economics: Economic Essays in the Spirit of Duncan Foley* (Basingstoke: Palgrave), pp. 394–404.

Mehrling, P. (2013b) 'Essential hybridity: A money view of FX', *Journal of Comparative Economics*, 41(2): 355–363.

Melander, I. (2017) 'France's Le Pen launches election bid with vow to fight globalisation', *Reuters*, 5 February, https://uk.reuters.com/article/uk-france-election-fn/frances-le-pen-launches-election-bid-with-vow-to-fight-globalisation-idUKKBN15K0M2.

Metcalf, S. (2017) 'Neoliberalism: The idea that swallowed the world', *The Guardian*, 18 August, https://www.theguardian.com/news/2017/aug/18/neoliberalism-the-idea-that-changed-the-world/.

Mirowski, P. (2013) *Never Let a Serious Crisis Go to Waste: How Neoliberalism Survived the Financial Meltdown* (London: Verso).

Mogato, M. (2009) 'Global financial market losses $50 trillion: ADB study', Reuters, March 9, https://www.reuters.com/article/us-financial-adb/global-financial-market-losses-50-trillion-adb-study-idUSTRE5281FN20090309/.

Montalban, M. and M. Sakinç (2013) 'Financialization and productive models in the pharmaceutical industry', *Industrial and Corporate Change*, 22(4): 981–1030.

Moran, M. (1984) *The Politics of Banking* (London: Macmillan).

Moran, M. (1991) *The Politics of the Financial Services Revolution: The US, UK and Japan* (Basingstoke: Palgrave).

Moseley, F. (1991) *The Falling Rate of Profit in the Postwar United States Economy* (Basingstoke: Macmillan).

Moseley, F. (1997) 'The profit rate and the future of capitalism', *Review of Radical Political Economics*, 29(4): 23–41.

Needham, D. (2014) *UK Monetary Policy from Devaluation to Thatcher, 1967–1982* (Basingstoke: Palgrave Macmillan).

Nelson, P. (2008) *Capital Markets Law and Compliance: The Implications of MiFID* (Cambridge: Cambridge University Press).

Nelson, R. and G. Wright (1994) 'The erosion of U.S. technological leadership as a factor in postwar economic convergence', in W. Baumol, R. Nelson, and E. Wolff (eds), *Convergence of Productivity: Cross-National Studies and Historical Evidence* (New York: Oxford University Press), pp. 129–63.

OECD (1989) *OECD Economic Surveys: United Kingdom, 1988/1989* (Paris: Organisation for Economic Co-operation and Development).

OECD (2020) 'Real GDP forecast' (indicator), https://data.oecd.org/gdp/real-gdp-forecast.htm.

Offe, C. (1976) '"Crisis of crisis management": Elements of a political crisis theory', *International Journal of Politics*, 6(3): 29–67.

ONS (2017) 'Housing affordability in England and Wales: 2016', *ONS Statistical Bulletin*, 17 March, https://www.ons.gov.uk/peoplepopulationandcommunity/housing/bulletins/housingaffordabilityinenglandandwales/1997to2016/.

Orhangazi, O. (2008a) 'Financialisation and capital accumulation in the non-financial corporate sector: A theoretical and empirical investigation on the US economy: 1973–2003', *Cambridge Journal of Economics*, 32(6): 863–86.

Orhangazi, O. (2008b) *Financialization and the US Economy* (Cheltenham: Edward Elgar).

Orphanides, A. (2015) 'What caused the crash? The political roots of the financial crisis', *Foreign Affairs*, July/August, https://www.foreignaffairs.com/reviews/review-essay/2015-06-16/what-caused-crash/.

Palley, T. (2013) *Financialization: The Economics of Finance Capital Domination* (Basingstoke: Palgrave Macmillan).

Pandit, N., G. Cook, and P. Ghauri (2006) 'Towards an explanation of MNE FDI in the City of London financial services cluster', in F. Fai and E. Morgan (eds), *Managerial Issues in International Business* (Basingstoke: Palgrave Macmillan).

Parkinson, C. (1992) *Right at the Centre: An Autobiography* (London: Weidenfeld & Nicolson).

Parr, H. (2006) *Britain's Policy Towards the European Community: Harold Wilson and Britain's World Role, 1964–1967* (London: Routledge).

Peck, J. (2010) *Constructions of Neoliberal Reason* (Oxford: Oxford University Press).

Peeters, J. (1988) 'Re-regulation of the financial services industry in the United Kingdom', *University of Pennsylvania Journal of International Business Law*, 10(3): 371–407.

Pickard, J. (2017) 'Corbyn lashes out at financial sector "speculators and gamblers"', *Financial Times*, November 30, https://www.ft.com/content/834527ba-d5f0-11e7-a303-9060cb1e5f44/.

Pimlott, G. (1985) 'The reform of investor protection in the UK—An examination of the proposals of the Gower Report and the UK government's White Paper of January, 1985', *Journal of Comparative Business and Capital Market Law*, 7: 141–72.

Pistor, K. (2013) 'A legal theory of finance', *Journal of Comparative Economics*, 41(2): 315–330.

Pitts, F. H. (2019) 'Value form theory, Open Marxism, and the New Reading of Marx', in A. C. Dinerstein, A. G. Vela, E. González, and J. Holloway (eds), *Open Marxism 4: Against a Closing World* (London: Pluto), pp. 63–75.

Plender, J. (1986) 'London's Big Bang in international context', *International Affairs*, 63(1): 39–48.

Postone, M. (1993) *Time Labour and Social Domination: A Reinterpretation of Marx's Critical Theory* (Cambridge: Cambridge University Press).

Rawlings, P., A. Georgosouli, and C. Russo (2014) *Regulation of Financial Services: Aims and Methods* (London: Queen Mary University of London).

Reid, M. (1982) *The Secondary Banking Crisis, 1973–75: Its Causes and Course* (London: Macmillan).

Riddell, P. (1979a) 'UK industry's profits fall', *Financial Times*, 21 June.

Riddell, P. (1979b) 'Exchange controls eased further but framework remains', *Financial Times*, 19 July.

Riddell, P. (1979c) 'Howe removes all exchange controls', *Financial Times*, 24 October.

Robinson, J. (1960) *An Essay on Marxian Economics* (London: Macmillan).

Rogers, C. (2009) 'From social contract to "social contrick": The depoliticisation of economic policy-making under Harold Wilson, 1974–75', *British Journal of Politics and International Relations*, 11(4): 634–51.

Rogers, C. (2012) *The IMF and European Economies: Crisis and Continuity* (Basingstoke: Palgrave Macmillan).

Rogers, C. (2013) 'Crisis, ideas, and economic policy-making in Britain during the 1970s stagflation', *New Political Economy*, 18(1): 1–20.

Roos, J. (2019) 'From the demise of social democracy to the end of capitalism: The intellectual trajectory of Wolfgang Streeck', *Historical Materialism*, 27(2): 248–88.

Rubenstein, W. D. (1993) *Capitalism, Culture, and Decline in Modern Britain* (London: Routledge).

Rubin, I. I. (1978) 'Abstract labour and value in Marx's system', *Capital and Class*, 2(2): 109–39.

Rubin, I. I. (2010) *Essays on Marx's Theory of Value* (New Delhi: Aakar Books).

Scarbrough, E. (2000) 'The two faces of urban democracy in Britain', in O. Gabriel, V. Hoffman-Martinot, and H. Savitch (eds), *Urban Democracy* (Opladen: Leske and Budrich), pp. 127–86.

Schenk, C. (2010) *The Decline of Sterling: Managing the Retreat of an International Currency, 1945–1992* (Cambridge: Cambridge University Press).

Schwartz, H. (2018) *States Versus Markets: Understanding the Global Economy*, 4th edn (London: Red Globe Press).

Scott, P. (1996) *The Property Masters: A History of the British Commercial Property Sector* (London: E & FN Spon).

Seabrooke, L. (2006) *The Social Sources of Financial Power: Domestic Legitimacy and International Financial Orders* (Ithaca, NY: Cornell University Press).

Shaikh, A. (1987) 'The falling rate of profit and the economic crisis in the U.S.', in R. Cherry, C. D'Onofrio, C. Kurdas, T. Michl, F. Moseley, and M. Naples (eds), *The Imperilled Economy, Book I: Macroeconomics from a Left Perspective* (New York: Union for Radical Political Economics), pp. 115–26.

Shaikh, A. (1992) 'The falling rate of profit as the cause of long waves: Theory and empirical evidence', in A. Kleinknecht, E. Mandel, and I. Wallerstein (eds), *New Findings in Long-Wave Research* (London: Palgrave Macmillan), pp. 174–94.

Shaikh, A. (2011) 'The first Great Depression of the 21st century', *Socialist Register*, 47: 44–63.

Shepherd, D., A. Silberston, and R. Strange (1985) *British Manufacturing Investment Overseas* (London: Routledge).

Shilliam, R. (2018) *Race and the Undeserving Poor: From Abolition to Brexit* (Newcastle: Agenda Publishing).

Simmel, G. (1971) 'The metropolis and mental life', in *George Simmel on Individuality and Social Forms: Selected Writings*, ed. D. Levine (Chicago: University of Chicago Press), pp. 324–449.

Singh, D. (2007) *Banking Regulation of UK and US Financial Markets* (Farnham: Ashgate).

Slobodian, Q. (2018) *Globalists: The End of Empire and the Birth of Neoliberalism* (Cambridge, MA: Harvard University Press).

Smith, A. (1999) *The Wealth of Nations, Books IV–V* (London: Penguin).

Smith, J. E. (2020) *Smart Machines and Service Work: Automation in an Age of Stagnation* (London: Reaktion Books).

Smith, M. (2019) *Invisible Leviathan: Marx's Law of Value in the Twilight of Capitalism* (Chicago: Haymarket Books).

Smith, N. (2010) *Uneven Development: Nature, Capital and the Production of Space* (London: Verso).

Smith, R. (2018) 'Mapped: Average house prices in London Boroughs', *City A.M.*, 16 April.

Sohn-Rethel, A. (1978) *Intellectual and Manual Labour: A Critique of Epistemology* (Atlantic Highlands, NJ: Humanities Press).

Solomon, R. (1982) *The International Monetary System, 1945–1981* (London: Harper & Row).

Stiglitz, J. (2010) 'Lessons from the global financial crisis of 2008', *Seoul Journal of Economics*, 23: 321–39.

Stockhammer, E. (2004) 'Financialization and the slowdown of accumulation', *Cambridge Journal of Economics*, 28(5): 719–41.

Strange, S. (1994) *States and Markets*, 2nd edn (London: Continuum).

Streeck, W. (2011) 'The crises of democratic capitalism', *New Left Review*, 71: 5–29.

Streeck, W. (2014) *Buying Time: The Delayed Crisis of Democratic Capitalism* (London: Verso).

Summers, L. (2013) 'IMF fourteenth annual research conference in honor of Stanley Fischer', *larrysummers.com*, http://larrysummers.com/imf-fourteenth-annual-research-conference-in-honor-of-stanley-fischer/.

Supple, B. (1994) 'Fear of failing: Economic history and the decline of Britain', *Economic History Review*, 47(3): 441–58.

Tabb, W. K. (2010) 'Financialization in the contemporary social structure of accumulation', in T. McDonough, M. Reich, and D. Kotz (eds), *Contemporary Capitalism and its Crises: Social Structure of Accumulation Theory for the 21st Century* (Cambridge: Cambridge University Press), pp. 145–67.

Talani, L. (2012) *Globalization, Hegemony and the Future of the City of London* (Basingstoke: Palgrave Macmillan).

Tebbit, N. (1989) *Upwardly Mobile* (London: Futura).

Telegraph, The (2010) 'David Cameron promises to "transform economy"', *The Telegraph*, 28 May, https://www.telegraph.co.uk/news/politics/david-cameron/7779372/David-Cameron-promises-to-transform-economy.html.

Temin, P. (2002) 'The Golden Age of European growth reconsidered', *European Review of Economic History*, 6(1): 3–22.

Temperton, P. (1991) *UK Monetary Policy: The Challenge for the 1990s* (London: Macmillan).

Teulings, C. and R. Baldwin (2014) *Secular Stagnation: Facts, Causes and Cures* (London: CEPR Press).

Thain, C. (1985) 'The education of the Treasury: The Medium Term Financial Strategy 1980–84', *Public Administration*, 63(3): 261–85.

Thatcher, M. (1993) *The Downing Street Years* (London: HarperCollins).

Thomas, W. A. (1978) *The Finance of British Industry* (London: Metheun & Co.).

Thompson, N. (2004) 'The centre', in R. Plant, M. Beech, and K. Hickson (eds), *The Struggle for Labour's Soul: Understanding Labour's Political Thought Since 1945* (London: Routledge), pp. 47–67.

Thompson, H. (2017) 'How the City of London lost at Brexit: A historical perspective', *Economy and Society*, 46(6): 211–28.

Thorpe, A. (1999) 'The Labour Party and the trade unions', in J. McIlroy, N. Fishman, and A. Campbell (eds), *British Trade Unions and Industrial Politics: The High Tide of Trade Unionism, 1964–79* (Aldershot: Ashgate), pp. 133–50.

Thorpe, A. (2001) *The History of the British Labour Party* (Basingstoke: Palgrave).

Tickell, A. (1999) 'Success and Failure in the UK Financial Sector: The Barings Crisis.' Paper presented at the ECPR Joint Sessions, Workshop No. 16: Mannheim, ECPR, https://ecpr.eu/Filestore/PaperProposal/e882c0c7-824c-4d4f-8c7c-90a8f3f7523a.pdf.

Tickell, A. (2000) 'Dangerous derivatives: Controlling and creating risks in international money', *Geoforum*, 31(1): 87–99.

Tomlinson, J. (2001) *The Politics of Decline: Understanding Post-war Britain* (Harlow: Pearson Education).

Tomlinson, J. (2005) 'Economic decline in post-war Britain', in P. Addison and H. Jones (eds), *A Companion to Contemporary Britain, 1939–2000* (Oxford: Blackwell), pp. 164–79.

Tomlinson, J. (2007) 'Mrs Thatcher's macroeconomic adventurism, 1979–1981, and its political consequences', *British Politics*, 2(1): 3–19.

Toniolo, G. (2005) *Central Bank Cooperation at the Bank for International Settlements, 1930–1973* (Cambridge: Cambridge University Press).

Tooze, A. (2018a) 'Tempestuous seasons', *London Review of Books*, 40(17).

Tooze, A. (2018b) *Crashed: How a Decade of Financial Crises Changed the World* (London: Allen Lane).

Treanor, J. (2013) 'Farewell to the FSA—and the bleak legacy of the light-touch regulator', *The Guardian*, 24 March, https://www.theguardian.com/business/2013/mar/24/farewell-fsa-bleak-legacy-light-touch-regulator.

Turner, J. (2014) *Banking in Crisis: The Rise and Fall of British Banking Stability, 1800 to the Present* (Cambridge: Cambridge University Press).

Van der Zwan, N. (2014) 'Making sense of financialization', *Socio-Economic Review*, 12(1): 99–129.

Vogel, S. (1996) *Freer Markets, More Rules: Regulatory Reform in Advanced Industrial Countries* (Ithica, NY: Cornell University Press).

Vonyó, T. (2008) 'Postwar reconstruction and the Golden Age of economic growth', *European Review of Economic History*, 12(2): 221–41.

Wainwright, T. (2012) 'Building new markets: Transferring securitization, bond-rating, and a crisis from the US to the UK', in M. Aalbers (ed.), *Subprime Cities: The Political Economy of Mortgage Markets* (Oxford: Blackwell), pp. 97–119.

Walker, S. (2018) 'Hungarian leader says Europe is now "under invasion" by migrants', *The Guardian*, 15 March, https://www.theguardian.com/world/2018/mar/15/hungarian-leader-says-europe-is-now-under-invasion-by-migrants/.

Wang, Y. (2015) 'The rise of the "shareholding state": Financialization of economic management in China', *Socio-Economic Review*, 13(3): 603–25.

Wass, D. (2008) *Decline to Fall: The Making of British Macro-Economic Policy and the 1976 IMF Crisis* (Oxford: Oxford University Press).

Watson, M. (2010) 'House price Keynesianism and the contradictions of the modern investor subject', *Housing Studies*, 25(3): 413–26.

Weber, M. (1978) *Economy and Society*, Volume 1 (London: University of California Press).

Weber, R. (2010) 'Selling city futures: The financialization of urban redevelopment policy', *Economic Geography*, 86(3): 251–74.

White, G. (2015) 'Why are Republicans so obsessed with the Gold Standard?', *The Atlantic*, November 11, https://www.theatlantic.com/business/archive/2015/11/gop-debate-gold-standard/415386/.

Whittingham, T. G. and B. Towers (1977) 'Strikes and the economy', in E. W. Evans and S. W. Creigh (eds), *Industrial Conflict in Britain* (London: Frank Cass), pp. 75–86.

Wilson Committee to Review the Functioning of Financial Institutions (1980) *Report* (London: Her Majesty's Stationery Office).

Wolf, M. (2019) 'Why rigged capitalism is damaging liberal democracy', *Financial Times*, 19 September, https://www.ft.com/content/5a8ab27e-d470-11e9-8367-807ebd53ab77.

Woodward, N. (2004) *The Management of the British Economy, 1945–2001* (Manchester: Manchester University Press).

Index

For the benefit of digital users, table entries that span two pages (e.g., 52–53) may, on occasion, appear on only one of those pages.